Demographic Dimensions of the
New Republic

American Interregional Migration,
Vital Statistics, and Manumissions, 1800–1860

This book provides the first comprehensive and consistent analysis of vital
statistics and migration patterns for the United States between the Revol-
tion and the Civil War. It is anchored in the one available source for nation-
wide estimates, the decennial censuses. It attempts to provide, for black
and white populations, a consistent set of estimates of birth and death rates,
rates of natural increase, and net international and interregional flows.
For the black population, it also estimates the changing pace of manumissions in the ante-bellum decades. The census estimates are also
conditioned by a wide range of historical evidence, both quantitative and
non-quantitative, ranging from evidence on slave smuggling to ship traffic
during the War of 1812.

The book therefore provides the demographic components too long
absent from the historical and demographic analysis of the period. The
results are two-fold: a set of data and a set of questions suggested by the
data that promise novel challenges for historians of the ante-bellum era.

Demographic Dimensions of the New Republic

American Interregional Migration, Vital Statistics, and Manumissions, 1800–1860

PETER D. McCLELLAND

and

RICHARD J. ZECKHAUSER

CAMBRIDGE UNIVERSITY PRESS

Cambridge
London   New York   New Rochelle
Melbourne   Sydney

Published by the Press Syndicate of the University of Cambridge
The Pitt Building, Trumpington Street, Cambridge CB2 1RP
32 East 57th Street, New York, NY 10022, USA
296 Beaconsfield Parade, Middle Park, Melbourne 3206, Australia

© Cambridge University Press 1982

First published 1982

Printed in the United Sates of America

Library of Congress catalogue card number: 82-9648

British Library Cataloguing in Publication Data

McClelland, Peter D.
Demographic dimensions of the new Republic.
1. United States—Population—History
I. Title   II. Zeckhauser, Richard J.
304.6'0973   HB3505

ISBN 0 521 24309 2

Table of contents

List of tables

Preface

This project originated when the authors decided to undertake a joint exploration of the growth experience of America in the ante-bellum period. Initially we had planned to borrow whatever demographic insights were needed from available literature. The unsatisfactory state of that literature is what prompted this study.

Many have helped us along the way. Much of the computer work was undertaken by Pamela Memishian. Her patience and innovative suggestions proved to be invaluable. For helpful comments, we are indebted to Nancy Jackson and Robert Klitgaard. We are most especially grateful to Michael Brown-Beasley. For culling sources and tracking down obscure and often incomplete citations few could rival Michael in skill and determination. Michael Haines was kind enough to read the entire manuscript with exceptional care, and offered a wide range of helpful comments and criticisms.

Although the typing of various sections was done by a number of secretaries, the assembling of the final version was ably accomplished by Patricia Paucke.

Map 1: Regions of the United States

1

Introduction and Summary

1.1 General

(a) The problem. Of all numerical series that document the progress of a nation, none is more fundamental than its population statistics. In the changing patterns of birth and death rates, population expansion and migration, can be found the quantitative strands indispensable to weaving any larger tapestry of the economic history of a people. Without them, the larger picture is incomplete. This study attempts the first comprehensive analysis of vital statistics and migration patterns within the United States between the Revolution and the Civil War. It is anchored in the one available source for nation-wide estimates, the decennial censuses, and supplemented wherever possible by other relevant data. It attempts to provide, for black and white populations, a consistent set of estimates of birth and death rates, rates of natural increase, and net international and interregional flows. For the black population, it also estimates the changing pace of manumissions in the ante-bellum decades. In short, the goal of this work is to provide the demographic components too long absent from the historical and demographic analysis of the period. The results are twofold: a set of data and a set of questions suggested by the data that promise novel challenges for historians of the ante-bellum era.

In the most aggregate of demographic data, puzzling patterns are not difficult to find. As indicated in Table A-1, the North American rate of increase was unequaled on any other continent during the first half of the nineteenth century. But how much of this population growth could be attributed to the influx of immigrants? Was the high rate of natural increase of the domestic population – if it was high – more the result of exceptionally low death rates or high birth rates? The absolute level and secular trend of the death rate is a key numerical input to any study of the impact of early industrialization and modernization on the welfare of Americans. Of similar importance to studies of changing family structure is the level and trend of birth rates. These variables, combined with estimates of interregional migration and manu-missions, should also provide valuable numerical inputs to the continuing debate concerning the lot of black men and women in the newly united states.

Three facts are striking. First, the only adequate data base to study such

1

problems at the national level is the census data. If the objective is to derive birth and death rates for the nation as a whole, parochial studies of plantation records or bills of mortality will not do. Second, the most obvious way to estimate net migration – the census survivor technique – blends naturally into a study of vital rates. Third, no consistent study of both migration and vital rates has been undertaken previously for the white and Negro populations of ante-bellum America, despite the importance of both and the logical connection between the two. These three considerations were the primary motivating force for this study.

Two problems had to be resolved at the outset. The first was methodological in nature, concerning the optimal way to deal with imperfections in historical data. The second was to choose a set of regions as a necessary first step for estimating interregional migration.

(b) The question of method. The basic problem is easy to state and difficult to solve: How should numerical estimates be corrected for imperfections in historical data, when the degree of imperfection remains largely unknown? Census data are merely a case in point. They are the indispensable ingredient for any study of vital statistics for the nation as a whole, but a flawed ingredient. Perhaps the most striking evidence of imperfections in the original data is the negative death rates they imply for certain age cohorts during various intercensal periods. Further confounding the accuracy of the estimates of this study is the complete absence of certain required data, such as slaves smuggled into America, overland migration from Canada, and the population in unenumerated territories. This absence of data can only be overcome by a variety of assumptions, some more tenuous than others.

How should the historian regard the numerical estimates generated by such procedures, anchored as they are in imperfect data and assumptions difficult to verify? Or to give the question a pragmatic twist, how useful are such numerical estimates likely to be to the historian who needs them to test a given hypothesis? The answer is perhaps best explored in the context of examples of specific imperfections and associated hypotheses.

The defects of early censuses are a familiar and frustrating topic: familiar because any study using these data must note that imperfections exist; frustrating because the magnitude of such imperfections generally remains unknown. So traditional have caveats become that their very repetition may dull the reader's sense of how perilous numerical ventures can be when launched from this uncertain data base. Writing about collection procedures in the South in 1850, for example, Frederick Olmsted described the census marshals as 'generally excessively lazy, and neglectful of their duty, among that class which was most ignorant or indifferent on the subject. I have seen an advertisement of a deputy census marshal, in Alabama or Georgia, announcing that he would be at a certain tavern in his district, on a certain day, for

the purposes of receiving from the people of the vicinity – who were re-
quested to call upon him – the information it was his duty to obtain from
them.'[1] From his vantage point as superintendent of the 1870 census Francis
Walker noted pessimistically the implications of such procedures. 'I cannot
but believe, upon full consideration of all the information which it has been
possible to gather on the subject, that the two practices of "farming out"
subdivisions, and of "taking the census" at elections and on court days, instead of through the visitation by the assistant marshal of each dwelling house
in his subdivision, in turn, were general throughout the Southern States in
1850 and 1860, and not infrequent elsewhere. . . Both are in the last degree
destructive of all accuracy of enumeration.'[2]

For the demographer and the historian, Walker has overstated the case.
The relevant issue is not whether census data are completely accurate. They
never are. Or to put the matter more cautiously, they can never be known to
be completely free of error. As will be argued repeatedly below, the likely
degree of accuracy must always be kept in mind in gauging whether or not
the results of numerical manipulation can be accepted as a reasonable confirmation or disproof of a particular hypothesis. To ascertain the secular
decline in white birth rates, for example, or the broad patterns of interregional migration, requires only the roughest accuracy in the data base. Accordingly, estimates of such general trends can be viewed with considerable
confidence. (Put another way, sensitivity analysis would reveal that our
conclusions are robust with respect to likely values for the data.)

Other estimates, however, require a high degree of accuracy in the underlying data. A case in point is the miscegenation estimate of Fogel and
Engerman.[3] Their calculation depends critically upon the estimated mulatto
population in 1850 and 1860. The probable degree of accuracy of the final
result is difficult to gauge, in part because (a) free mulattoes were concentrated in urban centers and subject to serious underenumeration,[4] (b) the
term 'mulatto' was never defined by the Census Office at this time, and (c)
no specific instructions were given in 1860 to record mulattoes at all.[5] Without a reasonably accurate count of the population concerned, any estimate of
miscegenation becomes highly conjectural.

The general problem is thus a tension between hypothesis testing and data
accuracy; between the probable degree of accuracy of numerical estimates
on the one hand, and, on the other, the degree of accuracy needed in those
numbers if they are to be used to test a given hypothesis. What the historian
therefore needs when confronted with any numerical series is some means of
gauging how accurate that series is likely to be. This is a tall order. Those who
generate numerical estimates can aid this gauging process, albeit imperfectly,
in five predictable ways.

First, and most predictable of all, the reader can be alerted to the tenuous
nature of the numbers before him. Without a vigorous warning, too many are

inclined to accept as demonstrated fact what is, at best, an approximation to the truth. Or as Alexis de Tocqueville preferred to put the matter, 'The mind is easily imposed upon by the affection of exactitude which marks even the misstatements of statistics; and it adopts with confidence the errors which are appareled in the forms of mathematical truth.'[6]

Second, the assumptions, procedures, and evidence that underlie the numerical estimates can be made explicit. This documentation, where possible, should be accompanied by an assessment of how well founded or precarious the assumption or procedure or evidence appears to be.

Third, sensitivity analysis can be used to indicate the impact upon numerical estimates of modifications in initial assumptions. Moreover, estimates can be reported contingent upon different values for estimated variables. Procedures such as these are particularly crucial for those assumptions that appear to be most tenuous.

Fourth, and perhaps most controversial, modifications in initial data can, in some sense, be kept to a minimum. The lurking problem is most easily seen by considering the alternative strategy. A data series of population age cohorts, for example, that is relatively unsmooth in its original form can always be converted into a smooth series by repeated modifications. The difficulty is that, as modifications multiply, the reader is hard pressed to evaluate the probable accuracy of the final product. And it is this evaluation that is central to the use of those data to test historical hypotheses.

Fifth, last, and most difficult of all, the authors can attempt to make summary judgments concerning the probable degree of accuracy of the numbers that they have generated. If steps two through four outlined above have been followed with considerable care and candor, readers will be better placed to undertake a similar assessment for themselves. The end product can hardly be exact. Neither author nor reader can expect to generate for each numerical estimate a range, or a confidence interval, in which the 'true' number is likely to lie with a precisely specified probability. But some sense of likely accuracy – be it as vague as 'high' or 'low' – is preferable to no sense whatsoever. Equally important, the effort to cultivate this sense should instill a degree of caution that is perhaps the best guardian against the mechanistic or unthinking use of numerical estimates for subsequent hypothesis testing.

Before any of these assignments can be broached, the one remaining task is to define the regions that will be the focus of much of this inquiry.

(c) Defining the regions. The word 'region' suggests a discrete geographic entity, defined according to specific objectives.[7] For the economist, a region can frequently be distinguished by the homogeneity of productive activities within given geographical boundaries. Few regions, however, produce a single good, and most goods were produced by many regions in nineteenth-century

America. The result is a distressing lack of tidiness in geographical boundaries, with any preliminary pattern based upon similarities in productive activities resembling 'an irregular layer of pieces of slate, carelessly flung down'.[8]

Several considerations dictated the flinging down process adopted for this study. The dominant priority was to assure that the resulting interregional migration estimates prove valuable for any subsequent analysis of American development in the ante-bellum years. The number of regions was kept to a minimum so that broad patterns could be more easily discerned.[9] The main criteria for choosing specific regional boundaries were (a) the location of the frontier at the start of the nineteenth century, and (b) the rough homogeneity of productive activities within a region.

The six geographic regions chosen for this study are (1) New England, (2) Mid-Atlantic, (3) Northwest, (4) Old South, (5) New South, and (6) Far West. Five of these regions are outlined on Map 1. The sixth region, the Far West, consists of the area west of the Mississippi minus the tier of states running from Louisiana in the south to Minnesota in the north. The Far West is comprised of residual territory judged to be of negligible economic significance before 1850, and of limited significance in the next decade. The remaining territory was divided along the Appalachian fall line, a division requiring the separation of New York, Pennsylvania, and West Virginia into eastern and western segments. Eastern states were then apportioned along traditional lines, New England and the Old South requiring little explanation,[10] with the intervening states labeled Mid-Atlantic. Territory west of the fall line was split along the cotton belt, Tennessee being the northernmost state of the New South and Kentucky the southernmost state of the Northwest.

This study proceeds in three stages. Principal numerical findings are outlined in sections 1.2 through 1.7. These are then reviewed in section 1.8, in which the authors attempt to indicate their summary judgments concerning the probable degree of accuracy of each. The remainder of the work then details the evidence, procedures, and assumptions used to generate each series.

1.2 Migration

(a) General. In the era between the Revolution and the Civil War, a key determinant of American economic development was the westward migration of its people. The importance assigned to this phenomenon by most economic historians makes all the more remarkable the comparative scarcity of migration estimates for this period.[11] Part of the explanation is the complexity of that task. As will be documented at length below, even a method as relatively uncomplicated as the census survivor estimation technique requires a host of adjustments, assumptions, and estimates that no historian would attempt before the advent of computers, and few would welcome even with such sophisticated mechanical assistance. Lurking in the previous sentence is a warning for those who would interpret the numerical estimates of this study. All migration estimates should be viewed as approximations. Further, *net* migration estimates – the only kind possible for this period given the nature of surviving data – invariably understate the total movement of people. The word 'net' indicates the exclusion of those whose arrival into a region has been offset by others leaving. Net migration estimates also fail to count the movement of a given migrant who enters and leaves a region within a given decade. The net migration estimates attempted here therefore do not measure total movement. They represent only the net difference between those who left and those who entered between two census dates. They are nevertheless indicative of important national trends, given the dominant direction of the flows. Even with a generous allowance for possible error and crosshauling, the data suggest a number of conclusions, some unsurprising and others startling.

(b) White population 1800–60. The dominant pattern of movement, as anticipated, was from East to West, but within this broader flow a number of unexpected developments were found. In the North, by far the most import-ant supplier of population to the Northwest was the Mid-Atlantic region: New Jersey plus those portions of New York and Pennsylvania to the east of the Appalachian fall line. West of that fall line, the North towers over the South in importance. The total influx of people into the New South was less than 15 percent of the inflow into the Northwest in the years 1800–60. As for changing patterns across decades in the North, the influx into the Northwest rises sharply in every decade with one curious exception. In the 1820s, despite the completion of the Erie Canal (and despite the inclusion of western New York in the Northwest region), net in-migration was roughly one third less than it had been in the previous decade. New England patterns raise fewer questions. The region's decade of greatest loss encompassed the War of 1812. The smallest exodus (actually a slight influx) was recorded in the 1840s, when railroad building and early industrialization are commonly viewed as producing a booming economy in that region.

The southern flows suggested by the data raise a range of new and chal-lenging questions for the ante-bellum historian. The anticipated movement from East to West, as noted previously, is readily confirmed. The greatest net influx into the New South, however, occurred during the decade 1810–20, well before the cotton boom of the 1830s, and even somewhat antedating the full development of steamboats on western rivers. Even more startling is the difference between eastern losses and western gains. In the first four decades of the century, the net loss of the Old South was almost three and a half times the net gain of the New South. Even allowing for the addition of Texas in the 1840s (included in the Far West region), this imbalance remains. In the 1840–60 period, the New South became a region of major exodus. If the net losses in these two decades of both southern regions (Old South and New South) are combined with the net gains of the Far West (which includes California), this three-region unit still loses a total of some 200,000 white persons in the twenty years before Lincoln's election. In short, to the common view of an East–West flow must now be added the uncommon view of a *major South–North flow throughout the entire 60-year period*. This raises in bold relief the question of motivation. Was this southern exodus a flight from slavery or a rush towards economic opportunity? If the latter was the dominant consideration, the loss of population suggests that throughout the ante-bellum years, the South was continually viewed by its own inhabitants – or at least by those who left – as promising less economic opportunity than did the North. This in turn raises doubts about those accounts that portray in glowing terms the southern economic performance in the 1840s and 1850s.[12]

Both the age and the sex composition of the South–North migrants appear to be in marked contrast to those of their northern counterparts. Among the migrants moving out of New England and the Mid-Atlantic states, males predominated over females (often by as much as 6:4 or 2:1), with the dominant age group those who were between 20 and 40 at the end of the decade of their exodus. The age and sex composition of those entering the Northwest, not surprisingly, were markedly similar. The population abandoning the South was noticeably different. From regions of out-migration – the Old South throughout the entire period and the New South after 1840 – came a migrant population in which the ratio of males to females was almost equal, with a far larger percentage of total migrants in the age group 10–20 at the end of the decade of their migration. This suggests the possibility that the South–North movement was dominated by entire family units. To be sure, these contrasts in migrant composition would be lessened if, within the South, death rates were actually much higher for a particular sex or age cohort than estimated for this study. It is hardly credible, however, that such a possibility could restructure the composition of South–North migrants to match closely that of East–West migrants within the North. Whatever the explanation, future studies of ante-bellum development must now address a new set of questions whose answers may reshape our views concerning the economic and demographic experience of Americans.

Last, and probably least from an American perspective, is the curious change in migration patterns from Canada into the northern states. In the period 1840–60, the willingness of Canadians to move south declined sharply. Once again, this numerical trend raises both economic and non-economic questions. Did the Canadian economy surge forward relative to that of the United States during these decades, or did the intensification of sectional strife temper the willingness of Canadians to migrate into states progressively less united? Here too are fresh topics for research.

(c) Negro population 1800-60. Migration flows conform to the expected
pattern: from East to West, mainly in the slave states, reaching a peak during
the cotton boom of the 1830s, and declining thereafter. (This contrasts
sharply with white migration, where movement into the New South reached
a peak two decades earlier.) Two features of the Negro migration are particularly striking. The first is the rough equality between the sexes in that net
migration. Females often slightly outnumbered males, but given imperfections
in the data and the smallness of the differential, it is difficult to say whether
this tendency is significant. The second striking feature is the dominance of
youth. Almost half of those who moved were in the age cohort 10-20 at the
end of the decade of their migration. This suggests that many of the slaves
subjected to forced interregional migration were younger than eighteen, the
traditional age of a 'prime field hand'. A further 25-30 percent were in the
20-30 age cohort. The magnitude of the two figures combined raises the
question of the impact of this forced migration upon the slave family.[13]
Could such preponderance of youth be consistent, for example, with Fogel
and Engerman's claim 'that about 84 percent of the slaves engaged in the westward movement migrated with their owners'?[14] If the age distribution of
migrants was so much more heavily concentrated among the young than was
the Negro population as a whole, does this imply that masters who moved
had a disproportionate share of young before moving? A third possibility is
that the estimate of 84 percent is incorrect, as Richard Sutch has documented
at great length.[15] Whatever the subsequent structure of the debate concerning
the interaction of slave migration and the slave family, the striking demographic fact that all arguments must now encompass is the preponderance of
the young among the migrants.[16]

1.3 From migration estimates to vital statistics and manumissions

The logical connections between migration estimates and vital statistics estimates are at the heart of this study. The standard method for calculating migration, the census survivor technique, requires the estimation of a death rate for
each age cohort for the ten-year period between American census dates. These
different cohort rates can then be combined into a single rate for the entire
population. The result is the first set of national crude death rates[17] for both
the white and Negro population for the 1800-60 period that are based upon
census data and refined international migration estimates.

Two problems complicated this conversion process, one associated with
the youngest age cohort (0-9), and the other necessitated by the need to
correct for the relative underenumeration of children apparent in the census
data. Both problems, although of minor importance for migration estimates,
had to be resolved if national death rates were to be estimated. The attempted

resolution, in turn, touched upon issues that were of the first importance for estimating national birth rates. At the national level, no adequate data exist on annual births for the ante-bellum years. The one possible method for estimating a crude birth rate is to convert those reported by the census in the youngest age cohort into an implied birth rate. This requires (a) the correction of census data for estimated relative underenumeration of children,[18] and (b) the conversion of observed children into implied births using estimates of death rates for children and the rate at which the number of births is changing. (A given distribution of surviving children might be the result of no change in the rate of births and a given death rate, or alternatively the product of a rising rate of births and a higher death rate.)

Estimates of birth and death rates normally lead to estimates of rates of natural increase. This was not the case in this study. Death rate estimates presented here exclude that portion of the population under 10 at the end of a given ten-year census period. The reasons for this exclusion are (a) the census survivor technique produces no death rates for this age cohort, and (b) alternative methods, with their attendant uncertainties, would threaten to undermine such conclusions as might be feasible concerning the secular trend of death rates for the rest of the population. Rates of natural increase were, however, a logical adjunct to our migration estimates. The latter required estimates of net international migration and population in unenumerated territories. With both of these estimates in hand, one can readily calculate the rate of natural increase for the domestic population in any intercensal period. The secular trend in these rates of natural increase can then be compared with secular trends in birth and death rates, both as a consistency check and as a means of detecting the proximate cause for declining rates of a natural increase in the ante-bellum period.

The final topic is manumissions. Until now, no serious attempt has been made to estimate the changing pace at which slaves were freed throughout the ante-bellum era. The stakes are high. Even an approximate estimate as to trend would have widespread implications for studies concerned with social values of the South, with the economics of Negro slavery, or with the economic structure of the region. To estimate the number of slaves freed in any ten-year period requires the following data: (a) the size of the domestic free and slave population at the beginning and end of the period, (b) the numbers of slaves smuggled into America each year, and (c) the death rates for both free and slave populations. The first two were available as the result of our migration estimates. Initially, we assumed equal death rates for free Negroes and slaves, allowing us to use the age cohort death rates produced by the census survivor technique. The resulting peculiarities – notably negative manumissions for certain age cohorts in certain decades – necessitated further refinements described in more detail in section 1.7.

1.4 Death rates

(a) General. Little is known about the level and trend of mortality in the United States in the ante-bellum years.[19] Sporadic studies based upon sources such as plantation records or local bills of mortality leave uncertain the relevance of their conclusions for the country as a whole. The 1850 census did collect information on deaths throughout the nation, but even the superintendent of that census could not take the results seriously. So pervasive and blatant was underreporting that he was forced to conclude that, 'The tables . . . of Deaths . . . can be said to have but very little value.'[20] In a masterful understatement of the problem, Maris Vinovskis concluded that 'The study of mortality rates and trends in the United States before 1860 has been rather unsystematic to date.'[21]

The estimates presented here are therefore among the very few that attempt, for the nation as a whole, to assess both the level and trend of mortality among both whites and Negroes throughout the ante-bellum years. The results are, of course, no better than the data and assumptions from which they spring. The frailties of both will be closely scrutinized in the analysis that follows. The estimates themselves nevertheless constitute a starting point for future demographic work, both in terms of their use of the only national data base available, and in the emphasis given to the intimate connection between data imperfections, attempts to remedy those imperfections, and the strength or weakness of conclusions derived about apparent numerical trends.

(b) White population 1800-60. The inadequacy of estimates of vital rates for this period is apparent in the conflict of opinion over likely secular trends. Thompson and Whelpton, for example, believe that mortality declined throughout the nineteenth century, while the Taeubers suggest little improvement prior to 1850.[22] Both opinions reflect little more than outright guesses. Subject to all the caveats about data imperfections, the most striking feature in all the death rate estimates presented here (male, female, and combined) is the absence of any clear secular trend. Indeed, it would take data errors of an unlikely magnitude to convert this apparent stability into a pronounced trend.[23] The absence of secular trend suggests that forces making for a decline in death rates, such as economic growth, were apparently counteracted by such negative influences as increased urbanization. It is entirely probable that neither influence was particularly strong during the period under review. A second, somewhat more tenuous conclusion is that women enjoyed a consistently lower death rate than men throughout the ante-bellum era. Such a differential is by no means uncommon as a demographic characteristic of a people.

(c) Negro population 1800–60. To begin at the end, both the level and trend of Negro mortality in the ante-bellum period threaten to be unsolvable riddles.[24] The problem is an apparent high degree of inaccuracy in the original census data, or at least in parts of these data. Underenumeration of children appears to be especially widespread. Peculiar cohort patterns also emerge in particular decades. Data for the 1830s, for example, suggest absurdly low death rates for the cohort that was 20–30 at the end of that decade. Death rates for the 10–20 cohort seem atypically high. One obvious possibility is that many of those who actually were 10–20 in 1840 were counted as being 20–30.

While the existence of imperfections is obvious, the best means of adjusting for them is not. The approach of this study, as noted, is to make a minimum of corrections for the most blatant defects and observe the resulting patterns. This procedure is in marked contrast to Eblen's methods,[25] which combine (a) arbitrary graphic smoothing, (b) adjustments based upon life tables, and (c) rather arbitrary corrections for underenumeration. Concerning the last of these, he writes 'The final data sets were raised by nearly ten percent on the assumption that the underenumeration of the black population was roughly fifty percent greater than the average estimated underenumeration of whites.'[26] The estimated underenumeration of whites, in turn, is taken from a study suggesting, on the basis of extremely limited information, that at the end of the nineteenth century white underenumeration averaged just over 6 percent.[27] Why 6 percent should be used to estimate white underenumeration in the ante-bellum years is unclear. Why Negro ante-bellum rates should be 50 percent higher than a rough estimate for whites at the end of the century remains totally obscure.

This single example merely underscores a general difficulty. All efforts to correct Negro census data must, in the last analysis, be arbitrary. Any correction procedure that repeatedly employs smoothing techniques will yield, not surprisingly, a relatively smooth result in terms of demographic tables. But the extent to which the smoothed results are a fabrication of the procedure used remains the crucial issue, and an unresolvable issue.[28]

A better sense of what is at stake may be gained by contrasting Eblen's conclusions with trends suggested by our data. Both studies indicate that Negro death rates were higher than those for whites.[29] There the similarity in conclusions ends. Eblen finds no secular trend prior to 1850, with a noticeable rise in death rates in the subsequent decade.[30] All of our estimates suggest that while 1860 mortality levels closely approximated those at the beginning of the century, Negro mortality deteriorated somewhat in the interim, especially in the 1830s, before improving between 1840 and 1860. Does this pattern reflect the impact of such factors as cholera and intensified migration in the 1830–40 period, or is it merely a result of data imperfections? The answer would have a crucial bearing on the debate concerning whether the lot of the slave changed significantly in the ante-bellum years. If instead Eblen's calculations are viewed as more correct, the implication, in the author's own words, is that 'The new estimates . . . reinforce the assertion that worsening mortality conditions accompanied the generally increased severity of slavery during the decades before the Civil War',[31] or, more correctly, during the last decade before the Civil War. This is partially attributed by Eblen 'to changes in the institution of slavery in the era of Sectionalism'.[32] In short, one set of estimates focuses the historian's attention upon the 1830s, migration and cholera; the other, upon the 1850s and the possibility of an institutional change in slavery that made for a worsening in mortality.

Concerning male–female differentials, our estimates suggest a differential in favor of females in the first thirty years of the century which subsequently disappears. Eblen finds a continuing differential in favor of females among both infants and adults.[33]

Finally, the matter of summary judgments. Eblen's summary bristles with numerical precision.

As can be seen from the foregoing tables, the life expectancy at birth for both sexes fluctuated between 33 and 34 years during the nineteenth century and declined to its lowest points in the decade before the Civil War and during the Civil War and early years of Reconstruction. Most of the fluctuation in life expectancy was due to changes in the infant and early childhood mortality rates. The infant death rates ($1000m_0$) of females ranged from about 222 to 237 per thousand. The male and female life expectancies at age 20 (e_{20}) varied only about six months in the period covered, the male expectation centering on 34.0 years and the female on approximately 34.5 years. . . The new estimates reflect a degree of stability which suggests that there were no extreme annual fluctuations in vital rates. According to the estimates [in this article], the intrinsic death rate (the crude death rate for a stable population) of the black population during the nineteenth century and the expectation of life at birth for both sexes oscillated between only 30 and 31 per thousand and 33 and 34 years, respectively.[34]

Our main conclusion concerning ante-bellum Negro mortality is that summary judgments such as the above are unacceptable. Given the apparent error in the original data base and the arbitrary element in all correction pro-cedures, the final results cannot be proffered as established fact, correct to the second decimal point. At the very least it is venturesome in the extreme to conclude that 'there were no extreme annual fluctuations in vital rates' on the basis of numerical estimates that are the product of repeated and some-what arbitrary smoothing. Such conclusions are hardly to be welcomed by historians whose research on slavery would greatly benefit from mortality estimates for the ante-bellum years. But at the risk of laboring the obvious, the census offers the only relevant national data, and that data base does not seem capable of supporting anything beyond the tentative conclusions ven-tured in this study.

1.5 Birth rates

(a) General. All efforts to estimate birth rates for the ante-bellum years confront the problem, by now only too familiar, that direct estimates of national trends are not possible for want of national data. The only solution is to employ census data on age cohorts to make an indirect estimate using the ratio of young children to women of childbearing age. To convert this ratio into a birth rate estimate requires an estimate of infant mortality, a number that historically has been both volatile and difficult to gauge, particularly in pre-industrial and early industrial societies. The more tentative are infant mortality estimates, the more birth rate estimates for this era must be regarded as rough approximations.[35]

(b) White population 1800-60. Two features of birth rate estimates for the white population are particularly striking, features that no reasonable corrections for probable data imperfections are likely to remove. First, by European standards, American birth rates were exceptionally high at the start of the nineteenth century.[36] Second, thereafter the secular trend was unambiguously down. This secular decline in the birth rate is not without its curious features. Little change apparently occurred between 1800 and 1810, followed by a moderate decline for three decades, a sharp drop in the fourth decade (1840-50), and then a complete reversal of the trend in the 1850s, with birth rates increasing either trivially or sharply depending upon which estimate one regards as most correct. The general pattern of decline accords with the secular trend suggested by all other major estimates for this period.[37] The reversal in the 1850s, whether large or small, directly contradicts the continued decline in that decade implied by the estimates of Yasuba, and Thompson and Whelpton.[38] The ever-present worry is that numerical curiosity may be a fabrication of imperfect data.[39] If this is not the case, demographers have a puzzle: Why should the secular decline in the birth rate of forty years, which was apparently accelerating in the 1840s, suddenly be reversed in the years immediately preceding the Civil War?[40]

(c) Negro population 1800-60. Attempts to estimate birth rates for the Negro population are repeatedly imperiled by imperfections in age cohort data and the uncertainty over likely infant mortality. The presumed degree of accuracy in all vital statistics estimates is, therefore, considerably less than that for the white population.

The estimates of this study suggest no clear trend prior to 1840. The average for the 1800-10 period is roughly equivalent to the crude birth rate estimated for 1840. Thereafter all estimates indicate a decline of roughly 15 percent in the next two decades, most of it occurring in the 1840s. Eblen also finds that 'a general decline in fertility set in between 1830 and 1840',[41] but the magnitude of the decline – from 53.1 per 1,000 in the 1830s to 51.3 in the 1850s – in percentage terms is less than a third of that suggested by our estimates. Eblen's crude birth rate calculations are simply the difference between a rate of natural increase (calculated from his smoothed population series on the assumption of no net slave imports) and a crude death rate (which is also the product of repeated smoothing adjustments). One reason for the more moderate decline in Eblen's crude birth rate estimate is the rise in his estimated death rate in the late ante-bellum period, a numerical trend questioned in the previous section.

Once again the questions suggested by the numbers differ depending upon which estimation techniques are viewed as more appropriate. In this case, the choice is between (a) a nearly trivial decline in the Negro crude birth rate in the ante-bellum years (less than 4 percent) and (b) a marked decline (roughly 15 percent), with much of the latter occurring in the 1840s. Why should Negro birth rates, particularly slave birth rates, fall sharply in the two decades before John Brown's raid? As documented below, demographers and historians have not been able to advance a convincing explanation.

Whatever the answer, one is hard pressed to accept Eblen's summary judgment that 'The decline in black fertility roughly paralleled the decline in white fertility during the nineteenth century.'[42] Every major estimate of the white crude birth rate, including all of the estimates of this study, suggests that secular decline began well before 1840.[43] In terms of Negro and white numerical trends, the estimates of this study suggest a parallel and a contrast that have no counterpart in Eblen's numbers. The decade of sharpest decline in the crude birth rate for both races during this period was the same: the 1840s. Thereafter, the white birth rate rose (according to some estimates, quite sharply), while that of the Negro population did not. According to all of our estimates, the Negro birth rate declined slightly in the 1850s. The reasons for this divergent trend in birth rates is not clear. Part of the explanation may be that the white population, because it was more concentrated in urban centers, suffered higher infant mortality from the epidemics that preceded the taking of the 1850 census.[44] The higher were actual death rates, the more the observed lower ratio of children to women of childbearing ages should be attributed to children dying rather than to fewer births. Reasonable allowances for distortions from this factor, however, would not remove the dominant secular contrast between the races: compared to the Negro crude birth rate, that of the white population began to decline much sooner and fell much further in the 1800–60 period.

1.6 Rates of natural increase

(a) White population 1800–60. The answer to one demographic question is unambiguous. The main reason for the rapid expansion in the American white population between that nation's two civil wars was the high rate of natural increase of the domestic population. If no immigration had occurred in the period 1800 to 1850, for example, our estimates suggest that the total population would have been almost 25 percent smaller than it actually was at mid-century. Also relatively unambiguous is the proximate cause of this exceptional growth: a birth rate which, by European standards, was high at the beginning of the century, fell thereafter, and thereby lowered the rate of natural increase. Whether American death rates were also low by European standards remains unclear. The evidence cited previously does suggest that American death rates remained relatively stable throughout the ante-bellum years. This pattern of falling birth rates and comparatively stable death rates resulted in a declining rate of natural increase. International migration to America, however, tended to rise during this period. So closely matched were these two offsetting forces that the remarkable result was a nearly constant decade-by-decade growth rate of the total population throughout the ante-bellum period.

(b) Negro population 1800-60. Data for the Negro population raise a puzzle that has yet to be solved by demographers and historians. The observed rate of increase of the population seems to fall, particularly after 1840. In theory, this decline might reflect a stable rate of natural increase and falling imports; that is, a decline in slave smuggling. Available evidence, however, does not support such a marked change in illegal importations. The inescapable conclusion is that the rate of natural increase of the American Negro population was declining in the decades immediately preceding the Civil War. The question is why.

Even the issue of proximate causes remains obscure. Eblen's data, for example, suggest almost perfect stability in both birth and death rates until 1840. Thereafter, according to his estimates, birth rates fell slightly for two decades; death rates were stable for one (the 1840s) and rose for one (the 1850s).[45] Our own calculations suggest a different pattern. By judiciously choosing among the various estimates presented below, one could argue (a) that death rates rose slightly between 1800 and 1840 (especially in the 1830s) and then declined thereafter, reaching by 1860 levels that were roughly similar to those of 1800, (b) that the birth rate remained stable until 1820, then rose sharply for one decade (the 1830s), and declined sharply for two (1840-60), and (c) that the overall decline in the birth rate between 1800 and 1860 explains the observed decline in the rate of natural increase during the same time period. Both explanations thus focus on declining birth rates, although Eblen gives a secondary emphasis to rising death rates in the 1850s.

Two considerations, however, make a facile explanation emphasizing declining birth rates somewhat suspect. The first is that no convincing historical evidence has yet been assembled that would explain why the Negro birth rate should have declined over this period. The second concerns the imperfections in the data base, and the susceptibility of all estimates to correction procedures used and assumptions made concerning such variables as slave smuggling. The historian therefore cannot rule out the possibility that much of the observed decline in population growth may have been the result of rising death rates, or, somewhat less plausibly, changing imperfections in the data.

1.7 Manumissions

The level and trend of manumissions are topics of the first importance in the history of the changing status of the American Negro in the ante-bellum years. Virtually no serious effort has been made to estimate either level or trend prior to this study. Two numbers, however, are widely cited in the literature. According to the census of 1860, 1,500 slaves were liberated in 1850 and 3,000 in 1860, the implication being that manumissions were on the rise immediately before the Civil War.[46] A sharp increase in the willingness of southerners to free their slaves at this time hardly seems probable. A modified trend and alternative explanation are suggested below.

Estimates of manumissions must be approached with particular caution. The most striking evidence of data imperfections is the presence of negative manumissions in our estimates, a result that remained for certain age cohorts in certain periods despite efforts to remove these negative signs by various correction procedures that seemed defensible. Devising a mechanical procedure to remove negative numbers is a trivial assignment. None of the possibilities that would remove *all* negative numbers seemed defensible to us. Consistent with the general approach of this study, we pursued only the minimum corrections that did seem defensible and observed the resulting patterns.

Across almost all years and all estimates, female manumissions had a slight edge over those for males. What is perhaps striking is that this edge was so slight. Certainly no strong numerical support is given to the assertion that pervasive miscegenation resulted in a widespread freeing of females. Also striking is the diffusion of manumissions through all age cohorts in the 1800–40 period. Part of the explanation is the freeing in northern states in response to laws outlawing slavery. In the 1830s, however, when most northern laws had long since had their effect,[47] this diffusion remains. The estimates do suggest a somewhat higher manumission rate for those in the upper age cohorts, giving some support – albeit mild support – to the old abolitionist charge of a southern bias for freeing the aged and the infirm. Finally, on the matter of secular trend, the rate of manumissions appears to decline markedly after 1840. Part of the explanation concerns the operation of northern laws to 1840, as noted previously. The data are also consistent with the hypothesis that the southern propensity to free those in bondage declined noticeably as sectionalism intensified along with pro-slavery arguments. All of our estimates suggest that manumission levels of the 1850s were *slightly* higher than those for the 1840s, but this trivial increase, even if not the product of data imperfections, in no way confirms the near doubling of levels implied by 1860 census data described at the start of this section. Should numerical trend accurately reflect historical reality, the explanation is just as likely to be improved efficiency in the Underground Railroad as a modification of southern views on the merits of manumissions.

One anomaly in the early years of the century should be noted. All estimates suggest that manumissions fell off sharply between 1810 and 1820 relative to levels achieved in the previous and subsequent decades. This finding is partly to be explained by the negative manumission estimate in the youngest age cohort, suggesting a miscount of children. (The alternative hypothesis of widespread re-enslaving is hardly credible.) The decline in these years is also evident in other age cohorts, however, suggesting that something was reducing the willingness of Americans to free slaves. Possible explanations include uncertainties associated with the War of 1812 and/or upheavals in the South connected with the dispute over Florida. Certainly no obvious modifications of the data would remove this numerical down-turn in the second decade of the nineteenth century.[48]

1.8 Major findings in review

(a) The approach

We are struck by how our confidence varies across the different numerical assertions ventured above. At best, major data errors appear unlikely, numerical cross-checking confirms initial findings, and these findings are consistent with other historical evidence. At worst, the basic data are obviously flawed (negative death rates are perhaps the most glaring example), numerical cross-checking is not possible, and historical evidence provides no clear guide to choosing among several possible assumptions, even though final numerical results vary significantly, depending upon which assumption is chosen.

To grapple with this problem, we have adopted the following procedure. Each of the major numerical findings will have appended to it one of three letters: H (high), M (medium), or L (low). These indicate our degree of confidence in the results. If, in our judgment, the probable range of error in the underlying calculations is relatively narrow, trend statements based upon those calculations can be made with a high degree of confidence. The wider the probable range of data error becomes, of course, the less confidence one has in trend statements based upon those data.

Birth rate data for the white population illustrate the problem and the approach. The drop in the estimated birth rate is pronounced, cross-checks using estimates of rates of natural increase and death rates are consistent with a pronounced drop in the birth rate, and other historical evidence can be marshaled to suggest why the white birth rate might have declined at this time. Accordingly, we assign this trend statement the letter (H). At the opposite extreme are trend statements about manumissions. The basic data apparently have major flaws (as indicated, for example, by negative manumission estimates for certain age cohorts at certain periods), numerical cross-checks are not available, and the historical evidence provides little guide as to which of several assumptions should be used to make manumission estimates. Accordingly, we assign to most of these trend statements the letter (L). The range of probable error in the underlying data is high, which raises the possibility that the 'true' manumission number for, say, 1840 might be well below our 1840 estimate, and the 'true' number for 1860 might be well above our 1860 estimate. In that case, the decline in manumissions suggested by our estimates might not be confirmed by actual events. Notice, however, that a far greater error in our data would be required if the 'true' trend in manumissions were to be the rough doubling suggested by the data in the 1860 census.

(b) The findings: white population

(i) *Migration.* Two major movements dominate the ebb and flow of population within this period. The first, by far the more pronounced of the two, was from East to West (H). The region of greatest loss in the East was the Mid-Atlantic (H). The region of greatest gain in the West was the Northwest, which towered over all other western areas in terms of total net in-migration (H). This influx into the Northwest was dominated by young adults, with males far more in evidence than females (H). The secondary flow was from South to North (H). Its composition differed sharply from the East–West flow, with young children more in evidence, and the ratio of males to females far more equal (H). A third trend of minor consequence for Americans but of major consequence for Canadians was the sharp drop after 1840 in overland migration into the United States from Upper and Lower Canada (H).

(ii) *Death rate.* The data suggest the absence of any clear secular trend (H) and the presence of a lower death rate for females than for males (M).

(iii) *Birth rate.* American birth rates began the century far above European rates (H) and thereafter declined sharply (H). Much of that decline appears to be centered in the period 1810–50 (H), with some signs that decline was momentarily halted or reversed in the decade 1850–60 (M).

(iv) *Rate of natural increase.* The principal reason for the exceptionally rapid expansion of the American population during this period was not international migration but the high rate of natural increase of the local population (H). International migration was a factor of secondary importance, contributing roughly one quarter of the total population increase in the first half-century (H). The main proximate explanation for the American rate of natural increase being so high relative to that of Europe was its high birth rate (H). There is no clear evidence that American death rates were, by European standards, exceptionally low.

(c) The findings: Negro population

(i) *Migration*. The dominant movement was from the Old South to the New South (H), a movement that peaked in the 1830s and declined thereafter (H). The migrating population was characterized by a dominance of youth (that is, those in the age cohort 10–20 at the end of the decade of their migration) (H), and rough equality between the sexes (H).

(ii) *Death rate*. The apparent defects in the original age cohort data (as evidenced, for example, by the negative death rate estimates implied by the uncorrected data) suggest that most of the inferences based upon these data must be tenuous in the extreme. The most defensible conclusion is that Negro death rates tended to be higher than those of the white population (H). As for secular trend, the 1860 Negro death rate appears to be roughly equivalent to what it was in 1800, with the intervening period marked by a slight rise for four decades, particularly in the 1830s, followed by a slight decline for two decades (L). For the first 30 years, there appears to be a small differential in the death rates between the sexes in favor of females that subsequently disappeared (L).

(iii) *Birth rate*. Here, too, apparent defects in the basic data series make generalizing about levels and trends a precarious venture. What appears to be fairly certain is that the Negro birth rate did not begin to match the secular decline in the white birth rate (H). The secular trend of the Negro birth rate seems to be one of little change to 1840, followed by moderate decline to 1860 (L).

(iv) *Rate of natural increase*. All reasonable estimates of international slave smuggling into the United States imply a decline in the rate of natural increase of the American Negro population in the ante-bellum period, particularly after 1840 (H). This decline appears to be more a function of a falling birth rate than a rising death rate (M).

(v) *Manumissions*. Again, the frailties of the original data make extreme caution advisable. What appears to be relatively certain is that manumissions did not rise sharply in the 1850s (M), contrary to what might be inferred from the data released in the 1860 census. The data also suggest that manumissions were reasonably well diffused through all age cohorts, although somewhat biased towards upper age cohorts, and roughly similar for males and females (L). The apparent secular trend includes a slump in the decade 1810–20, recovery for two decades, and then decline after 1840 (L).

2

Migration model: closed population

2.1 The model

The technique used to estimate *net* migration is the census survivor method outlined in the United Nations manual on demographic procedures.[49] In summary form, for a closed population this technique requires only population data and a single assumption. The data must be available for each region, by desirable age cohort, at the time of the census. The assumption is that the death rate, by age group, is constant across all regions.[50] Census data can then be used to calculate intercensal survival rates: the percentage of the total population of a given age, or age grouping, that survived to the next census. A survival rate for a particular age group can then be combined with the total population within a region who are within the age group in question to estimate the expected number of survivors at the time of the next census. The difference between the actual number of people enumerated in the next census and the expected number of survivors is the estimate of the net number of migrants in a particular age group who entered the region in question and survived until the next census. (If the net migration number is negative, it records the net number of individuals who would have survived to the next census who left the region.)

The technique is perhaps most easily explained using mathematical notation. Assume that the census was collected every ten years beginning in 1800, and that migration estimates are to be calculated for the six regions of Map 1. Let

x = the index of single-year age cohorts,

i = the index of regions[51],

j = the index of decades: e.g. [3] = 1830–40,

$P_x[t]$ = individuals of age x in year t,

$p_{i,x}[t]$ = individuals of age x in region i in year t,

20

$M_{i,x}[j]$ = net migrants to region i in decade j who survive and are of age x in the next census year,

$S_x[j]$ = survivor ratio for those of age x during the decade j.

The number of people of age x in region i who migrated during decade j is then given by

$$M_{i,x+10}[j] - p_{i,x+10}[t \mid 10] \quad S_x \, p_{l,x}[t], \tag{1}$$

where $t = 1800 + 10_j$

The survivor ratio for an intercensal period of n years for those who are x years of age at time t is simply the number of people of age $x+n$ at time $t+n$ (in a closed population); i.e., the number of survivors, divided by the number of people of age x at time t. Thus, equation (1) can be rewritten as

$$M_{i,x+10}[j] = p_{i,x+10}[t+10] - \frac{P_{x+10}[t+10]}{P_x[t]} \, p_{i,x}[t]. \tag{2}$$

This estimation procedure can also be translated into one employing age-specific death rates. Let

$D_x[j]$ = the decade death rate for those of age x over decade j.

Then the same estimate of net migration can be rewritten as

$$M_{i,x+10}[j] = p_{i,x+10}[t+10] - (1 - D_x[j])p_{i,x}[t]. \tag{3}$$

The latter will be found to be more useful in subsequent analysis.

This study is concerned with the movement of six age groupings of the population: 0-9, 10-19, 20-29, 30-39, 40-49, and 50 and older. Representing

K = the index (in Roman numerals) of these age cohorts; i.e., III = those aged 30-39,

the x subscript in equations (1), (2), and (3) can be replaced by a K subscript to obtain an equation that expresses the number of migrants of each age cohort; that is,

$$M_{i,K+1}[j] = p_{i,K+1}[t+10] - (1 - D_K[j])p_{i,K}[t]. \tag{3a}$$

If the United States population during the period 1800-60 had been closed, equation (3a) could be used to calculate the net movement of people among the six regions noted. All that would be required would be accurate population totals, by region, by race, by sex, and by age cohort. Unfortunately, most of the requisite data are either unavailable, or available in a form that must be modified before they can be used. To describe the attempts made to overcome these deficiencies is the task of sections 2.2 through 2.8.

2.2 Summary of imperfections in data available for migration model (closed population)

Early census enumeration was far from perfect, especially in the years prior to 1860.[52] A revised series correcting many of the initial errors was published in the census of 1870.[53] These estimates were in turn slightly modified, and the results published in *Negro Population in the United States, 1790-1915.*[54] Unfortunately, these improved series do not include age-specific data. As a result, the major source of age-specific population data is the original census records.

Three imperfections in this source are particularly worrisome. Under-reporting is the most obvious – pervasive in influence but quantitatively difficult to estimate.[55] Also complicating demographic analysis are the changes in age groupings that occurred in successive decades of early census enumeration. Finally, the persistence of a frontier shifting ever westward creates a special difficulty for migration studies of the period. As of 1800 the census enumeration covered the following geographic territory:

Maine, New Hampshire, Vermont, Massachusetts, Rhode Island, Connecticut, New York, New Jersey, Pennsylvania, Delaware, District of Columbia, Maryland, Virginia, West Virginia, North Carolina, South Carolina, Georgia, Kentucky, Tennessee, and, first enumerated in 1800, Ohio, Indiana, Illinois, Michigan, Wisconsin, and the south central parts of Alabama and Mississippi.[56]

Additions by decade were as follows:[57]

1810   The area now constituting Arkansas, the northern parts of Mississippi and Alabama, and all but the southwestern part of Louisiana and the northwestern part of Missouri.
1820   The extreme southern parts of Alabama and Mississippi, and the southwestern part of Louisiana. Florida was purchased in 1819, but was not enumerated in 1820.
1830   Florida.
1840   Iowa, northwestern Missouri, and northeastern Minnesota.
1850   Texas, Utah, California, that part of New Mexico Territory now constituting the State of New Mexico with the exception of a small portion of the Gadsden Purchase of 1853, and that part of the Territory of Oregon now constituting the states of Oregon and Washington.
1860   Dakota Territory, the remainder of Minnesota, Nebraska, Kansas, Colorado, Nevada, that part of Washington Territory now constituting Idaho and those portions of Montana and Wyoming lying west of the Rocky Mountains, that part of New Mexico Territory now consti-tuting the state of Arizona, and that part of the Gadsden Purchase which now forms the southwestern part of New Mexico.

What follows is a description, first for the white population and then for the Negro population, of attempts made to correct for (1) inconsistency in the recording of age-specific data, (2) the existence of unenumerated territories, and (3) variations in the relative underenumeration of different census years. In terms of the notation used previously, the goal is to adjust available census data to yield estimates of

$$P_K[j] \text{ for all } K \text{ and all } j;$$

that is, to yield decade estimates of the total population of the United States for ten-year age cohorts, and with the aid of these figures to derive estimates of

$$p_{i,K}[j] \text{ for all } i, K, j;$$

that is, decade estimates of the total population, by ten-year age cohorts, for each of the six regions of Map 1.

2.3 Adjusting white population data to produce uniform age categories

The age divisions used in census enumeration are as follows:

Year	Age categories for white population
1800	0–9, 10–15, 16–25, 26–44, 45+
1810	0–9, 10–15, 16–25, 26–44, 45+
1820	0–9, 10–15, 16–25, 26–44, 45+
1830	0–4, 5–9, 10–14, 15–19, 20–29, 30–39, 40–49, 50–59, 60–69, 70–79, 80–89, 90–99, 100+
1840	0–4, 5–9, 10–14, 15–19, 20–29, 30–39, 40–49, 50–59, 60–69, 70–79, 80–89, 90–99, 100+
1850	0, 1–4, 5–9, 10–14, 15–19, 20–29, 30–39, 40–49, 50–59, 60–69, 70–79, 80–89, 90–99, 100+
1860	0, 1–4, 5–9, 10–14, 15–19, 20–29, 30–39, 40–49, 50–59, 60–69, 70–79, 80–89, 90–99, 100+

For purposes of this study, these data had to be regrouped into six divisions: 0-9, 10-19, 20-29, 30-39, 40-49, 50 and older. Some of the published data are already in this form or are readily combined to correspond with these divisions. For the remainder, a 'polygon' adjustment procedure was used, so named because the simple geometry of a polygon constitutes the core of the estimation technique.

The method is perhaps best described by an example. Consider the age groupings used in the census of 1800: 0-9, 10-15, 16-25, 26-45, 45 and older. The objective is to transform recorded census data into the six age categories noted (0-9, 10-19, 20-29, 30-39, 40-49, 50 and older). The first step is to calculate the percentage of the total census represented by each recorded group; for example, the percentage in 1800 that was in the age group 16-25. If one could assume that the number of people in each age grouping were evenly distributed over the ages in the group, then the age structure data of

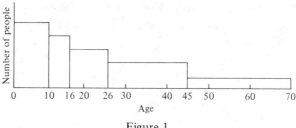

Figure 1

the 1800 population could be portrayed as illustrated in Figure 1. The area of each rectangle represents the total number of people recorded for that particular age grouping.

The obvious defect in such a representation is the discontinuities that occur at each of the age cohort divisions. The next step is to revise the graphic formulation to allow for a more uniform reduction in the size of each age cohort as the recorded age of the population increases. This transformation could be effected if one could calculate r_i, the growth rate of the size of successive yearly ages in age grouping i, so that (1) the number of people indicated at each age was unique and (2) the percentage of the population represented by each age cohort remained unchanged. Graphically, this amounts to transforming Figure 1 into Figure 2. The area of any given polygon in Figure 2 must be equal to the area of the corresponding rec-

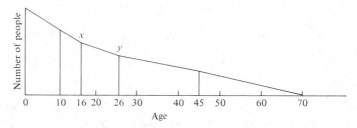

Figure 2

tangle in Figure 1. The slope of each of the age distributions in Figure 2 must equal the appropriate r_i. Thus, for example, the slope of the line from x to y represents the rate of change of the size of successive yearly ages from the age of 16 to the age of 26.

The remaining step is to determine r_i. This must be preceded by an arbitrary decision concerning the oldest age to enter the calculations, this being the extreme tip of the end triangle. The age chosen for this purpose was the conventional one of three score and ten. The rest of the procedure involves calculating (1) the area of each of the polygons of Figure 2, (2) the height of each vertical line in that figure, and finally (3) the value of each r_i. This requires solving a set of equations sequentially. Perpendicular lines are then drawn at each division desired but not used in the original enumeration (i.e., at 20, 30, 40, and 50); the area of each polygon so formed is calculated; and finally, the areas of different polygons are added together to achieve the age grouping desired. To determine the number of people ages 20–29, for example, one would sum areas A and B of Figure 3.

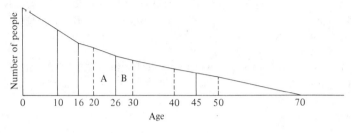

Figure 3

2.4 Adjusting white population data for unenumerated territories

The problems for census enumeration of a frontier expanding ever westward were outlined previously. The presumption is that migration calculations are improved by some attempt (rather than no attempt) to estimate the population in unenumerated territories, however crude that estimation procedure may be. Given the small size of population in question relative to that within the region as a whole, errors of any reasonable dimension should have a trivial effect on the final demographic calculations presented below.

Florida provides a case in point. Purchased in 1819, the state was not enumerated until 1830, at which time 18,385 white residents were reported. Not all 18,385 were net additions to the United States population. Some undoubtedly were former residents of other American states who migrated to Florida in the decade 1820/1830. The problem was to estimate the white population at each census date (1800, 1810, and 1820) prior to official enumeration. The general estimation procedure used was to assume that population growth in unenumerated territories was proportional to that of adjacent enumerated territories in the same time period. In the case of Florida, population growth was assumed to be proportional to that of the combined populations of Georgia and Alabama. That is, if

F_2 = Florida white population in 1820
F_3 = Florida white population in 1830
A_2 = Alabama white population in 1820
A_3 = Alabama white population in 1830
G_2 = Georgia white population in 1820
G_3 = Georgia white population in 1830,

then

$$F_2 = F_3 \frac{G_2 + A_2}{G_3 + A_3}. \tag{4}$$

Assumptions used for other enumerated territories are given in the notes to Table A-2.[58]

This type of calculation yielded an estimate of total population only. Age- and sex-specific data were derived by assuming that the unenumerated territory had the same age and sex distributions as the state reported when it was first enumerated. In the case of Florida, for example, it was assumed that the sex ratio of the entire white population in 1800, 1810, and 1820 was the same as that revealed when the state was first enumerated in 1830; namely, 56 percent male.

2.5 Adjusting white population data for variations in the relative underenumeration of census years

As noted above, underreporting of the population was undoubtedly a pervasive phenomenon, particularly in the early years of census taking. Fortunately, for most demographic estimates, including birth and death rates and migration patterns, what matters is not the absolute level of underreporting, but rather the underreporting of one census relative to another. If the percentage error remains constant over time, birth and death rates will remain unchanged, while migration figures will be understated by the same percentage as is the census as a whole.

The problem is therefore to adjust population totals in each census year to the same relative level. This was accomplished by introducing a relative underenumeration factor, $U[t]$, that describes the completeness of the census in year t relative to the census in the year $t+10$. All of the population data of the census in year t were then multiplied by the factor $(1+U[t])$.

In the period 1800 to 1860, there is no evidence to suggest that $U[t]$ should be negative; that is, that a later census was significantly worse than its predecessor. The only evidence that militated strongly in favor of a positive adjustment concerns the census of 1820. In 1828 John Quincy Adams noted the defects of beginning the census collection as of August 4 and continuing it for only six months. He advocated a more extensive period beginning in the spring, a suggestion subsequently incorporated into the 1830 census.[59] This change in procedure suggests that the 1820 census was relatively less accurate than that of 1830. How inaccurate it was in relative terms can only be guessed. The decision was made to make

$U[1820] = 0.005,$

a change that would seem to be adequate for an across-the-board adjustment pending further evidence.[60]

2.6 Adjusting Negro population data to produce uniform age categories

No data are available on the age or sex distribution of the Negro population prior to 1820. Thereafter the initial age categories chosen were somewhat broader than those used for the white population. Available census information can be summarized as follows:

Year	Age categories for Negro population
1800	No age distinctions
1810	No age distinctions
1820	0–13, 14–25, 26–44, 45+
1830	0–9, 10–23, 24–35, 35–54, 55+
1840	0–9, 10–23, 24–35, 36–54, 55+
1850	0, 1–4, 5–9, 10–14, 15–19, 20–29, 30–39, 40–49, 50–59, 60–69, 70–79, 80–89, 90–99, 100+
1860	0, 1–4, 5–9, 10–14, 15–19, 20–29, 30–39, 40–49, 50–59, 60–69, 70–79, 80–89, 90–99, 100+

The polygon method described previously can be used to convert age categories to those desired provided the census recorded some age data. The absence of age and sex information for the first two decades presents a major hurdle that can only be overcome by an assumption; in this case, the assumption that the regional age and sex distributions as first recorded for the free and slave population in 1820 could reasonably be applied to the years 1800 and 1810. Thus, for example, the age distribution of free male Negroes in the New England region was assumed to be the same in 1800, 1810 and 1820. The regional totals assumed for the 1800 and 1810 free and slave Negro populations were prepared from data published in *Negro Population in the United States, 1790–1915*, and estimates of the free and slave Negro populations of unenumerated territories.

2.7 Adjusting Negro population data for unenumerated territories

The size of the Negro population in unenumerated territories was determined by a procedure similar to that used for the white population. Specific assumptions used are summarized in the notes to Table B-4. Complicating the analysis is the necessity of dividing these estimates into slave and free populations. The procedure used was to determine the proportion of free and enslaved Negroes in each territory's total Negro population when it was first

enumerated. These proportions were then applied to the estimates of the
territory's Negro population when unenumerated to obtain free and slave
Negro population estimates. Similarly, age- and sex-specific data were derived
by applying the age and sex distribution of the free and slave Negro population
of the territory when it was first enumerated to the estimates of the free and
slave Negro populations in the territory when unenumerated.

2.8 Adjusting Negro population data for variations in the relative underenumeration of census years

No evidence could be found to support the hypothesis that the relative
underenumeration between successive censuses was significantly different
for the Negro and white populations.[61] The assumptions noted previously
were therefore used; that is, for all years other than 1820, $U[t] = 0$; for 1820,
$U[1820] = 0.005$.

One minor exception to these rules should be noted. The census of 1840
recorded 25,502 'free people of color' in Louisiana. In 1850 the count was
17,462. Subsequent historians, while noting the puzzle of the implied disappearance, have offered little by way of explanation.[62] The superintendent
of the 1850 census was also puzzled.

The decrease in the free colored persons of Louisiana . . . seems to be chiefly
in New Orleans, where the decline has been 9,321 since 1840 . . . All of this
is very extraordinary, and leads to the conviction that errors were committed
in one or the other period, (almost certainly the first) or that free mulattoes
have been passing into the white column, which is not shown, however, in the
increase of the whites in that municipality since 1840. The colored persons
who are known to have left the city will not account for this decline . . . not-
withstanding the natural increase.[63]

In 1853, the Louisiana census recorded 22,873 free Negroes in the state.[64]
The absence of an explanation for the severe decline implied by the 1850
data[65] and the presence of a higher number in 1853 suggested that the most
sensible procedure was to assume that the latter was correct. The 1850
population was therefore estimated by interpolation.

If

L_t = the size of the free Negro population of Louisiana in year t,

then one can determine a rate of increase, r, for the free Negro population of
the state such that

$$L_{1840}(1 + r)^{13} = L_{1853}. \tag{5}$$

This value of r can then be used to estimate the 1850 free Negro population
in Louisiana as

$$L_{1850} = L_{1840}(1 + r)^{10}.$$ (6)

This is the Louisiana figure used in all calculations requiring the 1850 free Negro population of the New South.

3

Migration model: adjustments for international migration

3.1 Modification of the model

The controlling objective, to review, is to estimate the net number of people of each sex, race, and age cohort who migrated into each region of Map 1 during each of the six decades in the period 1800 to 1860. The procedure described above is obviously flawed by its failure to correct for the effects of international migration. The purpose of this section is to outline the necessary modifications in the model. The following five sections then document data imperfections and attempts to overcome those imperfections.

The net number of migrants (who survive to the end of the decade) was estimated by the difference between the actual population at the end of the decade (as recorded by the census) and the estimated population, obtained by applying a survivor ratio to the recorded population at the beginning of the decade. In terms of notation previously defined[66]

$$M_{i,K+1}[j] = p_{i,K+1}[t+10] - \frac{p_{K+1}[t+10]}{P_K[t]} p_{i,K}[t] \tag{7}$$

or, using ten-year death rates,

$$M_{i,K+1}[j] = p_{i,K+1}[t+10] - (1-D_K[j]) p_{i,K}[t] \tag{8}$$

where $t = 1800 + 10j$.

Correcting these procedures for the arrival of international migrants obviously requires additional information on how many arrived and where they settled. A more difficult problem is to estimate the number who survived until the next census. This cannot be calculated by a direct application of a ten-year death rate, because most immigrants were not present during all ten years of the intercensal period in which they arrived. One possible solution is to transform the original immigration data into an equivalent number of immigrants entering exactly at the beginning of the decade. If one then assumes that immigrants had the same ten-year death rate as the domestic population, the computed ten-year death rate described previously[67] can then be applied to this revised immigration figure to obtain an estimate of the number of new immigrants who died before the next census.

An example may help to clarify the procedure used. Let

$f[j]$ = the average portion of decade j that new immigrants were within the country.

The number of immigrants entering the United States during decade j are then multiplied by this fraction. Assume that x immigrants arrive in decade j. Suppose further that one half of these enter on January 1 of the first year of the decade, and one half enter on December 31 of the last year of the decade. Then

$$f[j] = \tfrac{1}{2} \times 1 + \tfrac{1}{2} \times 0 = \tfrac{1}{2};$$

or the decade immigration pattern is equivalent to $(\tfrac{1}{2}x)$ people entering at the beginning of the decade.

To incorporate this procedure into the migration formula cited above will required some additional notation. Let

$H_K[j]$ = immigrants in decade j who will (if they do not die) join $P_K[j]$ of the most recent census year to make up members of $P_{K+1}[j+1]$ in the next census year,

$v_i[j]$ = the fraction of the immigrants in decade j who first settle in region i.

The number of new immigrants who join age cohort K in decade j and first settle in region i is then given by

$$H_K[j]\,v_i[j]. \tag{9}$$

Recall that

$f[j]$ = the average portion of decade j that an immigrant who arrived in decade j was in the country.

If one assumes that these immigrants have the same age-specific death rates as the domestic population, then the number of these new immigrants who survive the decade is given by

$$H_K[j]\,v_i[j] - H_K[j]\,v_i[j]\,f[j]\,D_K[j]. \tag{10}$$

Equation (10) can then be incorporated into the earlier migration model to obtain an improved model for estimating internal migration. The net number of migrants into region i in decade j is now given by

$$M_{i,K+1}[j] = p_{i,K+1}[t+10] - (1-D_K[j])p_{i,K}[t] + H_K[j]\,v_i[j]$$

$$- H_K[j]\,v_i[j]\,f[j]\,D_K[j]. \tag{11}$$

This model does not determine the exact number of people who migrated during the decade. It only estimates the net number of migrants who were alive at the end of the decade. For revealing basic migration patterns, however, the resulting calculations are eminently satisfactory for most purposes.

The variable $f[j]$ was not directly observable. The method of least squares was therefore used to determine the straight line that gave the closest fit to the actual yearly immigration data when those data were available.[68] Unfortunately, annual immigration data were often not collected, and those that were require further refinement for the purposes of this model. The remaining task is to describe available sources, modifications made in recorded data and estimation procedures used for those years for which no immigration data were recorded.

3.2 Available immigration data: white population - a summary

Reliable data on white immigration into the United States first became available for the years subsequent to 1819. Under the terms of an act passed in that year, the captains of incoming vessels were required to report to the local customs officer the age, sex, and occupation of all passengers on board plus 'the country to which they severally belonged'.[69] All estimates of immigration for the period before 1820 are purely conjectural.[70] Data simply were not collected at the official level.[71] Subsequent discussion is therefore divided into the two periods 1800–19 and 1820–60. The latter period is discussed first for reasons that will be apparent later on.

3.3 Immigration data: white population 1820–60

Although data on white immigration into the United States are available for the years 1820–60, the information is far from perfect. There was underreporting at Atlantic and Gulf ports where data were collected, immigrants arriving overland from Canada or Mexico were not counted at all,[72] and those arriving at Pacific ports were counted only after 1848.[73] Two of these omissions do not appear to have been critical. On the subject of the accuracy of the counts made, the Census of 1860 observed that 'There are some deficiencies, perhaps, in the returns of the first ten or twelve years, but the subsequent reports are considered reliable'.[74] The failure to include direct immigration into Pacific ports would also seem of little consequence in the first half of the nineteenth century. Oregon territory attracted few international migrants throughout this period,[75] and the precipitous rush for Californian gold only pre-dates the counting at Pacific ports by one year. The importance of overland immigration from Canada remains a subject of dispute. Potter, for example, emphasizes that homeward-bound Quebec timber ships carried many would-be immigrants to America,[76] but how many of these journeyed from Quebec to the promised land by overland routes is not clear.[77] (Those who transferred at New Brunswick or Nova Scotia to vessels bound for New England ports would have been included in American immigration reports.[78])

The above omissions tended to produce a final count of immigrants that was too low. These were at least partially offset by the inclusion in official counts of (a) transient aliens bound for territories outside the United States, and (b) second passages by 'merchants, factors, and visitors who go and come repeatedly, and are thus enumerated twice or more in the returns'.[79] Data on 'second passages' appear to become available only in the latter part of the 1850s, accounting for 2.9 percent of total alien arrivals between 1855 and 1860.[80] For the period 1856-60, temporary alien visitors constituted 1.5 percent of total alien passenger arrivals.[81] In the three decades prior to 1850, this group has been 'officially estimated' at 2 percent of total alien arrivals.[82]

The major difficulty is to combine all of the above information with an estimate of the number of Americans emigrating from their homeland to derive an estimate of net immigration into the United States for the period 1820 to 1860. What is the appropriate inflation or deflation of official immigration statistics necessary to derive an approximation for the net inflow of migrants into America from abroad? Almost every writer on the subject has a different answer. Rossiter suspects that emigration was negligible,[83] Ward would deflate official statistics by $1\frac{2}{3}$ percent,[84] and the Taeubers assert that 'It is commonly assumed that departures of aliens were perhaps 10 or 15 percent as numerous as alien arrivals in the decades from 1820 to 1870'.[85] The major estimates in support of this last contention appear to be two in number. The first of these is by Willcox.[86] Beginning with the assumption that the ratio of net to gross immigration was 65 percent for the decade 1891-1900, he then adds the further assumption 'that for each decade of the nineteenth century it was 5 percent above what it was in the next later decade'.[87] The implied deflations of official statistics for our period are as follows: 1821-30, 0 percent; 1831-40, 5 percent; 1841-50, 10 percent; 1851-60, 15 percent. What remains entirely without supporting empirical evidence is the procedure whereby 1891/1900 results are extrapolated backwards to cover the rest of the century.[88] The other major estimate in the 10 to 15 percent range is that of Potter, who deflated immigration data for the entire period 1820 to 1860 by 14.5 percent to estimate net inflows.[89] Potter's deflation is based upon a questionable calculation in the American census of 1860. The latter asserts that a deflation of 14.5 percent is required to adjust to a net basis the gross immigration estimates for the period 1800 to 1820,[90] apparently because surviving data for the period 1855 to 1860 suggest that 'the alien passengers should be diminished by 14.5 percent to determine the number of actual settlers from 1855 to 1860'.[91] The number of aliens arriving between 1855 and 1860 totalled 849,790.[92] Of these, 17,193 expressed their intention to reside outside the United States, and a further 24,848 of recorded alien arrivals were actually 'second passages'. The two combined constituted 5 percent of 849,790. To this total (17,193 + 24,848) the census then added the 50,901 whose intentions were 'not stated' plus an allowance for '30,000 emigrants to Canada via New York' to reach a figure of 122,942 or 14.5 percent of 849,790. As an estimate of net immigration, even for the period 1855/60, a deflation of 14.5 percent would seem wholly unacceptable. The assumption that all immigrants not stating their intentions would subsequently leave the United States is highly suspect. The same caveat applies to any assumed large *net* loss to Canada at this time.

Unfortunately, none of this resolves the problem of the relationship between recorded immigration and net immigration into the United States between 1820 and 1860. The problem can be summarized in terms of adjustments to the official count. To this official count one must add:

(1) immigrants arriving overland from British North America and Mexico,
(2) first and second class passengers not enumerated in the official counts,
(3) aliens arriving at Pacific ports (up to 1849), and
(4) immigrants arriving at Atlantic ports but not counted in the official tabulation.

From the resulting totals one must then subtract:

(1) transient aliens,
(2) second passages by aliens,
(3) aliens who have died on shipboard but are still included in official counts, and
(4) former residents of America who are leaving the country permanently.

Three of these factors – second passages, transient aliens, and overland immigration from the interior of Canada – have been estimated directly. The remaining upward and downward biases are assumed to be small in size and roughly offsetting. The unimportance of underenumeration, overland migration from Mexico and alien arrivals at Pacific seaports has been suggested above. Whether official counts excluded first and second class passengers and included would-be immigrants who died on shipboard is still a subject of dispute.[93] Overland migration from British territory other than Upper and Lower Canada can be assumed to have been negligible. The vast majority of movement south from Nova Scotia, New Brunswick, Newfoundland and Prince Edward Island was undoubtedly by sea, thereby insuring the inclusion of such migrants in American statistics. As for American residents with a propensity to migrate beyond American borders, their destinations appear to have been confined primarily to other areas within North America: either territory subsequently acquired by the United States or, to a minor degree, the British colonies of Upper and Lower Canada.[94] The first of these are included in the estimates of Table A-2; the second in the estimation procedures outlined below. No evidence could be found to suggest that the flows of

American residents to foreign territory other than those noted above were significant at any time during the first half of the nineteenth century.

Second passages and transient aliens were also comparatively minor flows, but data do exist to indicate their relative magnitudes. In the period 1855-60, second passages were approximately 3 percent of total alien arrivals; transient aliens about 2 percent.[95] Roughly three quarters of the latter group intended to reside in 'British America'. Those en route to Upper and Lower Canada are included in subsequent calculations. The reasonable assumption was therefore to deflate official United States immigration data not by the total combined effect of these two factors (5 percent) but by something less; namely, 4 percent.[96]

The final problem is to estimate net immigration from Upper and Lower Canada. For this purpose the following data are available:

(1) Departures from Great Britain for British North American Colonies, 1815 to 1860.[97]

(2) Immigrant arrivals at the ports of Montreal and Quebec City, 1827 to 1860.[98]

(3) The total population of Upper Canada for the years 1825, 1831, 1840, 1852, and 1861.[99]

(4) The total population of Lower Canada for the years 1825, 1831, 1844, 1852, and 1861.[100]

(5) The Catholic population of Lower Canada for the years 1831, 1844, 1852, and 1861.[101]

(6) Annual births and deaths for the Catholic population of Lower Canada, 1800 to 1860.[102]

In all cases the data appear to be relatively accurate.[103]

To estimate the *net* flow of immigrants into the United States using these data the following assumptions were made:

(a) The net inflow of immigrants into America from sources other than Upper and Lower Canada in any given year was 96 percent of the reported count of aliens arriving at American seaports in that year.

(b) The ratio of departures from Great Britain for British North America to arrivals at Montreal and Quebec was roughly the same for the years 1820 through 1826 – when no data are available on arrivals – as it was for the period 1827 through 1835 when data first became available.[104]

(c) Immigrants entering both Canadian and American seaports did so in a uniform flow throughout the year. Annual totals can therefore be regarded as entering at mid-year for purposes of estimating rates of natural increase.

(d) After their arrival, immigrants had a rate of natural increase equivalent to that of the domestic population of the area in which they resided.[105]

(e) The rate of natural increase for the Catholic population in any given period can be calculated (i) by assuming a constant population increase throughout the period, and solving for the population at mid-period, and

(ii) by calculating total births minus total deaths for that period, dividing this residual by the length of the period, and expressing the result as a percentage of the mid-period population.

(f) The rate of natural increase for the population of Upper Canada as well as that for the residual (non-Catholic) population of Lower Canada was midway between the rate of natural increase of the Lower Canada Catholic population and the estimated rate of natural increase for the United States population.

(g) The United States population can be approximated by the procedures outlined in the notes to Table A-2.

(h) The population of Lower Canada for the year 1840 can be approximated by interpolation, using the observed annual rate of increase between the two census dates of 1831 and 1844.[106]

(i) The Catholic population of Lower Canada for 1825 can be approximated by extrapolating back from 1831 the observed annual rate of increase of that population between 1831 and 1844. The remaining population can then be calculated by deducting the Catholic estimate from total population reported in the census of 1825.[107]

These assumptions can then be combined with available data to derive the desired estimates. Let

$P[t]$ = United States population in year t,

$Q[t]$ = Catholic population of Lower Canada in year t,

$N[t]$ = non-Catholic population of Lower Canada in year t,

$O[t]$ = Upper Canada population in year t,

$RDI[t]$ = recorded direct immigration into United States seaports in year t,

$CDI[t]$ = corrected direct immigration into United States seaports in year t, $CDI = 0.96\ RDI[t]$,

$MQA[t]$ = immigrants arriving at the ports of Montreal and Quebec City in year t,

$Y[j]$ = the percentage of immigrants arriving at the ports of Montreal and Quebec City that continue on to the United States in period j,

$R[j]$ = the United States rate of natural increase in period j,

$_{NO}R[j]$ = the rate of natural increase of the non-Catholic population of Lower Canada *and* the total population of Upper Canada in period j,

$_{Q}R[j]$ = the rate of natural increase of the Catholic population of Lower Canada in period j.

Assume for the moment that all census data were collected once every ten years on December 31, and that all immigration data were for the year ending December 31. With no net overland migration from Upper and Lower Canada, the American rate of natural increase $R[j]$ can be found by solving for $R[j]$ in

$$P[t](1 + R[j])^{10} + \sum_{T=1}^{10} (CDI[T + t])(1 + R[j])^{(10\frac{1}{2} - (T+t))} \tag{12}$$

$$= P[t + 10].$$

Once the possibility of an unrecorded influx from Canada is admitted, the problem becomes one of solving three equations for three unknowns: R, $_{NO}R$, and Y, where

$$_{NO}R[j] = \tfrac{1}{2}(R[j] + _{Q}R[j]), \qquad _{Q}R[j] > _{NO}R[j] > R[j] \tag{13}$$

$$(N[t] + O[t])(1 + _{NO}R[j])^{10} + Q[t](1 + _{Q}R[j])^{10}$$

$$+ (1 - Y[j]) \sum_{T=1}^{10} (MQA[T + t])(1 + _{NO}R[j])^{10\frac{1}{2} - (T+t)}$$

$$= N[t + 10] + O[t + 10] + Q[t + 10] \tag{14}$$

and

$$P[t](1 + R[j])^{10} + \sum_{T=1}^{10} (CDI[T + t])(1 + R[j])^{(10\frac{1}{2} - (T+t))}$$

$$+ Y[j] \sum_{T=1}^{10} MQA[T + t](1 + R[j])^{(10\frac{1}{2} - (T+t))} = P[t + 10]. \tag{15}$$

Actual calculations were complicated by variations in the time during which, or at which, data were collected.[108] The solutions for $R[j]$, $Y[j]$, and $_{NO}R[j]$ appear in Table A-7.

The variations in Y would seem to provide a new puzzle for Canadian economic historians. With extraordinary accuracy, Lord Durham estimated in the 1830s that 50 to 60 percent of immigrants arriving at Quebec and Montreal continued on to the United States.[109] More recent historians have tended, explicitly or implicitly, to extrapolate the Durham estimate to the remainder of the pre-Confederation era.[110] What is striking in the results of Table A-7 is the fall in Y that occurred shortly after Durham submitted his report. That document repeatedly emphasized 'the striking contrast which is presented between the American and the British side of the frontier line in respect to every sign of productive industry, increasing wealth, and progressive civilization'.[111] Was that contrast sharply modified in the two decades prior to the American Civil War? The United States economy certainly did not experience a prolonged slump. The shift that occurred in the rate of re-emigration from British North America may therefore be indicative of a Canadian upsurge.

3.4 Immigration data: white population 1800-19

The lack of official data on white immigration for the first two decades of the nineteenth century has engendered a host of unofficial estimates, the more important of which are reproduced in Table A-8. With two exceptions, all numbers in that table are nothing more than outright guesses.[112] Beginning in 1815 the British government collected data on passengers bound for countries outside Europe and the Mediterranean. Underreporting was undoubtedly widespread,[113] but the trends evidenced by these figures give some indication of the relative yearly flows of migrants to America in the period immediately following the War of 1812. The one attempt to count migrants who actually arrived in America was made by Adam Seybert. His sources were returns 'obtained from the records of the custom houses, except for Charleston which was made from the report of the harbor master'.[114] His final enumeration represented 'the number of the passengers who arrived in ten of the principal ports of the United States, from the 1st of January to the 31st of December, 1817'.[115] The two series are quite consistent, Seybert's count of the number arriving from Great Britain and Ireland (11,977) closely approximating the British count of the number sailing for America in 1817 (10,280).[116]

Fragmented British data and an American count for one year do not, of course, provide a sufficient basis for estimating the flow of immigrants over two decades. To these data must be added a variety of statistical and impressionistic evidence from contemporary sources. The end results can only be regarded as an informed guess concerning historical reality.

The major premise is that total net immigration for the first decade of the nineteenth century was slightly less than 100,000, and, for the second decade, slightly more than 100,000. All available evidence tends to support this hypothesis.[117] These totals are distributed annually by a series of further assumptions, the most important of which for the period 1801 through 1814 are the following:

　　(a) 1801 immigration was twice that of 1800.[118]

　　(b) From 1801 to 1807 the annual flow of immigrants was constant.[119]

　　(c) The effect of the Embargo Act was to reduce immigration in 1808 by roughly 25 percent.[120]

　　(d) From 1809 through 1811, immigration was slightly below 1801/1807 levels.[121]

　　(e) During the War of 1812-14, immigrant arrivals declined in proportion to the fall in the tonnage of ships entering American ports.[122]

The equations incorporating these five assumptions are presented in Table A-9.[123]

To estimate annual distribution of decade totals for the period 1815 through 1819, the following assumptions were made:

(a) Immigration for 1815 was quite low – roughly one quarter the level achieved in 1816.[124]

(b) For the years 1816 through 1819, overland immigration from Canada was equivalent to 50 percent of the number of immigrants arriving at St. Lawrence ports, the latter in turn being 90 percent of immigrants recorded as leaving British ports for British North America.[125]

(c) For 1816, net arrivals at American ports totalled 10,000.[126]

(d) From January 1817 through September 1819, immigrant arrivals at American ports were at the annual rate indicated by Seybert's count for 1817.[127]

(e) For the last quarter of 1819, the arrival of immigrants at American ports was at an annual rate of 8,385 – the total recorded immigration for the year ending September 30, 1820.[128]

The formulae in Table A-9 can be combined with the population totals of Table A-2 to yield a range of estimates for the period 1800–20, as indicated in Table A-11. The problem is to choose from a range of possibilities the most likely approximation to actual demographic variables.

The key variable in Table A-9 is Z: the number of immigrants in the years 1809, 1810 and 1811. Variations in Z have limited effect on the implied rate of natural increase for the decade 1810–20, but only because immigration estimates for that period are calculated by procedures largely independent of Z. The major problem, then, is to choose a value of Z that will yield believable immigration and natural increase estimates for the decade 1800–10. A value of 15,000 appears to be too high. The historical evidence suggests that in the first decade of the nineteenth century *net* immigration flows were below the implied magnitude.[129] A zero value for Z is also unacceptable. Implied immigration flows are at variance with other historical evidence, while the associated rate of natural increase borders on the incredible. The most likely value for Z seemed to be in the 5,000–10,000 range; for r_1, in the 2.88–2.98 range. The final choice, of necessity, must be somewhat arbitrary. The decision to set Z equal to 8,000 reflected the belief that the implied annual immigration flows were consistent with other historical evidence, and that the resulting rates of natural increase formed a credible pattern when combined with similar estimates for the 1820–60 period.[130]

3.5 Immigration data: white population – further adjustments

The principal immigration data for this study consisted of the following:

(1) Estimates of annual immigration, 1800–19. (See Table A-12.)

(2) Recorded immigration at seaports, 1820–60, corrected by procedures outlined above.

(3) Estimates of net overland immigration from Canada.[131]

Two other series that proved useful were:

(4) Passenger arrivals at U.S. seaports, 1855–60, by country of origin and intended destination. (See Table A-3.)

(5) Seaport arrivals, by age group and by sex, for the periods 1820–29, 1830–39, 1840–49, and 1850–55. (See Table A-6.)

These data still required adjustment to be useful for this study. For example, an eight-year old who immigrates three years before the next census would subsequently be enumerated in an age group different from that of a six-year old immigrating in the same year. The first goal was to obtain sex-specific five-year age data for all ages 0–70, and for all the years 1800–60.

Four assumptions were made:

(1) Immigrants entering during the years 1800–19, when no data were recorded, had the same sex and age patterns as those entering during the decade 1820–29, when data were first collected.

(2) The age and sex patterns of immigrants entering for the entire decade, 1850–59, were the same as the recorded patterns for the years 1850–55. (See Table A-6.)

(3) Immigrants from Canada had the same sex and age patterns as did recorded passenger arrivals at American seaports during the same decade.

(4) The small percentage of passengers who did not state their age were age 40 or older.

These assumptions were then used to estimate the size of the five-year age groupings for those forty years of age or older for the years 1820–55. Let

$$I_{x-y}[t] = \text{number of recorded passengers at American seaports ages } x \text{ to } y$$
inclusive for year t,

and

$$I_{x+}[t] = \text{the number of recorded passengers at American seaports of age } x$$
or older in year t.

Assume initially that the following equation holds:

$$\frac{I_{30-39}[t]}{I_{30+}[t]} = \frac{I_{40-49}[t]}{I_{40+}[t]} = \frac{I_{50-59}[t]}{I_{50+}[t]} = \frac{I_{60-69}[t]}{I_{60+}[t]}. \tag{16}$$

Given the number of passengers in the 30–39 age group for each of the relevant periods and the ease with which the total number of immigrants 30 or over can be determined for each of these decades, one can solve in turn for each of the ten-year age groupings over 40. These estimates can then be refined into five-year categories by assuming that the following equation holds:

$$\frac{I_{30-34}[t]}{I_{30-39}[t]} = \frac{I_{40-44}[t]}{I_{40-49}[t]} = \frac{I_{50-54}[t]}{I_{50-59}[t]} = \frac{I_{60-64}[t]}{I_{60-69}[t]}. \tag{17}$$

The final task was to convert five-year data into one-year data. The key problem was to determine a reasonable age distribution for each five-year category. Three assumptions were made:

(1) A linear relationship existed between the number of immigrants in a given age in a year and the number of another age within the same five-year age grouping.

(2) The number of immigrants in a given year whose age is at the mid-point of a five-year age grouping (for example, 2.5, 7.5, etc.) was the same as that indicated by an even age distribution.

(3) The distribution of immigrants in a five-year age group was related in a reasonable fashion to the number of immigrants in the adjoining five-year age groups.

The second assumption is all that is required to estimate the number of immigrants aged 2.5, 7.5, and so on, in a given year. These points can then be graphed for each year using age as the abscissa and number of immigrants as the ordinate. The next step was to determine the slope of the line joining the midpoints of two age groups that are five years apart; for example, the slope of the line that joins 7.5 and 17.5, the midpoints of the 5–9 age group and the 15–19 age group, respectively. This slope indicates the gain per average year during this ten-year span of time. The further assumption was made that the age distribution of immigrants in the intervening age group shows the same gain per average year as indicated by the calculations for the ten-year age interval. In other words, a line representing the age distribution of those 10–14 years of age will be parallel to the line extending from 7.5 to 17.5.

This procedure is presented graphically in Figure 4. The shaded area represents the age-distribution that would be used for the 10–14 age group if the

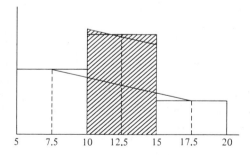

Figure 4

even distribution were as portrayed by the rectangles. The age-specific distribution is derived from this new formulation by dividing the new 10–14 age distribution into areas that represent the number of immigrants in each of the five ages of the age category. The area of each of the trapezoids of Figure 4 is then calculated.

The one age group to which this procedure cannot be applied is 0–4. In this case it is assumed that the slope of the line representing the age distribution of this particular cohort is the same as the slope of the line extending from the midpoint of this first cohort (i.e., from 2.5) to the midpoint of the next cohort (i.e., to 7.5).

The technique described could yield a negative estimate for the number of immigrants for one or more ages. Such an occurrence is most likely in the youngest and oldest age cohort. Should this occur, the endpoint of the cohort that is computed as negative would be corrected to zero.

One problem remains: to estimate where immigrants settled prior to the next census. Part of the difficulty was overcome by assuming that immigrants arriving by sea remained in the region of entry until the next census. This still leaves unresolved the questions of where immigrants arriving overland from Canada settled in the period 1820–60, and where all immigrants settled in the two decades 1800–19.

As is so often the case in this study, both problems can be overcome only by assumptions, conditioned where possible by supporting historical evidence. Concerning overland migration from Canada, the historical literature suggests that (a) almost all movement was into the Northwest region of Map 1,[132] (b) northern New England was relatively unattractive to new settlers, and (c) 'some' of the overland arrivals settled in the eastern part of New York and the eastern part of Pennsylvania (both of which are in the Mid-Atlantic region of Map 1). For each of the years 1800–60 it was therefore assumed that 5 percent of these overland immigrants settled in New England, 10 percent settled in the Mid-Atlantic region, and 85 percent settled in the Northwest.

The period 1800–19, as noted previously, is distressingly barren of clues as to the destination of foreign arrivals. To estimate the region of settlement, the two most obvious possibilities for those arriving at Atlantic seaports are:

(1) to use the 1817 data – the one year for which passenger data are available – and a variant of a previous assumption; that is, that immigrants arriving by sea remained in the region of entry until the next census; or

(2) to use the 1820–29 arrival data as indicative of the regional distribution of arrivals in the previous two decades, and the same assumption linking port of entry to region of settlement.

The second approach was pursued, mainly because the 1817 data omitted a number of ports. The arrival patterns implied by the two procedures were actually quite similar.

The distribution of those arriving overland from Canada in the period 1800-19 is determined in several steps. The first was to divide the period into two segments: 1800-14 and 1815-19. For the earlier segment the assumption was made that *net* overland immigration from Canada was zero. The principal justification is the negligible size of the square timber trade during this period. Only in the later stages of the Napoleonic Wars did this trade develop to major proportions in response to the Berlin Decree, a growing scarcity of Baltic timber in Britain, and the resulting increase in British preferential duties on colonial timber designed to stimulate colonial shipments.[133] Once it did develop, the excess cargo space on the return journey to North America resulted in low passage rates that in turn stimulated migration from Britain to St. Lawrence ports, especially Quebec City.

Data on emigration from the United Kingdom for the years 1815-19 were used as the basis for estimating overland migration from Canada during the same period. The following assumptions were made:

(1) 90 percent of the emigrants from the United Kingdom whose reported destination was British North America arrived at St. Lawrence ports.

(2) Net overland migration from Canada to the United States in any year equalled 50 percent of these arrivals.

The estimates of total net immigration presented in Table A-12 (which include Canadian immigration) can then be used to determine net overland immigration from Canada as a percentage of total net immigration.[134] Canadian immigration estimates can then be combined with other data to derive the pattern of settlement shown in Tables 3.5.1 and 3.5.2. The numbers in the second table are calculated from the first by adding the relevant regional percentage to the appropriate Canadian figure for a given year. For example, the total percentage of immigrants settling in New England in the decade 1820-29 (8.505) is calculated by adding 6.2 to the product (0.05 x 46.1).

Table 3.5.1 *United States immigration: estimated regional immigration as a percentage of total immigration*

	At ports in:					from Canada	Total
	New England	Mid-Atlantic	Old South	New South	Far West		
1800–09	11.5	67.4	12.9	8.2	0.0	0.0	100.0
1810–19	9.2	54.1	10.4	6.6	0.0	19.7	100.0
1820–29	6.2	36.3	7.0	4.4	0.0	46.1	100.0
1830–39	7.3	53.7	8.6	7.4	0.0	23.0	100.0
1840–49	11.3	67.6	5.1	10.4	0.3	5.3	100.0
1850–59	7.6	73.1	3.1	10.9	3.2	2.1	100.0

Source: see text.

Table 3.5.2 *Percentage of total immigrants settling in each region from outside the U.S.*

	New England	Mid-Atlantic	North-west	Old South	New South	Far West
1800–09	11.5	67.4	0.0	12.9	8.2	0.0
1810–19	10.2	56.1	16.7	10.4	6.6	0.0
1820–29	8.5	40.9	39.2	7.0	4.4	0.0
1830–39	8.5	56.0	19.6	8.6	7.4	0.0
1840–49	11.6	68.1	4.5	5.1	10.4	0.3
1850–59	7.7	73.3	1.8	3.1	10.9	3.2

Source: see text.

Table 3.5.3 *Average length of stay in decade* j *for a white immigrant arriving in decade* j

Decade	1800–10	1810–20	1820–30	1830–40	1840–50	1850–60
$f[j]$	0.4982	0.3539	0.4096	0.4947	0.3978	0.5751

Source: see text.

The final piece of information required is the average length of time new immigrants were in the country for each of the decades of our period, $f[j]$. This was calculated, as noted previously, by fitting a straight line to the actual yearly immigration data. The results are presented in Table 3.5.3.

The above can be used to estimate the total contribution of immigration to population growth within America.[135] The record in the first half of the nineteenth century is unimpressive. Had no migration occurred into the United States after 1800, the domestic population by 1850 would have been about 25 percent lower than it actually was.[136] This of course assumes that domestic growth was unaffected by the flow of immigrants. The much-debated Walker thesis postulates an inverse relationship between local rates of natural increase and the tide of immigration, overseas migrants not so much adding to the domestic population as displacing local growth that otherwise would have occurred.[137] Even if the hypothesis is false – and its merits appear to be dubious[138] – the basic conclusion remains: the major explanation of the rapid growth of the American population in the first half of the nineteenth century was the exceptional reproductive capacities of its local population.

3.6 Immigration data: Negro population

The paucity of data on Negro immigration is in sharp contrast to that available for the white population. The explanation is not difficult to find. By

1800, all of the states of the newly formed United States had outlawed the importation of slaves from abroad. From that date until the Emancipation Proclamation, this ban on imports remained in force, with two exceptions.

Late in 1803 the legislature of South Carolina voted to reopen the slave trade, a decision that remained in force until superseded by a Federal law that closed all American ports beginning January, 1808. The total of annual importations into South Carolina between 1804 and 1807 is still a subject of dispute, as indicated in Table B-5. Curiously enough, the count by the *Virginia Argus* would seem to be more accurate than that compiled by Donnan from the *Charleston Courier*, insofar as the *Argus'* total more closely approximates the four-year aggregate compiled in 1820 from Charleston custom house records.[139]

The other exception to the nineteenth century ban on slave imports into America concerns the territory of Louisiana. This particular maritime activity had been allowed by Spain, condoned by France, and never seriously challenged by Louisiana's Governor Claiborne. The change in status to American territory in 1803 appears to have had little initial restraining effect upon the trade.[140] In 1806 the United States attorney-general did give official approval to importations from other American states, a decision that appears to have stimulated rising importations in slave ships that first touched at the port of Charleston.[141] The Federal prohibition of 1808 met with limited initial success in Louisiana, as evidenced by the events of 1809. In that year, a large number of French subjects who had fled from Santo Domingo to Cuba to escape the ravages of a slave uprising, now found their status in Spanish-owned Cuba imperiled by Napoleon's invasion of Spain. The result was a second flight, this time to New Orleans. The city witnessed a total influx in 1809 of 3,305 whites, 3,429 free Negroes and 7,011 slaves – a migration that clearly contravened Federal law, raised a furor in New Orleans, but in the end was tolerated by local officials.[142]

These fragmentary counts for Louisiana and South Carolina appear to constitute all of the available data on slave imports into America during the nineteenth century. How many were smuggled in after 1808 – or indeed how many were smuggled in prior to 1808 to avoid payment of Charleston duties[143] – remains a matter of conjecture.

The American statutes prohibiting the importation of slaves suggest a growing effort to eradicate that trade during the first two decades of the nineteenth century. In 1808 the trade was outlawed; in 1818 rewards to informers were increased; in 1819 a naval squadron was authorized to implement suppression; in 1820 engaging in the slave trade was declared a capital offence.[144] Enforcement, however, was anything but rigorous. In the ante-bellum period, no one was executed under the 1820 statute. Nor is this failure surprising, given the prevailing administrative fabric of few officials commanding negligible forces and a southern public that was, at best, indifferent to their success. Typical of repeated complaints was that of a New Orleans customs officer that 'No efforts of officers of the customs alone can be effectual in preventing the introduction of Africans from the westward'.[145] Similar sentiments were echoed by his counterpart in Mobile: 'We have only a small boat with four men and an inspector to oppose the whole confederacy of smugglers and pirates'.[146] To the would-be slaver, the seacoast of America must have appeared more analogous to a sieve than a fortress. What appears above dispute is that some slaves were smuggled into southern states during this period.[147] The question remains: How many?

The four principal estimates of total imports by decade are given in Table B-6.[148] The Curtin estimate is labeled by its author as a 'shot in the dark',[149] a phrase that could apply with equal force to all attempts at quantifying the American slave trade of this period. The sensitivity of the rate of natural increase to variations in immigration estimates is indicated in Table B-7; a sensitivity underscoring the importance of the latter estimates in one's overall interpretation of the demographic history of this period.

Shipping tonnage data might offer one possible clue as to a reasonable upper bound. According to Howard, the average slaver was 200 tons, with an allowance of two slaves per ton proffered as a 'generous' estimate.[150] To hypothesize slave smuggling of the order of 10,000 per year is to imply that 5,000 tons of shipping could have skirted America's southern coast undetected. This tonnage in turn appears to be trivial when compared with the total maritime activity of the area. (See Table B-8.) The Howard estimate therefore cannot be used to rule out of court the more generous estimates of slave smuggling that appear in Table B-6.

Those who argue that 'large' numbers were smuggled in generally emphasize the lax enforcement of United States laws and the widespread outfitting of slave ships in northern ports.[151] Those who claim that imports were 'small'[152] point out that neither of the above two factors necessarily implies large-scale smuggling into American territory. Indeed, minimal smuggling seems to be the hypothesis most consistent with available evidence – or lack of evidence. Antislavery societies, for all their sound and fury, could not uncover more than a handful of examples of illegal importations.[153] The 1870 census, concerned with the same problem, could find only 1,984 Negroes who admitted to being 'born in Africa'.[154] Most persuasive of all – and most frequently cited by those who would minimize slave importations – is the fact that males constituted roughly 50 percent of the total American Negro population throughout the ante-bellum period,[155] a ratio that would seem to be inconsistent with widespread smuggling in ships that typically carried two males for every female.

The hypothesis that slave vessels carried males to females in the ratio of 2:1 is one of the most widely quoted and least well documented assertions about the Atlantic slave trade.[156] It does accurately describe the sex ratio of slaves recaptured by the British Squadron off the coast of Africa.[157] That ratio may still overstate the importance of males in the smuggling trade between the West Indies and America, because the former did not place much value on the breeding capabilities of females, and the latter did.[158] Some downward revision in the 2:1 ratio for the American trade is also suggested by the fragmentary data in Donnan, which indicate that in the period 1750–1808 slave vessels trading to mainland America carried males to females in the ratio of six to four.[159] Either of these ratios (6:4 or 2:1) when combined with available data on the proportion of males to females in the American Negro population can provide a means of testing the hypothesis that slave smuggling was not pervasive after 1808, provided that male and female death rates can also be estimated.

One final piece of evidence must be noted at this juncture. If the magnitude of illegal importations remains obscure, the dimensions of Negro emigration from America are well documented. In 1817 the American Colonization Society was founded for the express purpose of returning American Negroes to Africa. Its success in terms of numbers moved was inconsequential.[160] One obvious problem was the conflicting objectives of its white sponsors, ranging as they did from Quaker humanitarianism to the Jeffersonian desire to remove the Negro population 'beyond the reach of mixture'.[161] The primary difficulty, however, was the near universal opposition of American Negroes to the goals of the organization.[162] Emigration was therefore not to be a significant demographic influence for the black population throughout the first half of the nineteenth century.[163]

To review, available information on the net immigration of Negroes to America consists largely of (1) fragmentary counts for the years 1804–07 and 1809, (2) estimates of total importations by various scholars, all of which are fairly labeled shots in the dark, (3) impressionistic evidence that smuggling was limited, despite lax enforcement of federal laws, (4) quantitative data suggesting that the ratio of males to females on slave ships was 2:1 in the transatlantic trade, and 6:4 in the eighteenth-century trade between the West Indies and the thirteen colonies, and (5) a count of Negroes who emigrated to Africa.

To fill in the gaps in the statistical series, the following assumptions were made:

(a) For the period 1820–60, net immigration into America was 5,000 per year (i.e., smuggled slaves less migration from America to Africa).

(b) For the period 1800–19, net annual immigration was as presented in Table B-19.

(c) The sex ratio of males to females for these slaves was 6:4.

(d) Net immigration occurred at a uniform rate throughout the year.

(e) 90 percent of arriving slaves entered the New South region of Map 1, and 10 percent entered the Far West (mainly Texas).

Table 3.6.1 *Recorded age distribution of
slaves taken off captured vessels 1808–41*

Period	Percentage Recorded as 'adults'	'children'
1808–19	71	29
1820–29	65	35
1830–39	57	43
1840–41	61	39
1808–41	62	38

Source: See Table B-21.

Table 3.6.2 *Assumed age distribution for
imported slaves*

Age cohort	Percentage of total imported
0–4	1
5–9	3
10–14	10
15–19	30
20–24	20
25–29	15
30–34	10
35–39	7
40–45	3
45–49	1
	100

The first and second assumptions reflect the belief that, in the main, slave smuggling was limited throughout our period. The estimates in Table B-19 require a further word of explanation. For the period 1804–07, the count of the *Virginia Argus* was assumed to be the most accurate for reasons cited previously. These numbers were increased by 20 percent to adjust for unrecorded arrivals (i.e., smuggling into South Carolina, and arrivals not recorded elsewhere, notably at New Orleans). The assumption that dominates all other data is that the annual net inflow was 5,000 per year, with two exceptions. The 1809 arrivals at New Orleans (free and slave) were added to the figure of 5,000 to derive a total estimate for that year. The 1808 estimate of 8,000 reflects the belief that slave importations declined somewhat slowly in the first year during which such activity was again made illegal.

The third assumption concerning age distribution was conditioned by available data on 'adults' and 'children' among slaves recaptured by the British Squadron off the coast of Africa. (See Table 3.6.1.) The usual age of a 'prime field hand' was 18, so that the 'children' category probably refers to those under the age of 16 or 17. Because of the appalling conditions on board ship and the associated low survival probabilities for the very young, it is unlikely that a large percentage of these children were under 10 years of age. As for the 'adults', the most productive years were usually in the 17-35 age range (except in cases of unusual skills), and for that reason the vast majority of these importations were undoubtedly in that age cohort. This information tempered the estimates of Table 3.6.2, although of necessity the final choices by five-year age cohorts is somewhat arbitrary.

The fifth assumption permits the calculation of $f[j]$, the average portion of the decade that a slave who was imported in decade j was in the country.[164] Given the assumption that 5,000 slaves (net) were imported in each of the years 1810-60, then $f[j] = 0.5$ for $j = 1, 2, 3, 4, 5$. The fifth assumption when combined with the data of Table B-19 implies that $f[O] = 0.3794$.

The sixth assumption on the regional distribution of imports reflects the belief that given relative regional demands for additional slaves and relative population densities along the seacoast, most of the smuggled slaves would be landed on the coastline running between, and including, Georgia and Louisiana.

4

Interregional migration estimates
1800 – 1860

4.1 General

Estimates of net migration, by decade, are presented in Tables C-1 and D-1.
The numbers include only those migrants who survived to the next census
enumeration. Data are broken down by both region and age cohort for males,
females, and the two sexes combined. The row labeled 'Total immigration'
represents estimated net international migration into the United States for a
given age cohort during the decade in question.

4.2 White population 1800-60

If one focuses on migration data for both sexes, a number of patterns are
apparent for the different regions of Map 1, some of them unsurprising, and
some quite unexpected.

(a) New England. Throughout the period this region tended to be a net
loser of population, but several developments are curious. The largest
absolute loss occurred in the decade 1810-20, well before the completion of
the Erie Canal. If population movements are symptomatic of relative
economic strength, the decade 1810-20 was the worst for the region's
economy. By the same reasoning, the 1840s apparently were the best, at
least in the 1800-60 period. The pattern of in-migration in the youngest
cohort during the 1840s suggests the possibility of data imperfections in that
cohort, but the above inference is also supported by the sharp reduction in
the exodus of all other cohorts in the 1840s. Admittedly, the linkage of
population change to conclusions about economic welfare should perhaps be
tempered in this case by considerations relating to the influx of impoverished
Irish men and women, but the era in which New England railroad building
boomed was clearly atypical in terms of population flows.

(b) Mid-Atlantic. Emerging with startling clarity from the migration data is
a fact too often forgotten by historians: that the largest net loser of population throughout this period was the region comprised of those portions of
the traditional mid-Atlantic states (N.Y., N.J., and Pa.) *east* of the Appalachian
fall line. To cite but one comparison, the total exodus from this region for
the entire period 1800-60 exceeded the total net loss of the Old South by

more than 75 percent. Part of the explanation, of course, concerns the role of New York and Philadelphia as receiving ports for immigrants, particularly the former. (The more international migrants that disembark en route to the west, the higher will be the apparent net out-migration.) Part of the explanation lies in the way that the regions are divided, with both upper New York state and western Pennsylvania relegated to the Northwest region. The point of that division, however, was to emphasize the numerical trends noted above: that in the territory east of the Appalachians, the middle states were far and away the most important suppliers of population to the west. In terms of aggregate flows, the out-migration accelerated between 1800 and 1820, momentarily slackened, and then roughly doubled in every decade between 1830 and 1860. The loss for the entire period amounted to approximately two thirds of the total net in-migration into the Northwest region in the same sixty years.

(c) Northwest: Historians will hardly be surprised to learn that the region ga...ing the most population in the ante-bellum period was west of the Appalachians and north of Tennessee. The net influx between 1800 and 1860 was almost four million, an influx that exceeded the total in-migration into the combined regions of the New South and the Far West by a factor of six. Put another way, if one adds to the southern states west of the Appalachians and south of Kentucky (including Georgia and Florida) all of the territory west of the Mississippi (except for the single tier of states Missouri, Iowa, and Minnesota), the net influx of white population into this region in the period 1800–60 was only 15 percent of the in-migration into the Northwest. Here, too, the 1820s constitute the exception to a rising trend, with the 1850s being the years of greatest population movement by a handsome margin.

(d) Old South. Like the territories to the north of Virginia, the southern states of the eastern seaboard were, as one would expect, net losers of population. The total net loss for the Old South in the 1800–60 period was almost four times that of New England. Not surprisingly, the decade of greatest loss corresponds with the cotton boom of the 1830s. What is perhaps unexpected is the rapid decline thereafter in out-migration to levels significantly *below* any of the decade losses of the 1800–30 period.

(e) New South. Here also can be found an expected trend and several surprises. From 1800 to 1840, the region experienced a net influx of humanity. Curiously enough, however, the most pronounced influx occurred in the decade 1810–20, well before the cotton boom of the 1830s, and even antedating – at least to some degree – the full development of steamboats on western rivers. Even more curious is the net exodus in the two decades prior to the Civil War. Part of the explanation is undoubtedly the drawing power of Texas (included in the 'Far West' region). If one adds to the net loss of both the Old and New South in the 1840–60 period the total net gain of the Far West, these three regions combined lost a net of some 200,000 in the two

decades before Lincoln's election. The implication is a significant exodus from the South as the nation became progressively divided – an exodus even more pronounced than the above figures suggest, insofar as those who rushed to California are counted in the Far West. For all regions and all decades, the ratio of male to female migrants tends to fluctuate between 6:4 and 2:1. The most notable exceptions are (a) the youngest age cohort for all regions (b) the Old South across all age cohorts and (c) the New South across all age cohorts when it is losing population. In all three cases, the ratio is much closer to 50:50. In addition, there are a few marked departures, such as the extreme dominance of males in the Mid-Atlantic exodus, 1800–10, in the influx into the New South between 1830 and 1840, and in the migration into the Far West in the 1840s.

4.3 Negro population 1800–60

In terms of absolute magnitudes, the only migration of consequence for the Negro population was from east to west within the confines of the southern states. This flow tended to peak markedly in the decade of the 1830s – a pattern that contrasts sharply with white population movements within the same regions. Also somewhat at variance with white migration patterns is the limited flow of Negroes into the Far West before 1850, and the heavy influx in the next decade. Apparently the willingness to move slaves into Texas was minimal until the resolution of political and military issues in the 1840s. North of the Mason–Dixon line aggregate movement was – predictably – quite limited, with two exceptions. In the first two decades of the nineteenth century, the Northwest actually gained almost as many Negroes as did the New South. In the 1850s, the exodus from the Northwest for the first time became somewhat pronounced, lending empirical support to the contention that after the passage of the Fugitive Slave Act in 1850, free Negroes tended to migrate to Canada.

In terms of the age structure of migrants, one is struck by the dominance of youth. Almost half of those leaving the Old South (and those entering the New South) in the 1800–60 period were in the age cohort 10–20 at the end of the decade of their migration. This suggests that many of the slaves subjected to forced interregional migration were actually younger than eighteen: the tradition age of a 'prime field hand'. As for the ratio of males to females among migrating Negroes, except for the earliest decade (1810–20), it remained close to 50:50 across most age cohorts, with females having a slight edge in the youngest cohorts, and males a slight edge in the older ones. More significant than these slight variations, however, is the dominant impression that forced interregional movement affected both sexes about equally.

At the risk of laboring the obvious, all of the above conclusions are based upon estimates that must be viewed as only approximately correct. The abnormal death rates (in some cases, even negative death rates) are merely one indicator of the need for keeping this qualification ever to the fore. Despite such imperfections, these migration estimates would seem to be about the best possible, barring further data manipulation that would, in the final analysis, be arbitrary. Further, for purposes of estimating migrations, many data imperfections are of limited importance. For example, under-enumeration is not a crucial defect insofar as it remains roughly constant across time and age cohorts.

Many of these defects, however, become matters of the first importance if the task is to use census data to estimate the vital statistics of the white and Negro populations for the 1800–60 period. Despite such difficulties, calculating those estimates seemed a logical extension of this study. What follows, therefore, are estimates of death rates, birth rates, and rates of natural increase for both populations. In addition, manumission estimates for the Negro population will be found to be a natural derivative of demographic estimates. The overriding objectives are (a) to provide the best vital statistics possible using census data, and (b) to underscore the tenuous nature – in some cases, *extremely* tenuous nature – of vital statistics estimates for this period. To put the second point another way, historians are too frequently deceived into presuming an aura of objectivity and accuracy accompanies estimates that, *in all cases*, must be viewed as first approximations subject to a range of uncertainty. As will be documented below, those who ignore such uncertainties too often view as demonstrated fact what is actually a tenuous – and in some instances, indefensible – assertion about the level or trend of the vital statistics of this period.

5

White population: birth rates, death rates, and rates of natural increase

5.1 Overview: 1800-60

Among the puzzles raised by the demographic statistics for the American white population of this period, two are particularly noteworthy. The first, as indicated at the outset of this study, is how exceptional the growth record was by contemporary world standards. The main explanation of this record, as documented by previous immigration calculations, was the exceptional rate of natural increase of the local population. The second concerns the sharp discontinuity in estimated rates of natural increase,[165] a discontinuity that remains for all reasonable variations in the assumptions underlying these estimates. Why was the domestic rate of natural increase so atypical, and what caused it to change so dramatically in the period 1800-1860?

That American birth rates were exceptionally high in the latter part of the eighteenth century was a commonplace among contemporary observers. Their explanations stressed abundant land, high living standards and a propensity to marry early.[166] Death rates were 'low'. The rural and dispersed population was better fed and less subject to contagious and infectious diseases – or so the argument ran.[167] Whether death rates were considered to be unusually depressed by European or world standards is not clear. The exceptional nature of birth rates was never questioned.

American demographers are agreed that during the first half of the nineteenth century birth rates fell quite rapidly.[168] Such factors as urbanization, rising incomes, and changing land availability are usually cited as contributing to a rise in marriage age and a fall in the incidence of marriage.[169] Contraception techniques were by no means unknown in 1800, but during the next half-century the evidence suggests a growing diffusion, particularly in the northeast, and particularly after the beginning of the American birth control movement in the late 1820s.[170] About the trend in death rates there is much less agreement. Urbanization may have stimulated a rise, improved standards of living may have stimulated a decline, and both may have worked primarily through infant mortality.[171] Epidemics of cholera and yellow fever do appear to be more in evidence during the first half of the nineteenth century,[172] but the primary killers (even during epidemics) continued to be 'pulmonary tuberculosis, diarrheal disease of infancy, bacillary dysentery, typhoid fever, and infectious diseases of childhood, particularly scarlet fever, diphtheria, and lobarpneumonia'.[173]

The question of level and trend of both variables – birth and death rates – can be solved only by an appeal to available data. Regrettably, almost none have survived from the period in question. Information on death rates is largely confined to the following:

(1) Blodget's estimate of 25 per 1,000 for the turn of the century based upon the bills of mortality of a few communities and rural areas.[174]
(2) Elliot's estimate of 21.4 per 1,000 for 1855 based on 166 of 331 towns in Massachusetts.[175]
(3) Bills of mortality for a few eastern cities for the years following 1805.[176]
(4) Nation-wide data collected by the census of 1850.[177]

In no case are the data accurate enough and/or representative enough to permit a reliable inference concerning national death rates. The most obvious source – the census of 1850 – was subject to such widespread underreporting that the census itself was forced to concede that 'The tables . . . of Deaths . . . can be said to have but very little value.'[178]

The level and trend of death rates could still be inferred with confidence from reliable estimates of birth rates and rates of natural increase for the nation as a whole. Every census in the nineteenth century collected information on the age structure of the population. The ratio of children to women of child-bearing age can be used to estimate a national birth rate. The most notable of these estimates are reproduced in Table A-17. When combined with the rates of natural increase calculated above [179] they give the series of death rates presented in Table A-18. When compared with European vital statistics, these estimates would seem to confirm the impression of contemporaries that American birth rates of the early nineteenth century were exceptionally high, but leave in doubt the question of whether death rates were 'low'.[180] What would seem no longer in doubt is the proximate cause of the sharp decline in the American rate of natural increase after 1830. Falling birth rates, not rising death rates, were the explanation.

As noted in section 1.3, the logical connections between migration estimates and vital statistics estimates are at the heart of this study. With revised census and immigration data in hand plus national death rates implied by the census survivor technique, one is well on the way to the necessary ingredients for estimating vital statistics for the period. The following sections have two objectives: (a) to compute a revised series of crude birth and death rates for the period 1800–60, and (b), in making these calculations, to demonstrate some of the imperfections in, and puzzles raised by, the census data available for these years.

5.2 Calculation of death rates from census data: theory and model – closed population

The death rate in a given period for a defined population is simply the number of deaths in that population divided by the average number of people alive during the period in question. Calculating this death rate from ten-year census data is complicated by two problems. First, children who are born and then die during the intercensal period will never be recorded. Second, the average number of people in a given age group during a ten-year period will never be readily apparent from census data alone.

The first difficulty would not seem to admit to a solution. The second problem is circumvented by a rather straightforward estimation procedure.

Assume for the moment that the population is closed (i.e., that there is no emigration or immigration) and that age-specific census data were collected in consecutive years. Let

$$P_x[t] = \text{individuals of age } x \text{ at time } t.$$

The number of people in $P_x[t]$ who die before the next census is equal to the difference between the number of people of age x at time t and the number of people of age $x + 1$ at time $t + 1$;[181] that is, the difference

$$P_x[t] - P_{x+1}[t + 1]. \tag{18}$$

If

q_x = the proportion of people of age x who will not be alive one year hence,

it follows that

$$q_x = \frac{P_x[t] - P_{x+1}[t + 1]}{P_x[t]}. \tag{19}$$

This procedure can be used to estimate the death rate for the total population or for any segment. In subsequent discussion when the phrase 'death rate' is used without qualification, it refers to calculations derived by this technique.

If census data were collected annually, no problems would arise. The one-year death rate for the entire population, for example, could be calculated by

$$q = \frac{P[t] - (P[t + 1] - P_0[t + 1])}{P[t]}, \tag{20}$$

where

q = the one-year death rate for the population as a whole,[182]

$P[t]$ = the size of the population at time t,

$P_0[t + 1]$ = the number of children born between time t and time $t + 1$ who survive to year $t + 1$.

The problem is to calculate death rates when census data were collected every ten years. The most obvious starting point is to calculate a ten-year death rate for the whole population analogous to equation (19). To convert this to a one-year rate, two approaches are possible. The first of these begins with the number of people in the original group at time t, $P[t]$, and the number of people in the original group who are still living at time $t + 10$, $P'[t + 10]$. One can then estimate the probability $S[j]$ that someone in the initial population will survive the next ten-year span by

$$S[j] = \frac{P'[t + 10]}{P[t]},$$ (21)

where

$$t = 1800 + 10j.$$

Given the size of the population 10 years from time t, $P[t + 10]$, and the number of children ages 0 through 9 at time $t + 10$, $P_0[t + 10]$, one can calculate the numerator of equation (21) as

$$P'[t + 10] = P[t + 10] - P_0[t + 10].$$ (22)

The average survival rate, S, for any given year in the decade can then be calculated by

$$S = \left[\frac{P'[t + 10]}{P[t]} \right]^{1/10}.$$ (23)

(The probability of surviving all ten years would be calculated as S^{10}.) The average probability of death, q, in any given year is simply

$$q = 1 - S.$$ (24)

Hereafter the phrase 'one-year crude death rate' will refer to estimates derived by this procedure.

If any given age category is not enumerated to the same extent as others, making satisfactory adjustments for this deficiency is rather complicated – and, in the final analysis, rather arbitrary. Moreover, since death rates vary across age cohorts, one-year crude death rates could be made a function of the individual cohort death rates.

The logical way to create such a function is (a) to calculate ten-year cohort death rates by the procedure described earlier, (b) weigh the individual death rates in accordance with the number of people in the cohort, and then (c) sum the results. One preliminary difficulty is that the proportion of the population represented by any cohort varies over the ten-year period. This difficulty was overcome by averaging the proportions at the beginning and the end of the decade. Let

$P_K[t]$ = the number of people in the age cohort i to $i + 9$
        (inclusive) in year t,

$P[t]$ = the population at time t; i.e. $P[t] = \sum_K P_K[t]$,

q_K = the one-year death rate for $P_K[t]$,

z_K = the weight ascribed to cohort $P_K[t]$.

The method heretofore described sets

$$q_K = 1 - \left[\frac{P_{K+1}[t + 10]}{P_K[t]} \right]^{1/10}, \tag{25}$$

and

$$z_K = \frac{1}{2} \left[\frac{P_K[t]}{P[t]} + \frac{P_{K+1}[t + 10]}{P[t + 10]} \right]. \tag{26}$$

One problem remains. The sum of all the z_Ks may not equal one. Since these weights merely partition the variable population of the decade, it is necessary to normalize them by dividing each weight, z_K, by the sum of all the weights; that is,

$$W_K = \frac{z_K}{\sum_K z_K}. \tag{27}$$

Rewriting $\sum_K z_K$ using equation (26) and rearranging variables reveals that

$$\sum_K z_K = 1 - \frac{P_0[t + 10]}{2P[t + 10]}. \tag{28}$$

Combining equations (25), (27), and (28), one can then express the one-year crude death rate, q, as

$$q = \sum_K W_K q_K$$

$$= \sum_K \frac{1}{2} \left[\frac{P_K[t]}{P[t]} + \frac{P_{K+1}[t + 10]}{P[t + 10]} \right] \left[\frac{1}{1 - \frac{P_0[t + 10]}{2P[t + 10]}} \right] \left[1 - \left(\frac{P_{K+1}[t + 10]}{P_K[t]} \right)^{1/10} \right]. \tag{29}$$

Hereafter this will be referred to as the 'weighted average method'.

This second procedure will not generate estimates equivalent to those that could be calculated if one-year data were available. Of all the equivalency problems, those associated with infant mortality are particularly worrisome. If infant mortality is high – and it undoubtedly was during the period under review – then the cohort death rates computed by the weighted average method could greatly understate the true death rate for this age group. This is partly because a large number of deaths were never recorded. The uneven pattern of deaths produces a further complication that confounds the calculation of the true average death rate. In particular, the death rate for the first year is much larger than that for the second, and both of these are much larger than the death rates for children, say, between the ages of four and fifteen. The probability of surviving therefore increases sharply the longer the infant lives. The average survival rate, calculated for ten years, thus substantially overestimates the survival rate in the first year. In the calculation of a crude death rate, this underestimation of the first age cohort is slightly counterbalanced by trends in the other cohorts. For example, the age-specific death rates tend to rise after the age of eleven or twelve. Death rates for the latter are, however, still quite low when compared with those for the first two years of life. The net result is systematic underestimation – and one that would remain however perfect census enumeration might be.

The problem, then, is to devise a procedure to correct the children's death rate for this bias. Two procedures might be used:

(1) estimating the ratio of the true death rate of this cohort to the one obtained by the weighted average method, calculating by that method the death rate of this age group, and then multiplying this calculation by the ratio noted, or

(2) estimating the difference between the true children's death rate and the one computed by the weighted average method, calculating by this method the death rate of this age group, and then summing the two.

Experiments were conducted using stable population analysis to determine which method was likely to yield superior results.

For the American white population, the most accurate death rate estimates for this period appear to be those in Jacobson's life table for Massachusetts and Maryland of 1850.[183] The cross-check technique consisted of using the male rates in this table to generate a stable population for various growth rates r. From this, population death rates were then calculated for the youngest cohort to indicate the desirable correction factor for the two procedures cited previously.

The 1850 Massachusetts–Maryland life table indicates, for an original cohort of 100,000 newly born babies, the number who could expect to live to the age of 5, 10, 15, etc. It also indicates the probability of death at each of these five-year marks. The first problem was to generate one-year death rates. The most obvious procedure was to begin with the death rates indicated

for five- or ten-year spans and smooth these over the age cohorts. If, for example, the number of deaths for the 15–19 age cohort were 8.0 and the
deaths per thousand for the 20–24 age cohort were 15.0, one could inter-
polate as follows:

age	15	16	17	18	19	20	21	22	23	24
deaths/1,000	6	7	8	9	10	11.5	13	15	17	19

This procedure was checked for its sensitivity to the chosen method of interpolation. Results achieved by this 'smoothing' technique were compared with
results generated by the more extreme procedure of setting each age-specific
death rate equal to its corresponding cohort death rate. For example, if the
death rate for the age cohort 0–4 was 66.8 per thousand, then the death rate
for each of those ages was equated to 66.8 per thousand. *All* death rates computed for the population so generated were found to be quite close to those
computed for the smoothed set of age-specific death rates described above.
The implication was that results were relatively insensitive to interpolation
procedures. The smoothing technique was therefore used with no further
modifications.

One final problem concerned the unrealistic age structure of the population
implied by the foregoing procedures. The number of births for the year was
equated to the number of 0-year-olds at one point in time. This implies a
model in which (1) all births occur on the morning of January 1, (2) the
population is counted immediately after the births, and (3) all deaths are on
some day other than January 1. If there were 100,000 births in a year, one
would expect to find, on a given day, that the number of infants alive and
under one year old would be less than 100,000. For age groups in which deaths
were spread somewhat evenly throughout the year, the reasonable expectation
is that the number of people of age x would be halfway between the number
reaching age x in a year and the number of those who will reach age $x + 1$.
Thus, instead of using the number $P_x^s(t)$ directly (the superscript s indicates
a stable population), one might want to use the quantity

$$\frac{P_x^s[t] + P_{x+1}^s[t+1]}{2} . \tag{30}$$

Differences produced by such an alteration would be small, however, if the
death rates for the age cohorts are themselves small. Because the death rates
were low for most of the age range and there were relatively few people in
the older age groups, the decision was made to use the life table directly.
This procedure also facilitated the investigation of problems peculiar to the
youngest age cohort outlined below.

The next problem was to use the life table expanded by these techniques
to generate a population. The simplest approach was to use stable population

analysis, the crucial assumption of which is that, whatever the population growth rate, the fraction of people in each age category remains the same. Three further assumptions were necessary:

(1) emigration and immigration were trivial; i.e., the population was closed,

(2) age-specific birth and death rates were constant, and

(3) the number of births each year was growing at a rate r.

These assumptions and the expanded life table can then be used to generate age-specific data for the initial year, $t = 0$, and all subsequent years. Also easily determined is $P_x^s[t]$, the number of people aged x at their last birthday in year t, for all $t \geq 0$.

The key number in the expanded life table is q_x: the proportion of people reaching age x who will not reach age $x + 1$. If there were 100,000 births in the initial year, and if births increased at the rate r, then the number of births x years ago is given by

$$100{,}000/(1 + r)^x. \tag{31}$$

This means that the number of people of age x in the initial year $t = 0$ was

$$P_x^s[0] = \frac{100{,}000}{(1 + r)^x}(1 - q_0)(1 - q_1)\ldots(1 - q_{x-1}) \text{ for all ages } x > 0. \tag{32}$$

It is also true that

$$P_x^s[t] = P_x^s[0](1 + r)^t.^{184} \tag{33}$$

It therefore follows that

$$P_x^s[t] = (1 + r)P_x^s[t - 1] \tag{34}$$

and

$$P^s[t] = (1 + r)P^s[t - 1]. \tag{35}$$

Thus, once q_x, r and $P_0^s[0]$ are known, one can generate $P_x^s[t]$ for any year starting with $t = 0$. Not surprisingly, the structure of the population so generated is quite sensitive to the value of r.

The death rate of the stable population so generated can be computed simply by calculating the fraction of the initial population that is living one year hence and subtracting this number from one. In terms of notation previously defined, the death rate, q, is given by

$$q = 1 - (1 + r)\left[\frac{P^s[0] - P_0^s[0]}{P^s[0]}\right]. \tag{36}$$

A little arithmetic reveals that this is exactly the same as the sum

$$\sum_x (P_x^s[0]/P^s[0])q_x.^{185} \tag{37}$$

Since this is a very good approximation of the true crude death rate, it will hereafter be referred to as the true death rate.

Of particular interest is the comparison of the true crude death rate so generated and a one-year death rate computed from ten-year data using the weighted average method described earlier. Because all age cohorts in a stable population can be expressed in terms of the initial population, the equations for the weighted average method are somewhat simplified for a stable population. The cohort death rates, q_K, are given by

$$q_K = 1 - \left[\frac{(1+r)^{10} P_{K+1}^s [0]}{P_K^s [0]} \right]^{1/10} , \qquad (38)$$

and the weighting factors, w_K, are given by

$$w_K = \frac{z_k}{\sum\limits_K z_k} = \frac{\frac{1}{2}\left(\dfrac{P_K^s[0]}{P^s[0]} + \dfrac{(1+r)^{10} P_{K+1}^s[0]}{(1+r)^{10} P^s[0]} \right)}{\sum\limits_K \frac{1}{2}\left(\dfrac{P_K^s[0]}{P^s[0]} + \dfrac{P_{K+1}^s[0]}{P^s[0]} \right)} = \frac{P_K^s[0] + P_{K+1}^s[0]}{2P^s[0] - P_0^s[0]} . \qquad (39)$$

The expanded version of the 1850 Massachusetts–Maryland life table was used to generate death rates, using four different values for the growth rate, r, of the stable population; namely, $r = 0, 0.01, 0.02$, and 0.03. The results are presented in Table 5.2.1. As expected, the weighted average method produced death rate estimates that were consistently below the 'true' rates. The main explanation, as noted earlier, is the peculiar pattern of death rates for ages within the youngest cohort. An example may help to clarify the problem.

Table 5.2.1 *Computation of crude death rates*[186] *from Massachusetts–Maryland table (1850)*

	Rate of growth			
Method	0.00	0.01	0.02	0.03
'True'	24.4	23.1	23.0	23.7
Weighted average	21.5	18.2	15.8	14.3

Suppose that a stable population has a growth rate $r = 0$, and the parameters of the first few ages are as shown:

age = x	q_x	l_x
0	0.2	100,000
1	0.1	80,000
2	0.02	72,000
3	0.01	70,560

Let P_{0-1} = the two-year age cohort 0-1, and

P_{2-3} = the two-year age cohort 2-3.

Then

$$l_{0-1} = 180,000$$

$$l_{2-3} = 142,560.$$

If a true death rate is calculated for the first age cohort, one obtains the rate 0.156. However, the death rate estimated by using the survivor method is

$$1 - \left(\frac{P_{2-3}}{P_{0-1}}\right)^{1/2} = 1 - \sqrt{0.792} = 1 - 0.890 = 0.11.$$

Some idea of the magnitude of the errors induced by the youngest cohort can be obtained by making the same two calculations for the population ten years of age and older. The results are presented in Table 5.2.2. As expected,

Table 5.2.2 *Computation of crude death rates for population ages ten and over*

Method	Rate of growth			
	0.00	0.01	0.02	0.03
'True'	20.7	17.2	14.6	12.5
Weighted average	23.5	19.8	16.9	14.7

the weighted average method now overstates the 'true' death rate. One possible solution would be to attempt an adjustment for every age cohort. The general strategy of this study, however, is to make only those adjustments that are unavoidable, and, where possible, to minimize the total number made. For this reason only the youngest age cohort was corrected. The problem remains: How great should the correction be?

The estimate in question was derived by (a) using the Massachusetts-Maryland life table to generate, for the youngest age cohort, a 'true' one-year death rate and (b) comparing this rate with one computed from ten-year data. The results appear in Table 5.2.3. If the death rate for the youngest cohort is first computed using ten-year data and then adjusted (a) by a multiplication using the appropriate ratio in Table 5.2.3, or (b) by adding the appropriate difference given in Table 5.2.3, the bias created by the peculiarities of the youngest cohort will be largely removed. If these corrected rates are then used to calculate a crude death rate by the weighted average method, the results are as shown in Table 5.2.4. These results indicate that these correc-

tion procedures, designed to remove a downward bias, will yield estimates
that tend to overstate the one-year death rate for the entire population – an
upward bias that will need to be borne in mind in the interpretation of later
calculations.

Table 5.2.3 *Computations of death rates for youngest cohort*

	Method	Rate of growth			
		0.00	0.01	0.02	0.03
(1)	'True'	40.7	41.8	42.9	44.0
(2)	Using ten-year data	12.9	13.1	13.3	13.6
	Ratio of 'true' and weighted	3.16	3.19	3.21	3.24
	Difference between 'true' and weighted	27.8	28.7	29.6	30.4

Table 5.2.4 *Crude death rates using 'corrected' children's death rates*

Method	Rate of growth			
	0.00	0.01	0.02	0.03
'True'	24.4	23.1	23.0	23.7
Corrected weighted average	26.9	25.2	24.7	25.1

The above cross-check procedure suggests that if the growth rate is between
zero and three percent, an acceptable adjustment to the children's one-year
death rate is either to multiply it by three or add 0.28 to the computed death
rates for this cohort. The former was chosen because it allows for changes in
scale, whereas an additive factor would not.

Even if a perfect correction factor were devised to transform calculations
from ten-year data into one-year statistics, the end product would still be
imperfect, insofar as the census data underlying these calculations were subject to underenumeration. One correction for relative underenumeration has
already been made by multiplying *all* data from a given census by the correction factor $U[t]$.[187] This leaves unresolved those problems arising from the
underenumeration of one age cohort relative to another within a given
census. Calculations from unmodified data of death rates for the age cohort

0-9 yielded results that could only be viewed as extraordinarily low – or, more correctly, low to the point of suggesting serious relative underenumeration of this cohort.

Once again stable population analysis and the 1850 Massachusetts-Maryland life table were used to indicate the magnitude of the problem. The structure of the stable population in any given census year was estimated by setting the rate of increase, $r[t]$, of this stable population equal to the average annual rate of increase in the number of children under ten in the intercensal decade prior to that year. In terms of notation defined earlier, where

$P_K[t]$ = the number of people in cohort K in year t,

the calculation in question sets

$$r[t] = \left(\frac{P_0[t]}{P_0[t-10]}\right)^{1/10} - 1 \quad \text{for } t \geqslant 1810. \quad (40)$$

The value of $r[1800]$ was set equal to $r[1810]$. Unfortunately the rates $r[t]$ obtained in this manner are affected by the underenumeration of children in one year relative to another. If the percent relative underenumeration of children with respect to the population as a whole was the same in each of these census years, then the rates $r[t]$ would still constitute a close approximation to the true rates of increase. However, if the percent relative underenumeration of children varies from census to census, the $r[t]$s will have corresponding errors since, as noted earlier, the population is quite sensitive to the rate of increase chosen. These errors will be reflected in the age distribution of the stable population.

The assumption was made that the stable population so generated gave a reasonable approximation to the actual population. For each stable population generated (one for each of the $r[t]$s), an estimate was derived for the number of people in the age cohorts 0 through 9 and 10 through 19. The superscript 's' will be used to distinguish these estimates from the actual size of these cohorts as determined from the original census data (or more correctly, from census data modified by procedures described above). The crucial comparison will involve the ratio $P_0^s[t]/P_1^s[t]$ for the stable population for a given year t, and the corresponding ratio $P_0[t]/P_1[t]$ for census population data. If

$$\frac{P_0^s[t]}{P_1^s[t]} = \frac{P_0[t]}{P_1[t]}, \quad (41)$$

the implication is that the relative underenumeration of children for that year is negligible. If instead these ratios diverge sharply, that divergence will be used to measure the relative underenumeration of children. In this latter case, the correction factor, $C[t]$, will be given by

$$C[t] = \frac{P_0^S[t]/P_1^S[t]}{P_0[t]/P_1[t]} . \tag{42}$$

If $P_0[t]$ is multiplied by $C[t]$ – the relative underenumeration factor for children for the year t – the result should be an age structure similar to the age structure of the stable population; that is, the youngest age cohorts of the population are now calculated as

$$P_0[t]C[t] = P_0^S[t]\left(\frac{P_1[t]}{P_1^S[t]}\right) . \tag{43}$$

The associated calculations of $C[t]$ are presented in Table 5.2.5.

Table 5.2.5 *Computed underenumeration factors for children*

Year	$r[t]$	$C[t]$
1800	(1.031)	1.08
1810	1.031	1.08
1820	1.027	1.06
1830	1.027	1.06
1840	1.028	1.08
1850	1.022	1.13
1860	1.031	1.20

5.3 Calculation of death rates from census data: corrections for international migration

The above calculations are not without their deficiencies. Problems with the $r[t]$ estimates have already been noted. In addition, some of the assumptions of stable population analysis are highly questionable when applied to the American demographic experience of this period. Three problems are particularly worrisome.
(1) The number of births probably did not increase at a constant rate.
(2) The age-specific death rates probably did not remain constant over time.
(3) The population was clearly not closed; i.e., unaffected by international migration.

The first and second of these are unlikely to produce large distortions. If age-specific birth and death rates vary gradually in time, the effects of trends will be most marked in the older age groups. In populations with high death rates, these older age groups are a relatively small fraction of the population. Hence, gradual variations in both age-specific birth and death rates will not greatly affect the birth and death rates computed for the population as a whole.

The effect on calculations of the population not being closed is more difficult to determine.[188] As indicated in Table 5.2.5, the value of $C[t]$ rises sharply in the two decades 1840-60 – a period during which total immigration rose sharply,[189] and birth rates fell sharply, as indicated by subsequent calculations. An awareness of this divergence from the assumptions of stable population theory will necessarily temper subsequent interpretations of estimates for this period.

Solving another difficulty created by international migration can no longer be postponed. Estimated death rates must allow for new arrivals. As was true for migration calculations, complications arise because each immigrant in a given decade was not necessarily in the United States for the full duration of the decade. The correction technique used in the migration model consisted of transforming immigration data into an equivalent number of immigrants entering at the beginning point of the decade. This was accomplished by multiplying the actual number of immigrants by the fraction $f[j]$: the average portion of decade j that an immigrant who arrived in decade j was in the country. The same solution was used in death ratio calculations to estimate the probability that someone in age group $P_K[t]$ will die by the year $t + 10$. To determine this probability, one simply divides the number of deaths by the number of people at the beginning of the decade. The ten-year death rate, $D_K[j]$, is thus given by

$$D_K[j] = \frac{P_K[t] + H_K[j] - P_{K+1}[t + 10]}{P_K[t] + f[j]H_K[j]} , \qquad (44)$$

where

$$t = 1800 + 10j.$$

The final problem, easy to solve and of limited consequence, concerns the uneven length of some of the early census periods. The actual lengths for the period under review were as follows:

Decade:	1800-10	1810-20	1820-30	1830-40	1840-50	1850-60
Length:	$10\frac{2}{365}$	$10\frac{1}{365}$	$9\frac{298}{365}$	10	10	10

The calculation of one-year death rates from ten-year rates is easily adjusted for these variations by substituting the reciprocal of the length of the decade in place of the value 1/10 in equation (29). If

$$L[j] = \text{the length of the intercensal decade } j,$$

then the one-year death rate is given by

$$q_K = \left[\frac{P_K[t] + H_K[j] - P_1[t + 10]}{P_K[t] + f[j]H_K[j]} \right]^{1/L[j]} . \qquad (45)$$

The weighting factor is given by

$$w_K[t] = \left[\frac{P_K[t]}{P[t]} + \frac{P_{K+1}[t+10]}{P[t+10]}\right] \left[\frac{1}{2 - \dfrac{P_0[t+10]}{P[t+10]}}\right]. \tag{46}$$

The cohort death rates can then be weighted and the results summed to obtain a one-year death rate, $q[t]$, for the whole population by

$$q[t] = \sum_K w_K[t] q_K[t]. \tag{47}$$

The resulting one-year and ten-year death rates computed for the white population are given in Tables C-2 through C-13. Given the apparent imperfections in the original data and the various correction procedures used, it seemed advisable to present a range of results. For example, the multiplicative correction factor of three produced significant changes in the death rates for the youngest cohort. These changes, in turn, alter the death rate for the population as a whole. If a further correction is made for underenumeration of children (the correction factor $C[t]$), the crude death rates for the white population are higher than those calculated from uncorrected data by approximately 11 deaths per thousand.

These rates appear to be somewhat high, perhaps in part because of the upward bias that is still present in the other age cohorts. Several specific figures also appear to be highly suspect. The death rates for those in the white population who will be 20–30 at the end of the decades 1820–30, 1830–40, and 1840–50 seem to be uncommonly low. Moreover, the death rate produced by the 1850–60 data for the youngest cohort in the white population is considerably lower than corresponding figures in other years. There is no reason to believe that infant mortality declined in this decade. In fact, the observed result may indicate the opposite. A low number could be produced by an extremely high infant mortality, so high that many children were born and died in the intercensal period.

Despite such deficiencies, the modified crude death rates would seem to be about the best possible, given the priorities of (a) minimizing changes in the original data, (b) correcting those data for the most glaring deficiencies, and (c) achieving death rates that are, in the main, within a believable range. Almost all of the series calculated support two inferences. First, there are no clear secular trends. Indeed, what is striking is the apparent stability in death rates through the first half of the nineteenth century. Second, and somewhat more tenuous, there is an apparent differential in death rates in favor of females, a differential that seems to remain relatively constant during the period under review.

5.4 Birth rates

The two most common birth rate measures are (a) the number of births per thousand population, and (b) the number of births per thousand women of childbearing age, the latter normally incorporating the range 15–44. The first is normally called the 'crude' birth rate. Hereafter the second will be referred to as the 'refined' birth rate (what demographers usually call the general fertility ratio).

Any calculation of the second for the period 1800–60 must overcome two numerical difficulties. For some census years the age categories 15–19 and 40–44 were not recorded. In such cases the trapezoidal method described earlier was used to estimate the female population in these two age cohorts. More serious is the total absence of information on the births for the nation as a whole. This statistical hiatus was overcome by the following procedures:

(1) A stable population was generated for both male and female children using the Massachusetts–Maryland life table and growth rates $r[t]$ equal to the average rate of increase of children 0–9 in the decade preceding the census year. (These growth rates are the same as those used to determine $C[t]$ above.)

(2) The number of births of each sex was estimated by assuming that the ratio of births to children of that sex in the youngest age cohort in year t would be the same as an equivalent ratio in the corresponding stable population; that is, the stable population generated from the Massachusetts–Maryland life table and a growth rate of $r[t]$. For simplicity the number of births of each sex in the corresponding stable population in year t was assumed to be 100,000.

(3) For census years in which children ages 0–4 are recorded (1830, 1840, 1850, and 1860) the ratio of births to children in this age category was equated to an equivalent ratio in the corresponding stable population. For census years in which the age category was 0–9, the ratio was changed accordingly.[190]

In summary the equation that determines the number of births is given by

$$\frac{B[t]}{P_{0-x}[t]} = \frac{100,000}{P_{0-x}^s[t]}, \tag{48}$$

or

$$B[t] = \frac{100,000}{P_{0-x}^s[t]} P_{0-x}[t].$$

To solve this equation one needs to know $P_{0-y}[t]$, the number of children aged 0–y in year t (where y depends on the census year),[191] and $P_{0-y}^s[t]$, the number of children aged 0–y in the corresponding stable population in year t.

The first of these figures can be determined from the census data,[192] and the second is generated by procedures noted below.

In all birth rate computations, the relative underenumeration factor $U[t]$ was equated to zero for all years except 1820, where it was equated (as before) to 0.005. Two sets of data were generated, one with no correction for underenumeration of children and one correcting all children's data by the $C[t]$s computed previously. The number of children aged $0-y$ in the corresponding stable population was calculated as follows. The Massachusetts–Maryland life table was used to determine how many of the initial 100,000 males and 100,000 females in the stable population would survive to age 10. The table also reveals how many of the initial population would survive to each of the ages $0-5$. The remaining four numbers were obtained by extending both the female and male survivor data in the manner outlined previously for stable population calculations.[193] This extended life table was then used to establish the age structure of the corresponding stable population in year t. Equation (32) suggests that

$$P_{x+1}^s[t] = \frac{P_x^s[t](1 - q_x)}{1 + r[t]}.$$ (49)

One can obtain $1 - q_x$ from l_x, the number of people in the original population who survive to the age of x. All the required l_x values are given in the extended life table. Mathematically,

$$1 - q_x = 1 - \frac{l_{x+1}}{l_x}.$$ (50)

Since $P_0^s[t] = 100,000$ in the corresponding stable population, one can determine the age-structure of the original population by applying equation (49) sequentially. When these calculations are completed the results can be summed to obtain $P_{0-y}^s[t]$. A crude birth rate is then given by

$$\frac{B[t]}{P[t]} = \frac{100,000 \, P_{0-x}[t]}{P_{0-x}^s[t] \, P[t]}.$$ (51)

The method is analogous to the one employed by Yasuba to obtain his birth rates presented in Table A-17. His calculations differ from ours in only a few respects. When Yasuba constructs his representative stable population he assumed that the rate of increase of yearly births in this population is the same as the rate of increase of women of childbearing age. In contrast, we assume that the rate of increase, $r[t]$, of the corresponding stable population in year t is equal to the average annual rate of increase in the number of children under ten in the intercensal decade prior to that year. (The values used for $r[t]$ appear in the birth rate tables under INC.) His 'A' estimate uses the same life table as a source of survivor estimates. However, he does have a different estimate of the extent of the underenumeration of children. He assumes that there was a 5 percent underenumeration of children under the age of five. We vary the underenumeration estimate from 6 to 20 percent (see above, Table 5.2.5), and in addition apply this factor to all data for the youngest cohort, not simply to those children under the age of five.

The results of our calculations are presented in Tables C-14 through C-19. The column labeled DIFF is a multiplicative correction factor for the age-specific death rates supplied by the life table. In addition to this across-the-board correction, a function was introduced that raised the death rates according to the age of the child. A separate correction factor A, for children of age 0, is specified and then decreased as the age of the child increases.

If

L_x = the life table death rates (corrected by DIFF) for a child of age x, then the new adjusted death rate q_x is given by

$$q_x = \left[1 + A \left(\frac{10 - k}{10}\right)\right] L_x . \tag{52}$$

Given the use of the children underenumeration factors, $C[t]$, the most reasonable estimates may well be those without further corrections with DIFF or A.

The various estimates suggest that at the beginning of the nineteenth century the crude birth rate of the white population was, by world standards, unambiguously high. All calculations suggest a rate in the 50 to 55 per 1,000 range in the period 1800-10. Thereafter, the secular trend is down, but the nature of the trend depends crucially upon the estimates chosen. Between 1810 and 1850 all estimates drop by 12 to 13 per 1,000, with the biggest part of that decline – indeed, almost half – occurring in the 1840s. The 1850s, according to all estimates, were a decade of rising birth rates. The size of the increase, however, varies markedly across estimates. In some cases the increase is trivial; in others, it roughly offsets the sharp declines of the 1840s. The total decline in the half century 1810-60 therefore varies from 7 to 12 per 1,000, depending upon which estimation procedure is used. While this variation across estimates appears trivial if the issue is overall secular trend – clearly it was downward – it becomes a matter of some consequence in assessing demographic trends immediately prior to the Civil War. By one interpretation, there was merely a respite from the sharp birth rate declines of previous decades. According to other estimates, there is clearly a puzzle to be explained: Why should the secular decline of 40 years have been dramatically reversed in the decade 1850-60?[194]

5.5 Rates of natural increase

If the data of Tables A-7 and A-11 are combined, the estimated annual rates of natural increase for the white population are as follows:

1800–10	2.92
1810–20	2.83
1820–30	2.81
1830–40	2.53
1840–50	2.23
1850–60	1.99

From previous analysis it should follow that this observed decline is the result of changing birth rates (which fell) but not of changing death rates (which remained stable). A rough consistency check is possible, insofar as the fall in the crude birth rate (or more correctly, in the average birth rate for a given decade[195]) should roughly match the decade decline in the rate of natural increase. This match does seem to be in evidence except for the decade of the 1820s, when the rate of natural increase changed but little, while the birth rate fell by roughly 2 or 3 per 1,000. Consistency is very much in evidence for the period as a whole. Between 1800 and 1860 the annual rate of natural increase declined from 2.92 percent to 1.99 percent, or by 9.3 per 1,000, while the estimated decline in the crude birth rate ranged from 9.5 to 12 per 1,000. This rough match, in turn, lends further credence to the hypothesis that the death rate changed very little in the ante-bellum period.

6

Negro population: birth rates, death rates, rates of natural increase, and manumissions

6.1 Overview 1800-60

The marked decline in the observed rate of growth of the American Negro population in the period 1800-60 has been a continual puzzle for historians and demographers. From a high of 38 percent in the decade 1800-10, the growth rate declined to 22 percent in the decade 1850-60. (See Table B-1.) 'Neither demographic data nor contemporary accounts of living conditions satisfactorily explain why the growth rate tapered off.'[196] The explanation can only be in terms of falling immigration, rising death rates or declining birth rates. Section 3.6 indicated the tenuous nature of the historical evidence concerning the magnitude and trend of slave smuggling. Evidence on vital statistics is almost as elusive.

The birth rate of slaves was undoubtedly 'high' throughout the ante-bellum period. Historians have not infrequently claimed that their housing arrangements and loose family structure favored 'widespread sexual promiscuity',[197] a tendency that was hardly discouraged by white owners who had, in the discreet wording of Ulrich Phillips, 'everywhere and at all times an interest in the multiplication of their slaves'.[198] This interest occasionally manifested itself in specific incentives offered to prospective mothers: labor exemptions during pregnancy sometimes with the added bonus of better food and clothing; in some cases, complete exemption from field work for women with six or more healthy children.[199] Two conclusions follow. The first is that slave birth rates were probably close to the biological maximum throughout the south, which in turn suggests a crude birth rate in the vicinity of 50 to 55 per 1000.[200] The second is that charges of 'forced breeding' repeatedly leveled at certain eastern states were somewhat beside the point. Undoubtedly many plantation owners did raise slave children with an eye to future sale, but that phenomenon was hardly confined to the eastern seaboard. What is suspect is the connotation of force when applied to births.[201]

Zelnik has argued that the crude birth rate of the Negro population (free plus slave) was subject to a secular decline from 'around 60' in 1830 to 'about 54' in 1860.[202] His one piece of evidence in support of this contention is the

73

slight decline in the percentage of the population under 10 during the same
time period. This particular age group appears to have been especially subject
to underenumeration in the census, of which more below. Zelnik's explanation for this supposed decline in the birth rate appears to be somewhat
tenuous: a rise in the age of cohabitation and 'a slightly increasing disruption
of couples with the settlement of new slave territories'.[203] The historical
literature offers no significant corroboration for either point.

Impressionistic evidence suggests that the crude death rate of slaves was
probably 'high' relative to that of the American white population as a whole.
Contemporary opinion not infrequently cited as one relevant factor the con-
centration of slaves in the South. Higher temperatures favored insect life
associated with malaria, yellow fever and typhoid.[204] Heat also complicated
sanitation, made food preservation more difficult, and encouraged the
absence of footwear, thereby raising the incidence of hookworm infection.[205]
The extent to which the institution of slavery *per se* fostered higher death
rates is still a subject of dispute. Dietary deficiencies and malnutrition were
probably not widespread. The slave was too valuable a capital asset to be
deliberately underfed, and most plantations raised supplies of food adequate
for their own labor force.[206] Contemporary observers took for granted that
infant mortality among slaves was considerably higher than for whites.
Repeatedly cited were the primitive practices of Negro midwives, especially
the improper dressing of the umbilical cord with the associated high incidence
of trismus nascentium or tetanus.[207]

Farley's estimated crude death rate for the Negro population as a whole of
31 per 1000 for the period 1830 to 1850 is probably a lower bound.[208] The
estimate is based on the assumption of zero net immigration which undoubtedly gives it a downward bias. Certainly a crude death rate of 30 per
1000 would seem to constitute a probable lower bound for American slaves
of this period, given the evidence on contemporary European and Quebec
death rates, and the American white population death rate estimated above.[209]
A more precise estimate will be attempted below.

Evidence concerning the demographic statistics of free Negroes in the ante-
bellum period is almost non-existent, although most observers suspect that
their rate of natural increase was considerably below that of their enslaved
brethren.[210] The practice of manumitting the aged, infirm and unproductive
no doubt explains why the free colored population contained relatively more
older persons than did the slave population.[211] A surprising number of free
Negroes were located in urban centers. By 1850, for example, 28 percent
resided in 'major cities'. Within the north, by 1860 44 percent of all free
Negroes lived in urban centers of 5,000 or more; within the south, 29 percent.[212] The comparable figures for the slave population were 5, 4 and 3 percent, respectively.[213] Both factors – age structure and urbanization – should
have tended to produce lower birth rates among free Negroes than among

slaves. Whether a significant differential in economic welfare between the two groups existed is not clear. Slaves at least had the economic protection that came from being a valuable asset to some member of the white community. The fate of most free Negroes, north and south, was well summarized by Tocqueville: they '[performed] the meanest offices, and [led] a wretched and precarious existence'.[214] Between Tocqueville's visit and John Brown's raid little occurred to mitigate these circumstances. Progressively deprived of legal and political rights, victimized by growing hostility on both sides of the Mason–Dixon Line, the free Negro by mid-century was not so much a second-class citizen as *persona non grata* throughout American society.[215]

Any analysis of the vital statistics of the free Negro population is complicated not only by a scarcity of data but also by manumissions and by inter-marriages of free Negro with slave and free Negro with white. A union between free Negro and slave was relatively common, the offspring taking on the legal status of the mother.[216] What remains obscure is whether a majority of those offspring were free or slave.[217] Miscegenation was also assumed to have been relatively common, although growing white hostility attending any union between Negro male and white female makes one suspect that at least this aspect of racial mixing was very much the exception throughout America.[218] Most offspring of miscegenation would probably have been labeled as 'colored' by census marshals, thereby giving a significant upward bias to the free Negro birth rate. Offsetting that bias, at least in part, was the difficulty of finding a mate that many of the free Negroes scattered throughout the north in small numbers undoubtedly experienced.[219] The net bias remains unclear.

The magnitude and secular trend of manumissions are also unclear. According to the census of 1860, 1,500 were liberated in 1850 and 3,000 in 1860, the implication being that manumissions were on the rise immediately prior to the Civil War.[220] The real trend was probably the exact opposite. At the turn of the century, white Americans, imbued with the ideals of the Revolution, came to regard manumission as downright fashionable.[221] The enlightened instincts of the northern citizenry also received a significant prod from state laws and court decisions outlawing slavery either overnight or gradually over a limited number of years.[222] In the south, the same instincts may have been reinforced by depressed conditions in tobacco growing.[223] All this would change. In northern states the bulk of manumissions had been completed by 1830. Within the south, the rate of liberation slowed for very different reasons. Cotton became King, and the price of slaves rose sharply in every decade except the 1840s.[224] That rise in turn accentuated the opportunity cost of manumissions for white masters and complicated the task of Negroes anxious to buy their own freedom or that of their relatives.[225] The main deterring forces, however, may well have been non-economic. In the 1820s for the first time slavery began to be defended as a positive good.[226]

The 1830s brought the traumatic impact of Nat Turner's rebellion, with the rise to prominence of northern abolitionist societies further intensifying southern hostility towards the free Negro.[227] By mid-century, southern anti-slavery societies had all but vanished, and with them went the sentiments that had characterized the post-Revolutionary era. In 1785, Gresset Davis of Petersburg, Virginia, had freed his slave Ishmael 'being fully persuaded that freedom is the natural right of all men agreeable to the Declaration of the Bill of Rights'.[228] The time would come when citizens of the same community would lash a white man and order him to leave town for merely suggesting that 'Black men have, in the abstract, a right to their freedom'.[229] Impression-istic as such evidence is, it does lend credibility to the hypothesis that the rate of manumissions fell off sharply in the 1830s and was little more than a trickle for the remaining decades of the ante-bellum period.[230]

6.2 Death rates

One-year death rates for the Negro population were calculated using the same equations developed for the white population.[231] The results include a number of curiosities, the most startling of which are negative death rates for various age cohorts at various times. The obvious inference is that errors were made in the original data, or in the slave importation estimates, or in both. Various corrections were experimented with, including:

(a) multiplying the children's one-year death rates by three,
(b) introducing a correction factor of 10 percent for the relative under-enumeration of children,
(c) combining (a) and (b)
(d) introducing a higher correction factor of 15 percent for the relative underenumeration of children in the earlier years; viz., 1810 and 1820, and finally
(e) inflating the estimates of slave smuggling.

The first of these is an attempt to correct for the strong downward bias in the children's one-year rate produced by calculating rates from ten-year data. (The multiplicative factor is the same as that chosen for the white population.) The second reflects the belief that because data on slave children were collected from slave owners rather than from parents, their relative under-enumeration was worse than that encountered in white population data. Even with both of these adjustments, the death rates for the youngest cohort in the first two decades of the nineteenth century appear to be unreasonably low. Much of the problem may be traced to the absence of age specific data for 1800 and 1810, with age structure inferred by extrapolation from later census data. To bring these unreasonably low rates more into line with death rates of later years would require either (a) inflating estimates of slave smuggling by roughly 50 percent, or (b) assuming that the relative underenumeration of children was higher in 1810 and 1820 by roughly 15 percent instead of 10 percent, the latter being the figure deemed reasonable for subsequent years. Of the two possibilities, the second seems far more believable.

Even with all these modifications, including varying slave importations within a believable range, the resulting pattern of death rates is somewhat curious. Nor is this surprising. The enormous variation in the death rates in the unadjusted data – particularly in the youngest cohort – means that any correction that is applied to all decades will produce some strange results in some of those decades. All of these anomalies could of course be removed by adopting different adjustment procedures for different decades and different age cohorts. The difficulty with this solution is that there is no apparent justification for the smoothed series beyond the demographer's desire for smoothness. Worse, if data completely revised by such procedures are then used to make inferences about historical reality, the legitimacy of such inferences would seem – to use the kindest possible phrase – tenuous in the extreme.

A scanning of the various death-rate series calculated does suggest a number of tentative conclusions, but – to labor the point – all of them are no better than the data (plus modifications) from which they spring. The first is the absence of a distinct secular trend in any of the estimates. Thus, for those who wish to argue that slaves were becoming better off, or worse off, during the ante-bellum years, the death rates implied by census data offer no conclusive confirmation or disproof of their more general hypothesis. The 1830s appear to have been exceptionally bad years for mortality. This could be the result of (a) the cholera epidemic of that decade (b) increased deaths accompanying the mass migration from the Old to the New South, or (c) data imperfections. The second conclusion from scanning the various estimates is that while males had a higher death rate than females in the early decades of the nineteenth century, by the 1840s the two were roughly equal, and by the 1850s the balance had swung slightly against females. Here, too, the worry persists that an interesting secular development may in fact reflect changing data imperfections rather than changing historical reality – a doubt that is particularly strong when the differences in question are relatively small. Finally, on the matter of contrasts with the white population, the crude death rates for Negroes appear to be, on the average, roughly 30 percent higher than those for the white population. As for the youngest age cohort, the death rates for the two races differ by widely varying margins. The most telling conclusion would seem to be this: that only those inferences that require the roughest accuracy in the underlying data are defensible. Inferences that require a high degree of accuracy should never be made – or at the very least, should be made in the most tentative of terms, as subjects worthy of further investigation.[232]

6.3 Birth rates

Birth rates for the Negro population were estimated by using the same basic
equations as those employed for the white population. Once again the
Massachusetts-Maryland life table was used to generate the requisite stable
population. The rates of increase $r[t]$ for the stable population were determined by using Negro census data.[233] The basic procedure, as before, was to
set

$$r[t] = \left(\frac{P_0[t]}{P_0[t-10]} \right)^{1/10} - 1 \quad \text{for } t \geq 1810,$$

and $r[1800] = r[1810]$.

The calculation of a refined birth rate (the number of births per thousand
women of childbearing age) was complicated by a scarcity of data for the age
category 15-44. The age categories for the 1830 and 1840 census were 0-9,
10-23, 24-35, 36-54, 55 and over. The trapezoidal method could be used to
estimate the number of women 15-34, but could not be used to solve for the
missing cohort, 36-44. This difficulty was overcome by referring to the first
census in which Negro women were recorded in ten-year age categories for
the years 50-80. The trapezoidal method was used to determine the percentage of those 55 and over in these data who were included in the ten-year age
group 55-64. This computed ratio was then applied to the number of women
in the '55 and over' category in the 1830 and 1840 census to estimate the
number of those (in 1830 and 1840) who were 55-64. The trapezoidal
method was applied to these new data to estimate those in the ages 36-44.

To infer a birth rate from census data on surviving children the demographer must estimate an appropriate death rate, and that is extremely difficult in this case for reasons outlined in the previous section. Even if a retreat
is made into stable population analysis (which seemed the best of available
strategies), doubts persist as to whether observed movements in estimated
birth rates are in fact the result of variations in the true (as opposed to the
estimated) death rate. And, as always, doubts persist about the estimated
number of children, however the original census count is subsequently modified.

Various experiments were made in an attempt to remove census imperfections, including:
(a) the use of a function (A) to raise the death rate according to the age of
    child, with the correction decreasing as age increased,
(b) employing a multiplicative correction factor (DIFF) to the age-specific
    death rates supplied by the life table, and
(c) corrections for the relative underenumeration of children (applied first
    uniformly across all decades, and then more sharply to the first two
    decades).
The final estimates, not surprisingly, proved to be more sensitive to variations

in the third than to variations in the other two. A more compelling case can be made for using the first and second types of corrections for the Negro population than for the white population. Our calculations indicate that the former had a higher death rate than the latter. This suggests that some increase in the life table death rates is required. Moreover, insofar as the death rates for the youngest of the youngest age cohort were higher than those for the older ages in this cohort, some additional small A ,factor correction is called for. As to the final choice of actual corrections, the numbers chosen are, of necessity, somewhat arbitrary. Our inclination is to favor an A adjustment of 0.03 and a DIFF equal to one.

Most or all of the series generated by these modifications suggest several conclusions. The implied secular trend is somewhat curious, the crude birth rate remaining roughly stable in the period 1800–20, rising sharply in the 1820s, falling sharply in the 1830s (to roughly the 1800–20 level), falling again sharply in the 1840s (by roughly the same amount as in the 1830s), and then changing very little in the 1850s. Notice, however, how central the 1830 estimate is to these inferences. If the sharp rise in the birth rate of that year is a product of data imperfections (for example, improved enumeration of children), and if the true birth rate was little changed from earlier levels, then the implied secular trend becomes considerably modified: little change for four decades (1800–40), a sharp drop for one decade (the 1840s), and then little change thereafter. Finally, if enumeration of children became progressively worse as southern hostilities to census collection increased, the decline in the immediate ante-bellum years may reflect growing data imperfections more than declining fertility. The foregoing merely illustrates once again that the tenuous nature of the data confounds the easy identification of changes in numerical series with changes in the actual southern demographic experience in ante-bellum years.

If the secular trend noted at the outset is correct, the obvious puzzles to be explained are the sharp increase between 1820 and 1830, and the sharp decline in the next two decades. Changing interregional migration (contrary to Zelnik's suggestion[234]) offers no easy explanation in terms of associated disruption of families. The 1820s – a period of vigorous movement – was also a period of rising birth rates. Similarly, the migration of the 1850s was every bit as massive as that of the 1840s, but the birth rate remained relatively stable in the first period while dropping sharply in the second.

An explanation for birth rate changes might also be sought in the apparent differential in the birth rates of free and enslaved Negroes. This differential appears in the 1820s and remains relatively stable in magnitude after 1830.[235] As an explanation for the apparent decline in the total Negro birth rate after 1830, however, one cannot refer to a rising proportion of free Negroes for the simplest of reasons: that proportion actually declined from 14 percent in 1830 to 11 percent in 1860.

What, then, can the historical demographer conclude? The answer would seem to parallel closely the conclusions offered for death rates. Given the imperfections in the underlying census data, only those inferences requiring the roughest kind of numerical accuracy would seem to be defensible. As argued above, even the basic issue of secular trend – perhaps the most fundamental issue of all – is far from clear, although the case for a decline would seem to be more persuasive for birth-rates than for death-rates.

6.4 Manumissions

One of the unsolved puzzles in the historiography of American Negro slavery is the level and trend of manumissions between 1800 and 1860. The above calculations can be combined with available data to give a rough estimate of both. Let

$SP_K[t]$ = the number of slave Negroes in cohort K in year t,

$FP_K[t]$ = the number of free Negroes in cohort K in year t,
(i.e., $FP_K[t] + SP_K[t] = P_K[t]$),

$MAN_K[j]$ = the number of slaves manumitted in decade j who survive and are included in cohort K in the next census year.

The number of manumissions is given by either

$$MAN_{K+1}[j] = FP_{K+1}[t+10] - FP_K[t](1 - D_K[j])$$ (53)

or

$$MAN_{K+1}[j] = SP_K[t](1 - D_K[j]) + H_K[j](1 - f[j]D_K[j])$$
$$- SP_{K+1}[t+10].$$ (54)

All estimates are critically affected by two assumptions: (1) the level of illegal importations, and (2) the relative death rates of free Negroes and slaves. The most obvious starting point was to assume that free Negroes and slaves had the same age-specific death rate. This assumption was brought into question when the results gave negative manumissions for certain age groups in certain decades. The two most obvious corrections were either to abandon the assumption noted or to modify the original data. Both were the subject of subsequent experimentation.

If the number of immigrants in each of the years 1800–03 and 1807–60 is increased by 1,000, the figures improve only slightly, and many large negative numbers remain. If the death rates for free Negroes are assumed to have been significantly higher than those of the slave population, the estimates of implied manumissions become more plausible. Specifically, the slave population was assumed to have the age-specific death rates previously

calculated for the entire Negro population. (Given the overwhelming pre-
dominance of slaves in this population, the assumption did not seem to do
undue violence to reality.) The death rate for free Negroes was then increased
by various amounts, with manumission calculated using the equation that is
based upon census data for free Negroes.

Tenuous as the numerical foundations are, they do support the hypothesis
that the freeing of slaves fell off sharply in the 1830-60 period. They also
suggest that even if some northerners were selling their slaves southward in
the 1800-30 period to avoid impending legal compulsions to free them, a
significant number were given their liberty during the early years of the
nineteenth century. The data also suggest that total manumissions in the
second decade, 1810-20, contrasted sharply with that of either the first or
third. Part of the explanation may have been a reluctance to free slaves
during the military upheavals of the War of 1812, and perhaps even later
during the squabbles over Spanish Florida. Finally, all estimates suggest an
on-going bias to free relatively more females than males – a bias that became
more pronounced as the Civil War approached and total manumissions
declined.

6.5 Rates of natural increase

Table B-7 demonstrates two points: (a) that estimates of rates of natural increase are critically dependent upon assumptions concerning slave smuggling,
and (b) all of the more noteworthy smuggling estimates imply a decline – in
most cases, a sharp decline – in the rate of natural increase of the Negro population in the 1800-60 period. As noted previously, this decline has been an
on-going puzzle for demographers.

The first question is whether the decline is real or a product of imperfect
estimates. The adjusted Negro population data of this study and the net
smuggling estimates noted earlier imply rates of natural increase as shown in
Table 6.5.1.

Table 6.5.1 *United States Negro population:
estimated rate of natural increase 1800-60*

Decade	Annual rate of natural increase
	%
1800–10	2.4
1810–20	2.4
1820–30	2.5
1830–40	2.0
1840–50	2.1
1850–60	1.9

Is the sharp decline after 1830 real or a fabrication of data defects? Another way of asking that question is: By how much would estimated smuggling in earlier years need to be increased to lower the implied rate of natural increase to levels roughly equivalent to those of later years? To lower the estimated annual rate of natural increase for the first three decades to 2.1 percent, the *annual* smuggling estimates would need to be increased as follows: 1800-10, by 3,407; 1810-20, by 4,291; 1820-30, by 8,362. This would imply annual smuggling of the order of 10,000 to 13,000 – a range that cannot be ruled out of court as absurd, for reasons outlined in section 3.6. In the same vein, if the 1860 census were one percent less perfect than that of 1850 (for example, because of growing anti-Federal sentiment), then the estimated annual rate of natural increase in that decade should be revised from 1.9 to 2.0 percent.

All of the foregoing is merely one way of emphasizing the sensitivity of rate of natural increase estimates to changing assumptions. A second approach is to ask whether birth- and death-rate data support the hypothesis of a secular decline in the Negro rate of natural increase between 1800 and 1860. As noted in section 6.2, the various death rate estimates do not support the hypothesis of a secular rise in this period. Data considered in section 6.3 do suggest that a case might be made linking a fall in the rate of natural increase to a decline in the birth rate of the order of 4 or 5 per 1000. (For example, such a decline would, other things being equal, explain a fall in the rate of natural increase from roughly 2.4 percent to slightly less than 2.0 percent.) Relying ever more heavily upon the accuracy of the data, the demographer might even explain the slight rise of the 1820s in terms of a slight rise in the birth rate, and then trace the sharp decline of the 1830s to a falling birth rate (to previous levels) and a rising death rate (from such factors as the cholera epidemic in the early years of that decade). Stability in the 1840s might then be traced to offsetting declines in birth and death rates. The further decline in the 1850s, however, would remain a mystery, at least for those who sought in the birth- and death-rate estimates presented here evidence of tendencies that would explain such a decline. The temptation at this point is to resolve the mystery by an appeal to data imperfections; specifically, the decline in the accuracy of Southern census counts in 1860.

Three facts, however, give one pause. The first is that the total magnitude to be explained – a decline of 4 or 5 per 1,000 over 60 years – is relatively small. The second is the unambiguous evidence of data imperfections. (Clearly, a negative death rate will not do.) And finally, the evidence – again unambiguous – of the extreme sensitivity of birth- and death-rate estimates to changing assumptions. The word 'extreme' refers to the magnitude of change relative to the magnitude of that which is to be explained: the supposed decline in the Negro rate of natural increase in the ante-bellum years. Where, then, does the truth lie? The question is perhaps better rephrased to read: Which approach does one find more appealing: (a) one that assumes a high degree of accuracy in the estimates, thereby explaining the decline in terms of birth- and death-rate changes, or (b) one that spurns any conclusion because of a subjective judgment about the wide range of possible error? The answer, in the last analysis, is a matter of personal preference. What is perhaps worth emphasizing is that any historian who takes the first approach and lets the numbers determine the key demographic questions (Why the rise in death-rates in the 1830s? Why the fall in the birth rate? etc.) always is haunted, or should be haunted, by doubts that he is pursuing a false scent – that the puzzle he would explain is a fabrication of imperfect data, not historical reality.

As noted some time previously, this exploration of vital statistics for the Negro population in the ante-bellum period was prompted as a logical extension of interregional migration estimates. No one is less pleased than the present authors that the bottom line of that pursuit should include such a heavy dose of agnosticism. The historian, however, would seem subject to the same ethical imperative as baseball umpires; to call things as he sees them.

7

Conclusions

The substantive conclusions of this study have been summarized in chapter 1. The central methodological point deserves further scrutiny because it has been so frequently ignored.

The point concerns the linkage between data accuracy and hypothesis testing. The pioneering work of Conrad and Meyer illustrates the problem.[236] Their primary objective was to measure the profitability of slavery. This required comparing the rate of return from owning slaves with the return available on investment alternatives. Finding the average rate of return for slave owning to range from $4\frac{1}{2}$ to 8 percent[237] and that available on alternative investments to vary between 6 and 8 percent (101), the authors concluded that 'Slavery was profitable to the whole South.' (121)

One of several numerical inputs needed to calculate the rate of return from owning slaves is the value of land required per field hand, a number that bulks large in the final calculation. This was apparently derived by Conrad and Meyer from two sources:[238] (a) Lewis Gray's estimate of $35 per acre for a large plantation devoted to upland cotton 'say, in the Mississippi alluvium'[239] and (b) the report of a single farmer in Barbour County, Alabama, to *The Southern Cultivator* in 1846 concerning his operating costs during the previous two years, the relevant entry reading, 'Say, 360 acres poor pine land at $6 per acre.'[240] Taking these two numbers ($6 and $35) as representative of the end points of a distribution assumed to be uniform in structure, Conrad and Meyer calculated the average land price as midway between the two.

As an estimate of the average price of land throughout the ante-bellum South, this procedure yields a figure that cannot be presumed to be exactly correct. That is not, however, the key difficulty. The task of making estimates using imperfect data is typical of much of the research in economic history and historical demography. Because it is typical, the critical question in the Conrad and Meyer example is whether the final hypothesis testing – the comparison of two rates of return – can presume the high degree of accuracy needed in the underlying data if that comparison is to be meaningful. If the true rate of return from owning slaves was below the estimated rate, for example, then Conrad and Meyer's conclusion about the profit-ability of slavery would have to be reversed.

The question of whether slavery was or was not profitable is not at issue here. The above example has been cited to underscore the need to temper the use of numerical estimates with a sense of the probable degree of accuracy in the underlying data. Too often those who generate estimates present their results with an aura of precision that belies the tenuous nature of many of their data inputs. Demographic studies of ante-bellum America merely illus-trate this tendency. Despite a data base often fraught with imperfections, numerical conclusions not infrequently bristle with precision. A few examples illustrate the pervasiveness of the practice.

in the antebellum period, 1800-60, 68.5 percent of the fall in the total [white] fertility rate can be traced to a decline in marital fertility rates [Sanderson (1979) 340].

the birth rate [of the Negro population] declined from 53.2 [per 1,000] early in the [nineteenth] century to about 43.8 at the end [Eblen (1974) 301].

The instantaneous rate of increase for the population with declining fertility was adjusted . . . to provide an estimate of the intrinsic rate of increase as of 1850. The adjustment indicated an intrinsic rate of growth of 18.71 for Negro females [Zelnik (1966) 83].

Since the probate data are more representative of the ante-bellum slave popu-lation we conclude that the better estimate of mean age at first birth is the probate data figure of 20.6 years [Trussell and Steckel (1978) 492].

Our hope is that future work will be conditioned, as our study has been, by several methodological concerns. Most, if not all, historical data cannot be presumed to be absolutely accurate, but rather must be regarded as subject to a probable range of inaccuracy that varies, depending upon such factors as the nature of the original collection procedures and the accuracy of the recording methods. Moreover, to convert raw data into aggregate estimates usually requires assumptions that add a further tenuous element, and thus further possible error. This probable range of inaccuracy, which can vary from narrow to broad, should constrain the uses of numerical estimates in the testing of hypotheses. An hypothesis, such as that of Conrad and Meyer which requires highly accurate data, cannot be convincingly tested by using numerical estimates which are likely to be highly inaccurate. The likelihood of considerable inaccuracy in a given data set, however, does not make that set prima facie useless. As demonstrated by this study, the same data set may yield conclusions that vary from highly probable to extremely tentative. What appears as a reversal of the secular decline in the white birth rate in the 1850s, for example, may be the product of a rise in infant mortality ac-companying the cholera epidemic of the late 1840s. No probable degree of inaccuracy in the data, however, would undercut the assertion concerning the secular decline of the white birth rate in the first half of the nineteenth century.

We cannot claim to have found the optimal way for handling such problems, but one of our major goals has been to address them candidly. The central issue is the degree of accuracy needed to test a given hypothesis relative to the likely errors in the estimates. Our hope is that this work, by underscoring that issue, will lead to a revision in how numerical estimates are published and how they are used by economic historians and historical demographers.

Appendixes

Table A-1. *Estimated population increase 1800-50*

Geographic area	Annual Rate of Increase per 1000	
	Carr-Saunders	Willcox
World	5.1	3.4
Asia	4.3	2.0
Africa	1.1	0.0
Oceania	0.0	0.0
Europe and U.S.S.R.	7.1	7.0
Latin America	11.1	7.2
North America	29.8	29.8
United States	29.9	29.9

Sources: D.V. Glass and E. Grebenik, 'World Population, 1800-1950', in *The Cambridge Economic History of Europe* (Cambridge: Cambridge University Press, 1965) Vol. VI, p.58. United States data estimated from U.S. Bureau of the Census, *Historical Statistics of the United States* (Washington, 1960), p.8.

Table A-2. *United States white population: estimated population in territories not enumerated 1800-50*

	1800	1810	1820	1830	1840	1850
Recorded population	4,306,446	5,862,073	7,866,797	10,532,060	14,189,705	19,553,068
Estimated population in territories not enumerated (a)						
Miss. (b)	4,592					
Mo. (c)	3,853					
La. (d)	14,576					
Fla. (e)	934	3,113	10,378			
Iowa (f)	411	1,369	4,564	15,214		
Tex. (g)	774	2,579	8,598	28,660	95,533	
New Mex. (h)	273	909	3,029	10,098	33,661	
Utah (i)	50	167	558	1,860	6,199	
Oreg. (j)	29	96	319	1,064	3,546	
Cal. (k)	201	670	2,235	7,449	24,830	
Minn. (l)	103	342	1,139	3,798	12,661	42,203
Dak. (m)	2	6	20	66	220	734
Kans. (n)	} 148					
Neb. (o)		494	1,646	5,486	18,286	60,953
Col. (o)	49	164	547	1,824	6,080	20,268
Nev. (p)	5	16	52	173	577	1,923
Estimated gross population	4,332,446	5,871,998	7,899,882	10,607,752	14,391,298	19,679,149

Notes to Table A-2:

[a] The procedures used to estimate the population of a given state for the census year immediately preceding the first census enumeration of that state are noted in subsequent footnotes. Thus, the method used to calculate the Florida population of 1820 is described in note [e]. All other estimates for the beginning of a decade are 30 per cent of the estimated population at the end of that decade. The population of Florida in 1810 is therefore calculated as (0.30 x 10,378 = 3,113). The latter procedure was suggested by observing the rate of growth of population in frontier areas such as Illinois, Arkansas, and Michigan, for which census data are available for a number of decades.

[b] Calculated by assuming that the growth of Mississippi population between 1800 and 1810 was the same as that for Tennessee between 1800 and 1810. Part of Mississippi was enumerated in 1800. The estimate of 4,592 is therefore the difference between estimated total population of 9,781 and reported population of 5,189.

[c] Calculated by assuming that the growth of Missouri population between 1800 and 1810 was the same as that for Indiana between 1800 and 1810.

[d] Calculated by assuming that the growth of Louisiana territory (Louisiana plus Arkansas) between 1800 and 1810 was the same as that for Tennessee between 1800 and 1810.

[e] Calculated by assuming that the growth of Florida population between 1820 and 1830 was the same as that for the combined populations of Georgia and Alabama between 1820 and 1830.

[f] Calculated by assuming that the growth of Iowa population between 1830 and 1840 was the same as that for Missouri population between 1830 and 1840.

[g] Calculated by assuming that the growth of Texas population between 1840 and 1850 was the same as that for Louisiana between 1840 and 1850.

[h] Calculated by assuming that the growth of New Mexico population between 1840 and 1850 was the same as that for Missouri between 1840 and 1850.

[i] Calculated under the same assumptions as [h].

[j] Calculated by assuming that the growth of population in Oregon territory between 1840 and 1850 was the same as that for the combined populations of California and Oregon territory between 1850 and 1860.

[k] Calculated under the same assumptions as in [j].

[l] Calculated by assuming that the growth of Minnesota population between 1850 and 1860 was the same as that for Iowa between 1850 and 1860. Part of Minnesota was enumerated in 1850. The estimate of 42,203 is therefore the difference between estimated total population of 48,241 and reported population of 6,038.

[m] Calculated by assuming that the growth of population in Dakota territory between 1850 and 1860 was the same as that for Iowa between 1850 and 1860.

Notes to Table A-2 (contd)

[(n)] Calculated by assuming that the growth of the population in Kansas and Nebraska between 1850 and 1860 was the same as that for the combined populations of Iowa and Missouri between 1850 and 1860.

[(o)] Calculated by assuming that the growth in Colorado population between 1850 and 1860 was the same as that for the combined populations of Utah and New Mexico between 1850 and 1860.

[(p)] Calculated by assuming that the growth in Nevada population between 1850 and 1860 was the same as that for Utah population between 1850 and 1860.

Source: of recorded population, U.S. Bureau of the Census, *Negro Population, 1790-1915* (Washington: 1918), pp.44-5.

Table A-3. *Passenger arrivals at United States seaports by country of origin and intended destination 1855-60*

Country	Mean to reside in-			Born in-
	Males	Females	Total	Males and Females
United States	551,095	357,395	908,490	126,794
British America	7,682	4,044	11,726	25,443
Great Britain and Ireland	2,207	1,037	3,244	407,429
Azores	544	133	677	1,954
Spain	389	65	454	4,997
West Indies	271	72	343	5,170
France	130	47	177	19,338
Germany	140	36	176	279,957
Other countries specified	329	67	396	82,185
Not stated			50,901	23,317
Total of 5 years, 1855 to 1860			976,584	976,584

Source: U.S.Bureau of the Census, *Eighth Census of the United States 1860. Population,* p.xxi.

Table A-4. *Population of Upper and Lower Canada 1825-61*

	1825	1831	1840	1844	1852	1861
Lower Canada						
Total population	479,288(a)	553,134	644,351(b)	697,084	890,261	1,111,566
Catholic	353,206(a)	412,717	514,788(b)	572,439	746,854	943,253
Non-Catholic	126,082(a)	140,417	129,563(b)	124,645	143,407	168,313
French Canadian	–	–	–	524,244	669,528	847,615
Born in U.S.A.	–	–	–	–	12,482	13,648
Upper Canada						
Total population	157,923	236,702	432,159	–	952,004	1,396,091
Catholic	–	–	–	–	167,695	258 151
Non-Catholic	–	–	–	–	784,309	1,137 940
French Canadian	–	–	–	–	26,417	33 287
Born in U.S.A.	–	–	–	–	43,732	50 758

Notes:

(a) Estimated by extrapolating back from 1831 the observed annual rate of increase of the Catholic population between 1831 and 1844. The non-Catholic population was calculated by deducting the Catholic estimate from 479,288 – the total reported population.

(b) Calculated by interpolation, using the observed annual rates of increase between the two census dates of 1831 and 1844.

Source: Dominion Bureau of Statistics, *Census of Canada, 1871*, Vol. IV.

Table A-5. *Immigration (cabin and other passengers) through the ports of Quebec and Montreal by country of origin 1817-61*

Year	England	Ireland	Scotland	Continental Europe (a)	Lower ports (b)	Total
1817 -26	–	–	–	–	–	10,000- 12,000 annually
1827	–	–	–	–	–	15,862
8	–	–	–	–	–	12,697
9	3,565	9,614	2,643	–	123	15,945
1830	6,799	18,300	2,450	–	451	28,000
1	10,343	34,133	5,354	–	424	50,254
2	17,481	28,204	5,500	15	546	51,746
3	5,198	12,013	4,196	–	345	21,752
4	6,799	19,206	4,591	–	339	30,935
1835	3,067	7,108	2,127	–	225	12,527
6	12,188	12,590	2,224	485	235	27,722
7	5,580	14,538	1,509	–	274	21,901
8	990	1,456	547	–	273	3,266
9	1,586	5,113	485	–	255	7,439
1840	4,567	16,291	1,144	–	232	22,234
1	5,970	18,317	3,559	–	240	28,086
2	12,191	25,532	6,095	–	556	44,374
3	6,499	9,728	5,006	–	494	21,727
4	7,426	9,498	2,174	–	217	20,142
1845	8,511	14,060	2,011	–	160	25,375
6	3,851	26,186	1,632	1,084	–	32,753
7	31,505	54,310	3,747	–	–	74,408
8	6,034	16,582	3,086	1,395	842	27,939
9	8,980	23,126	4,984	436	968	38,494
1850	9,887	17,976	2,879	849	701	32,292
1	9,677	22,381	7,042	870	1,106	41,076
2	9,276	15,983	5,477	7,256	1,184	39,176
3	9,585	14,417	4,745	7,456	496	36,699
4	18,175	16,165	6,446	11,537	857	53,180
1855	6,754	4,106	4,859	4,864	691	21,274
6	10,353	1,688	2,794	7,343	261	22,439
7	15,471	2,016	3,218	11,368	24	22,097
8	6,441	1,153	1,424	3,578	214	12,810
9	4,846	417	793	2,722	–	8,778
1860	6,481	376	979	2,314	–	10,150
1	7,780	413	1,112	10,618	–	19,923

Notes:

(a) Primarily Germany and Norway.

(b) Primarily New Brunswick, Nova Scotia, and ports in the St. Lawrence River.

Sources to Table A-5

1817-26 : Estimate of A.C. Buchanan, Chief Agent, Emigration Department,
          Quebec; in Great Britain, *Parliamentary Papers*, IV (*Report from
          Committees*, Vol. 2), May, 1826, 'Report from the Select Committee
          on Emigration from the United Kingdom', p.169.

1827-28 : From the table compiled by Imre Ferenczi in Walter F. Willcox (ed.),
          International Migrations (National Bureau of Economic Research,
          1929), Vol. I, p.360.

1829-48 : Ferenczi, *op. cit.* p.360. The Ferenczi data can be found in the
          British *Parliamentary Papers* as follows:

Immigration year	Year	Parliamentary Papers Vol.	Paper No.
1829	1831-2	XXXII	724
1830	1831-2	XXXII	724
1831	1831-2	XXXII	724
1832	1833	XXVI	141
1833	1835	XXXIX	87
1834	1835	XXXIX	87
1835	1836	XL	76
1836	1837	XLII	132
1837	1837-8	XL	389
1838	1842	XXXI	373
1839	1842	XXXI	373
1840	1842	XXXI	373
1841	1842	XXXI	373
1842	1843	XXXIV	109
1843	1844	XXXV	181
1844	1846	XXIV	706
1845	1846	XXIV	706
1846	1847	XXX	809
1847	1847-8	XXVI	961
1848	1849	XXII	1082

1849-61 : Ferenczi, *op. cit.*, p.360. Ferenczi's original source was
          'Information supplied by the Canadian Government'. The British
          Parliamentary Papers do not give a complete set of data on
          Canadian immigration for all of the years 1849 to 1861, inclusive.

Table A-6. *Age distribution of passengers arriving at United States seaports 1820-55*

	Number of passengers					Percentage of total				
	1820-29	1830-39	1840-49	1850-55	Total	1820-29	1830-39	1840-49	1850-55	Total
Males										
Under 5	4,444	25,515	64,989	88,192	183,140	4.8	7.4	7.5	6.7	7.0
5-10	3,769	22,121	58,342	86,945	171,177	4.0	6.4	6.7	6.6	6.5
10-15	3,243	23,473	59,030	83,259	169,005	3.5	6.8	6.8	6.3	6.4
15-20	9,364	35,834	99,511	172,108	316,817	10.0	10.3	11.5	13.0	12.0
20-25	22,618	72,186	190,827	265,938	551,569	24.2	20.8	22.0	20.1	21.0
25-30	20,078	63,627	153,928	232,274	469,907	21.5	18.3	17.7	17.6	17.9
30-35	10,370	38,746	91,785	151,213	292,114	11.1	11.2	10.6	11.4	11.1
35-40	8,119	29,136	61,713	94,313	193,281	8.7	8.4	7.1	7.1	7.3
40 and over	11,438	36,280	88,937	146,676	283,331	12.2	10.5	10.2	11.1	10.8
Total	93,443	346,918	869,062	1,320,918	2,630,341	100.0	100.0	100.0	100.0	100.0
Females										
Under 5	4,057	21,527	57,908	83,228	166,720	10.9	11.5	9.8	9.3	9.8
5-10	3,389	18,506	51,291	80,630	153,816	9.1	9.9	8.6	9.1	9.0
10-15	2,535	16,896	51,023	74,018	144,472	6.8	9.0	8.6	8.3	8.5
15-20	5,289	25,542	92,315	145,758	268,904	14.2	13.7	15.6	16.4	15.7
20-25	6,781	34,064	124,211	187,729	352,785	18.2	18.2	20.9	21.1	20.6
25-30	5,840	24,307	79,159	111,548	220,854	15.7	13.0	13.3	12.5	12.9
30-35	2,906	15,622	49,111	72,086	139,725	7.8	8.4	8.3	8.1	8.2
35-40	2,541	12,543	34,000	44,252	93,336	6.8	6.7	5.7	5.0	5.5
40 and over	3,900	17,823	54,534	91,586	167,843	10.5	9.5	9.2	10.3	9.8
Total	37,238	186,830	593,552	890,835	1,708,455	100.0	100.0	100.0	100.0	100.0
Age not stated										
Male	2,727	12,399	7,648	60,816	83,590	1.8	2.2	0.5	2.7	1.9
Female	722	3,069	4,328	3,631	11,750	0.5	0.5	0.3	0.2	0.3
Sex not stated	17,506	23,500	4,888	2,807	48,701	11.5	4.1	0.3	0.1	1.1
Total arrivals	151,636	572,716	1,479,478	2,279,007	4,482,837	100.0	100.0	100.0	100.0	100.0
Aliens	128,502	531,078	1,427,337	2,118,404	4,205,321	84.7	92.7	96.5	93.0	93.8
Born in U.S.A.	23,134	34,335	52,141	160,603	270,213	15.3	6.0	3.5	7.0	6.0
Not stated	-	7,303	-	-	7,303	-	1.3	-	-	0.2

Source: William J. Bromwell, *History of Immigration to the United States* (New York: Redfield, 1856).

Table A-7. *United States white population*

Estimates of the United States rate of natural increase (*r*), the rate of natural increase of the Catholic population of Lower Canada (*q*), the rate of natural increase of the non-Catholic population of Lower Canada and the population of Upper Canada (*p*), and the percentage of immigrants arriving at Montreal and Quebec City that re-emigrate to the United States (*Y*): 1820–60.

Variable	Estimate	Period Covered
r_3	2.81	Aug. 8, 1820 – June 1, 1830
r_4	2.53	June 2, 1830 – June 1, 1840
r_5	2.23	June 2, 1840 – June 1, 1850
r_6	1.99	June 2, 1850 – June 1, 1860
Y_3	0.64	Jan. 1, 1820 – Feb. 1, 1831
Y_4	0.60	Feb. 2, 1831 – June 1, 1840
Y_5	0.22	June 2, 1840 – Jan. 12, 1852
Y_6	0.18	Jan. 13, 1852 – Jan. 14, 1861
q_3	2.84	Feb. 1, 1825 – Feb. 1, 1831
q_4	2.62	Feb. 2, 1831 – Feb. 1, 1840
q_5	2.87	Feb. 2, 1840 – Jan. 12, 1852
q_6	2.61	Jan. 13, 1852 – Jan. 14, 1861
p_3	2.82	Feb. 1, 1825 – Feb. 1, 1831
p_4	2.57	Feb. 2, 1831 – Feb. 1, 1840
p_5	2.54	Feb. 2, 1840 – Jan. 12, 1852
p_6	2.31	Jan. 13, 1852 – Jan. 14, 1861

Source: See section 3.3; *r* corresponds to $R(j)$; *q* corresponds to $Q^{R(j)}$; and *p* corresponds to $NO^{R(j)}$

Table A-8. United States white population: immigration estimates 1800-20*

Year	Annual estimates Blodget(a)	Annual estimates Seybert(b)	Annual estimates Tucker(c)	Decade Estimates 1860 Census(d) Gross	Decade Estimates 1860 Census(d) Net	Decade Estimates Seybert(e)	from U.K. only(f)	Actual counts From all countries Seybert(g) Unadjusted	Actual counts From all countries Seybert(g) Adjusted	Actual counts Official(h)
1800	4,000	6,000								
1	4,000	6,000								
2	4,000	6,000								
3	4,000	6,000		↑	↑	↑				
4	4,000	6,000								
1805	4,000	6,000		70,000	59,850	Never over 10,000 per year				
6	4,000	6,000								
7		6,000								
8		6,000		↓	↓					
9		6,000								
1810		6,000	10,000	↑	↑					
1			0							
2			0							
3			0							
4										
1815			10,000	114,000	97,470		1,209			
6			10,000				9,022			
7			21,000				10,280			
8			21,000	↓	↓	↓	12,429	22,240		
9			21,000				10,674		20,083(i)	
1820			21,000				6,745			8,385

Notes to Table A-8:

* All estimates are for gross immigration unless otherwise specified.

(a) Samuel Blodget, *Economica: A Statistical Manual for the United States of America* (Washington, 1806), p.75. Blodget estimates gross immigration at 4,000 per year 'while it is known that above half that number have migrated from the United States'.

(b) Adam Seybert, *Statistical Annals* (Philadelphia: Thomas Dobson, 1818), p.29.

(c) George Tucker, *Progress of the United States* (New York: Hunt's, 1855), p.82.

(d) U.S. Bureau of the Census, *Eighth Census of the United States. 1860 Population* I, p.xviii. The census estimate of 114,000 appears to be a summation of Tucker's estimates for the years 1811 to 1820, inclusive.

(e) Seybert, *op. cit.*, p.28.

(f) Walter F. Willcox (ed.), *International Migrations* (New York: N.B.E.R., 1929), Vol.I, p.627.

(g) Seybert, *op. cit.*, p.29.

(h) U.S. Bureau of the Census, *Historical Statistics of the United States* (Washington, 1960), p.57.

(i) In the period 1820-30, inclusive, total alien arrivals were 105 per cent of arrivals at the ten ports enumerated by Seybert. In the same time period alien arrivals were 86 per cent of total arrivals. Seybert's count of 22,240 'passengers arriving' was therefore multiplied by (1.05 x 0.86 = 20,083).

Table A-9. *United States white population: assumed immigration pattern 1800-20 (for year ending December 31)*

$L_{1800} = Z(0.55)$

$L_{1801} = Z(1.1)$

$L_{1802} = Z(1.1)$

$L_{1803} = Z(1.1)$

$L_{1804} = Z(1.1)$

$L_{1805} = Z(1.1)$

$L_{1806} = Z(1.1)$

$L_{1807} = Z(1.1)$

$L_{1808} = Z(0.8)$

$L_{1809} = Z$

$L_{1810} = Z$

$L_{1811} = Z$

$L_{1812} = Z\lceil (T_{1812})(\frac{263}{365}) + (T_{1813})(\frac{102}{365})\rceil \div \lceil (T_{1811})(\frac{263}{365}) + (T_{1812})(\frac{102}{365})\rceil$

$L_{1813} = Z\lceil (T_{1813})(\frac{263}{365}) + (T_{1814})(\frac{102}{365})\rceil \div \lceil (T_{1811})(\frac{263}{365}) + (T_{1812})(\frac{102}{365})\rceil$

$L_{1814} = Z\lceil (T_{1814})(\frac{263}{365}) + (T_{1815})(\frac{102}{365})\rceil \div \lceil (T_{1811})(\frac{263}{365}) + (T_{1812})(\frac{102}{365})\rceil$

$L_{1815} = (0.25)(L_{1816})$

$L_{1816} = (0.9)(0.5)(G_{1816}) + 10,000$

$L_{1817} = (0.9)(0.5)(G_{1817}) + (0.96)(20,083)$

$L_{1818} = (0.9)(0.5)(G_{1818}) + (0.96)(20,083)$

$L_{1819} = (0.9)(0.5)(G_{1819}) + (0.96)\lceil (20,083)(0.75) + (8,385)(\frac{92}{365})\rceil$

$L_{1820} = (0.9)(G_{1820})\lceil (0.5)(\frac{219}{365}) + (0.64)(\frac{146}{365})\rceil \div (0.96)\lceil (8,385)(\frac{273}{365})$

$\qquad\qquad + (9,127)(\frac{92}{365})\rceil$

Source: See section 3.4.

Table A-10. *Net tonnage capacity*
of vessels entering United States
ports 1790-1830

Year	Tons	Year	Tons
	(000)		(000)
1790	606	1810	989
1	604	1	981
2	659	2	715
3	611	3	351
4	609	4	108
1795	637	1815	918
6	722	6	1,136
7	681	7	992
8	610	8	917
9	732	9	869
1800	804	1820	880
1	1,007	1	847
2	944	2	889
3	951	3	895
4	944	4	952
1805	1,010	1825	974
6	1,135	6	1,048
7	1,203	7	1,056
8	586	8	1,019
9	705	9	1,004
		1830	1,099

Source: U.S. Bureau of the Census,
Historical Statistics of the United
States (Washington: 1961), p.451.

Table A-11. *United States white population: estimates of rates of natural*
increase for different estimates of net immigration 1800-20

Values for Immigration Constant Z [a]	Implied rate of natural increase	
	1800-10 (r_1)	1810-20 (r_2)
Z = 0	3.08	2.87
= 1,000	3.07	2.86
= 2,000	3.05	2.86
= 3,000	3.03	2.85
= 4,000	3.00	2.85
= 5,000	2.98	2.85
= 6,000	2.96	2.84
= 7,000	2.94	2.84
= 8,000	2.92	2.83
= 9,000	2.90	2.83
= 10,000	2.88	2.82
= 15,000	2.78	2.80

Note:

[a] Formulae using (Z) are given in Table A-9.

Source: see section 3.4.

Table A-12. *United States white
population: estimated immigration
1800-20*

(Z = 8,000)

1800	4,400	1810	8,000
1	8,800	1	8,000
2	8,800	2	5,411
3	8,800	3	2,498
4	8,800	4	2,950
1805	8,800	1815	2,879
6	8,800	6	11,517
7	8,800	7	23,688
8	6,400	8	26,091
9	8,000	9	27,079
		1820	17,197

Source: see section 3.4.

Table A-13. *United States white population:
estimated rates of natural increase 1800-60*

Period	Rate of natural increase
1800-10	2.92
1810-20	2.83
1820-30	2.81
1830-40	2.53
1840-50	2.23
1850-60	1.99

Source: see section 5.5.

Table A-14. *United States white population: contribution of immigration to total population increase 1800-60*

Time period	Population increase [a]	Immigration contribution	
		Number	% total increase
1800-10	1,539,552	95,785	6.2
1800-20	3,567,436	262,092	7.3
1800-30	6,275,306	581,634	9.3
1800-40	10,058,852	1,524,804	15.2
1800-50	15,346,703	3,639,574	23.7
1800-60	22,590,091	7,390,694	32.7

Note:

[a] Calculated from Table A-2.

Source: See section 3.5.

Table A-15. *Reported deaths in Boston and Massachusetts 1811-50*

	Boston				Massachusetts			
	Total(a)	Cholera	Smallpox	Consumption	Total	Cholera	Smallpox	Consumption
1811	892	–	2	221				
2	634	–	1	190				
3	750	–	–	193				
4	695	–	–	153				
1815	830	–	4	190				
6	873	1	–	180				
7	875	–	–	231				
8	925	–	–	138				
9	995	2	–	174				
1820	1,014	9	–	220				
1	1,304	1	–	192				
2	1,088	–	–	166				
3	1,045	–	1	183				
4	1,208	–	1	242				
1825	1,362	1	–	220				
6	1,167	6	–	231				
7	939	1	3	178				
8	1,159	2	2	217				
9	1,156	1	–	203				
1830	1,025	20	5	193				
1	1,353	21	4	203				
2	1,675	93	1	246				
3	1,374	19	–	240				
4	1,440	30	4	246				
1835	1,819	30	6	208				
6	1,648	30	5	233				
7	1,743	80	13	212				
8	1,799	61	3	256				
9	1,722	42	58	222				

1840	1,841	55	115	240			
1	1,783	29	57	256			
2	2,260	43	40	307	7,454	118	13	1,530
3	2,008	57	53	249	8,267	120	12	1,607
4	2,054	67	n.a.	305	8,201	115	11	1,634
1845	2,340	60	31	426	8,569	156	5	2,072
6	3,086	138	92	485	9,102	298	32	2,104
7	3,853	25	23	544	10,667	316	12	2,397
8	3,664	66	21	579	11,203	218	21	2,387
9	5,079	718	21	644	20,423	1,548	114	3,606
1850	3,667	44	192	586	16,606	317	334	3,527

Note:

(a) Excludes stillborn.

Sources: Lemuel Shattuck, *Bills of Mortality, 1810–1849, City of Boston* (Boston, Registry Department, 1893); Massachusetts, Secretary of State, *Annual Reports Relating to the Registry and Returns of Births, Marriages and Deaths.*

Table A-16. *Crude death rates for Boston, New York, and Philadelphia 1805-50*

	Boston			New York		
	Total deaths(a)	Total population(b)	Crude death rate (per 1,000)(c)	Total deaths(a)	Total population(b)	Crude death rate (per 1,000)(c)
1805				2,297		
1806				2,174		
1807				2,236		
1808				1,950		
1809				2,038		
1810	892	33,787 (49,654)	26.4(d) (18.0)	2,073	96,373 (119,734)	22.6(e) (18.2)
1811	892			2,431		
1812	634			2,442		
1813	750			2,207		
1814	695			1,881		
1815	830			2,405		
1816	873			2,651		
1817	875			2,409		
1818	925			3,106		
1819	995			3,008		
1820	1,014	43,298 (63,247)	25.5(e) (17.5)	3,226	123,706 (152,056)	25.9(e) (21.1)
1821	1,304			3,368		
1822	1,088			3,026		
1823	1,045			3,221		
1824	1,208			4,091		
1825	1,362			4,774		
1826	1,167			4,671		
1827	939			4,890		
1828	1,159			4,843		
1829	1,156			4,734		

Philadelphia

	Total deaths(a)	Total population(b)	Crude death rate (per 1,000)(c)
1805			
1806			
1807	1,961		
1808	2,145		
1809	1,884		
1810	1,897	53,722	37.4(e)
1811	2,249	(112,210)	(17.9)
1812	2,017		
1813	2,223		
1814	2,041		
1815	1,943		
1816	2,225		
1817	2,107		
1818	2,609		
1819	2,979		
1820	3,189	63,802	43.5(e)
1821	2,161	(137,097)	(20.2)
1822	3,334		
1823	4,372		
1824	4,284		
1825	3,539		
1826	3,845		
1827	3,659		
1828	3,971		
1829	4,001		

Table A-16 (*contd.*)

	Boston			New York		
	Total deaths(a)	Total population(b)	Crude death rate (per 1,000)(c)	Total deaths(a)	Total population(b)	Crude death rate (per 1,000)(c)
1830	1,025	61,392 (88,354)	19.3[e] (13.3)	5,198	202,589 (242,278)	26.2[e] (21.9)
1831	1,353			5,991		
1832	1,675			9,975		
1833	1,374			5,354		
1834	1,440			8,590		
1835	1,819			6,608		
1836	1,648			7,508		
1837	1,743			8,182		
1838	1,799			7,503		
1839	1,722			7,314		
1840	1,841	85,000 (124,037)	21.0[e] (14.4)	7,868	312,710 (391,114)	25.3[e] (20.2)
1841	1,783			8,531		
1842	2,260			8,503		
1843	2,008			7,933		
1844	2,054			8,127		
1845	2,340			9,886		
1846	3,086			10,079		
1847	3,853			14,441		
1848	3,664			14,553		
1849	5,079			22,373		
1850	3,667	136,881 (208,972)	26.8[f] (17.5)	15,377	515,547 (696,115)	29.8[f] (22.1)

Table A-16 (*contd.*)

	Philadelphia		
	Total deaths(*a*)	Total population(*b*)	Crude death rate (per 1,000) (*c*)
1830	3,948	80,462	52.1(*e*)
1831	4,623	(188,797)	(22.2)
1832	6,425		
1833	4,128		
1834	4,765		
1835			
1836			
1837			
1838			
1839			
1840	4,593	93,665	49.0(*f*)
1841		(258,037)	(17.7)
1842			
1843			
1844			
1845			
1846			
1847			
1848			
1849			
1850		121,376	
		(408,762)	

Notes to Table A-16.

$^{(a)}$Excludes stillborn.

$^{(b)}$Figures not in brackets for city proper; figures in brackets for city plus suburbs.

$^{(c)}$Figures not in brackets are the ratio of deaths to city population; figures in brackets, the ratio of deaths to the population in city plus suburbs.

$^{(d)}$1811 deaths divided by 1810 population.

$^{(e)}$Three-year average for deaths divided by census population.

$^{(f)}$Deaths for a single year divided by population for a single year.

Sources: Population data from George Rogers Taylor, 'Beginnings of Mass Transportation in Urban America: Part I', *Smithsonian Journal of History*, I (Summer, 1966), 36.
 Deaths: Boston data, see Table A-15; New York data from *Hunt's Merchants' Magazine*, XXVI (1852), 768; *Hazard's United States Commercial and Statistical Register*, IV (1841), 78; Philadelphia data from *Hazard's Register of Pennsylvania*, III, 126-8; V, 126; VII, 80; IX, 174; XI, 109; XIII, 104; XV, 135; *Hazard's United States Commercial and Statistical Register*, IV (1841), 208.

Table A-17. *Estimates of United States birth rates for white population 1800-60*
(per 1,000 of population)

	1800	1810	1820	1830	1840	1850	1855	1860
I Yasuba: A	52.9	52.7	51.1	49.8	47.9	42.9		42.1
II B	47.6	47.3	45.9	44.7	43.0	38.4		37.7
III Thompson and Whelpton	55.0	54.3	52.8	51.4	48.3	43.3		41.1
IV Coale and Zelnik							42.8	41.8

Sources:

(1) Yasukichi Yasuba, 'Birth Rates of the White Population in the United States, 1800-1860', *Johns Hopkins University Studies in Historical and Political Science*, LXXIX, (1961), p. 99. ('Estimate A is based on Jacobson's United States life table for 1850. Estimate B is based on the modified Jacobson's life table.')

(2) Warren S. Thompson and P.K. Whelpton, *Population Trends in the United States* (New York: McGraw-Hill, 1933), p.263.

(3) Ansley J. Coale and Melvin Zelnik, *New Estimates of Fertility and Population in the United States* (Princeton: Princeton University Press, 1963), p.21.

Table A-18. *Estimated death rates for Quebec Catholic population and white population of the United States 1800-60*
(per 1,000 of population)

Period	American estimates			Quebec estimate
	I[a]	II[a]	III[a]	
1000 10	23.6	18.3	25 5	29.1
1810-20	23.6	18.3	25.3	27.1
1820-30	22.4	17.2	24.0	27.5
1830-40	23.6	18.6	24.6	27.9
1840-50	23.1	18.4	23.5	23.4
1850-60	22.6	18.2	22.5	19.4

Note:

[a] See Table A-17.

Sources: American death rates calculated by averaging the birth rate estimates of Table A-17 and deducting the rate of natural increase of Table A-13. Quebec death rates from M.C. Urquhart and K.A.H. Buckley, *Historical Statistics of Canada* (Toronto: 1965), p.54.

Table A-19. *Birth and death rates for selected European countries*
(crude rates per 1,000)

Country		End of eighteenth century[a]	Mid nineteenth century[b]
England and Wales:	birth rate	37	33
	death rate	25	22
France:	birth rate	33	27
	death rate	n.a.	24
Germany:	birth rate	n.a.	36
	death rate	n.a.	27
Italy:	birth rate	n.a.	38
	death rate	n.a.	30
Belgium:	birth rate	n.a.	30
	death rate	n.a.	23
Netherlands:	birth rate	38	33
	death rate	n.a.	26
Denmark:	birth rate	31	31
	death rate	25	20

Notes:

[a] England and Wales 1781-1820; France 1801-05; Netherlands 1813-24; Denmark 1771-1830.

[b] 1841-60; except Italy 1862-70.

Source: Simon Kuznets, *Modern Economic Growth* (New Haven: 1966), pp.42-3.

Table A-20. *U.S.A. white population: regional distribution of arriving immigrants 1820-59*

	Percentage of total estimated to arrive						Total estimated arrivals		
	By sea at ports of[a]					Overland from Canada	At U.S.A. seaports	Overland from Canada	Total
	New England	Mid-Atlantic	Old South	New South	Far West				
	%	%	%	%	%	%			
1820-29	6.2	36.3	7.0	4.4	-	46.1	123,362	105,502	228,864
1830-39	7.3	53.7	8.6	7.4	-	23.0	516,846	154,445	671,291
1840-49	11.3	67.6	5.1	10.4	0.3	5.3	1,370,244	77,330	1,447,574
1850-59	7.6	73.1	3.1	10.9	3.2	2.1	2,701,972	56,903	2,758,875

Note:

(a) It was assumed that the pattern for American seaports for the period 1850-59 was the same as the 1850-55 pattern (data source: William J. Bromwell, *History of Immigration to the United States*).

Source: Data for American seaports calculated as 96 percent of recorded immigration. (See sections 3.3 and 3.5.) Canadian data calculated by procedures described in the text. All data revised to a year ending December 31, assuming a uniform rate of inflow throughout the year.

Table A-21. *U.S.A. population: immigrant arrivals*

Region	Port	Total recorded arrivals			
		1817	1820-25	1826-30	1820-30
New England	Boston	2,200	2,747	5,716	8,463
Mid Atlantic	New York	7,634	17,774	62,581	80,355
	Perth Amboy	637	88	105	193
	Philadelphia	7,085	4,070	10,966	15,036
Old South	Wilmington	558	–	65	65
	Baltimore	1,817	3,082	7,470	10,552
	Norfolk	520	427	982	1,409
	Charleston	747	1,824	1,030	2,854
New South	Savannah	163	220	8	228
	New Orleans	879	2,153	8,414	10,567
	TOTAL: above ports	22,240	32,385	97,337	129,722
	TOTAL: all ports	na	35,691	100,295	135,986

Percentage of total arrivals

	1817 %	1820-25 %	1826-30 %	1820-30 %
New England	10	8	6	7
Mid-Atlantic	69	68	76	74
Old South	16	16	10	11
New South	5	7	9	8
TOTAL: 10 ports	100	100	100	100

Sources: 1817 data from Adam Seybert, *Statistical Annals* (Philadelphia: Thomas Dobson, 1818), p.29; other data from William J. Bromwell, *History of Immigration to the United States* (New York: Redfield, 1856), passim.

Table A-22. *Indicators of transatlantic migration 1800-30*

	U.K. timber imports from British North America (loads: 000)	U.K. emigration to: British North America	U.S.A.
1800	2		
1	3		
2	5		
3	10		
4	13		
1805	10		
6	12		
7	21		
8	52		
9	85		
1810	108		
1	130		
2	150		
3	n.a.		
4	45		
1815	115	680	1,209
6	140	3,370	9,022
7	154	9,797	10,280
8	236	15,136	12,429
9	297	23,534	10,674
1820	216	17,921	6,745
1	291	12,955	4,958
2	313	16,013	4,137
3	351	11,355	5,032
4	386	8,774	5,152
1825	428	8,741	5,551
6	402	12,818	7,063
7	296	12,648	14,526
8	327	12,084	12,817
9	345	13,307	15,678
1830	348	30,574	24,887

Sources: Timber data from Great Britain, *Parliamentary Papers*, XIX (1835), Report from the Select Committee on Timber Duties, pp.384-5; emigration data from Walter F. Willcox (ed.), *International Migrations* (New York: N.B.E.R., 1929), Vol. I, p.627.

Table A-23. *U.S.A. white population: estimated immigration from Canada 1800-29*

	I Emigration from U.K. to British North America	II Arrivals at St. Lawrence Ports (I) x (0.9)	III Overland migrants to U.S.A. (II) x (0.5)	IV Canadian immigration as a % of total U.S.A. immigration (III) ÷ (data of Table A-12)
1800-15	-	-	-	-
1816	3,370	3,033	1,517	13.2%
1817	9,797	8,817	4,409	18.6%
1818	15,136	13,622	6,811	26.1%
1819	23,534	21,181	10,590	39.1%
1820-29				46.1%

Source: see sections 3.4 and 3.5.

Table A-24. *United States white population: estimated net annual immigration 1800-60*

Year (ending Dec. 31)	Net number of immigrants	Year (ending Dec. 31)	Net number of immigrants
1800	4,400	1830	40,142
1801	8,800	1831	58,269
1802	8,800	1832	77,422
1803	8,800	1833	69,346
1804	8,800	1834	81,311
1805	8,800	1835	51,075
1806	8,800	1836	89,826
1807	8,800	1837	89,307
1808	6,400	1838	39,317
1809	8,000	1839	69,810
1810	8,000	1840	89,113
1811	8,000	1841	83,256
1812	5,411	1842	110,145
1813	2,498	1843	74,199
1814	2,950	1844	88,554
1815	2,879	1845	125,068
1816	11,517	1846	174,936
1817	23,688	1847	239,897
1818	26,091	1848	240,671
1819	27,079	1849	293,243
1820	17,197	1850	290,783
1821	15,688	1851	373,324
1822	15,723	1852	363,842
1823	13,017	1853	360,505
1824	13,203	1854	420,292
1825	14,980	1855	196,671
1826	19,732	1856	196,458
1827	30,330	1857	247,031
1828	33,236	1858	120,507
1829	32,018	1859	118,011
		1860	149,321

Source: see section 3.5.

Table B-1. United States Negro population 1800-60

	1800	1810	1820	1830	1840	1850	1860
Population: Free (000)	108	186	234	320	386	434	488
Slave (000)	894	1,191	1,538	2,009	2,487	3,204	3,954
Total (000)	1,002	1,378	1,772	2,329	2,874	3,639	4,442
% Increase: Free		72	25	37	21	12	12
Slave		33	29	31	24	29	23
Total		38	29	31	23	27	22
Population in territories when first enumerated							
Free (000)		8.4		0.8	0.2	1.6	1.0
Slave (000)		54.8(a)		15.5(b)	-	58.2(d)	-
Total (000)		63.2(a)		16.3	0.2(c)	59.8(d)	1.1(e)
% of females: Free		-	51.7	52.0	51.7	52.0	52.0
Slave		-	48.9	49.6	49.9	50.0	49.9
Total		-	49.3	49.9	50.1	50.2	50.0
% Under 10 years old							
Free: Male		-	-	15.2	14.6	13.6	13.0
Female		-	-	14.8	14.3	13.8	13.2
Total		-	-	30.0	28.8	27.4	26.2
Slave: Male		-	-	17.6	17.0	15.8	15.4
Female		-	-	17.3	16.9	16.0	15.7
Total		-	-	34.9	33.9	31.8	31.1
Negro: Male		-	-	17.3	16.7	15.5	15.2
Female		-	-	17.0	16.6	15.7	15.4
Total		-	-	34.2	33.2	31.2	30.6

Notes to Table B-1.

[a] Miss., Mo., La.

[b] Fla.

[c] Iowa.

[d] Tex., New Mex., Utah, Oreg., Cal.

[e] Minn., N. Dak., S. Dak., Kans., Neb., Colo., Nev.

Source: Population totals from U.S. Bureau of the census, *Negro Population in the United States, 1790-1915* (Washington, 1918), p. 57. Other data from original census reports.

Table B-2. *United States free Negro population by regions 1800-60*

	1800	1810	1820	1830	1840	1850	1860
United States	108,435	186,446	233,634	319,599	386,293	434,495	488,070
New England	17,313	19,488	20,782	21,331	22,634	23,021	24,711
Me.	818	969	929	1,190	1,355	1,356	1,327
N.H.	852	970	786	604	537	520	494
Vt.	557	750	903	881	730	718	709
Mass.	6,452	6,737	6,740	7,048	8,669	9,064	9,602
R.I.	3,304	3,609	3,554	3,561	3,238	3,670	3,952
Conn.	5,330	6,453	7,870	8,047	8,105	7,693	8,627
Mid-Atlantic (coastal)	27,962	52,442	65,974	91,621	105,281	108,663	133,393
N.Y.-east(a)	10,166	24,286	26,761	40,071	43,591	41,342	40,499
N.J.	4,402	7,843	12,460	18,303	21,044	23,810	25,318
Pa.-east(b)	13,394	20,313	26,753	33,247	40,646	43,511	47,576
North-West	2,736	8,924	16,205	30,908	53,011	77,651	98,538
N.Y.-west (a)	251	1,047	2,518	4,799	6,436	7,727	8,506
Pa.-west (b)	1,170	2,179	3,449	4,683	7,208	10,115	9,373
Ohio	337	1,899	4,723	9,568	17,342	25,279	36,673
Ind.	163	393	1,230	3,629	7,165	11,262	11,428
Ill.	–	613	457	1,637	3,598	5,436	7,628
Mich.	–	120	174	261	707	2,583	6,799
Wis.	–	–	–	–	185	635	1,171
Minn.	–	–	–	–	–	39	259
Iowa	–	–	–	–	172	333	1,069
Mo.	–	607	347	569	1,574	2,618	3,572
Ky.	739	1,713	2,759	4,917	7,317	10,011	10,684
W.Va.-west	76	353	548	845	1,307	1,613	1,376

Table B-2 (contd.)

	1800	1810	1820	1830	1840	1850	1860
Old South	58,914	94,649	114,609	148,912	166,901	191,998	211,945
Del.	8,268	13,136	12,958	15,855	16,919	18,073	19,829
Md.	19,587	33,927	39,730	52,938	62,078	74,723	83,942
D.C.	783	2,549	4,048	6,152	8,361	10,059	11,131
Va.	19,598	29,292	35,470	45,181	46,809	51,251	55,269
W.Va.-east(c)	450	925	865	1,322	1,726	1,469	1,397
N.C.	7,043	10,266	14,712	19,543	22,732	27,463	30,463
S.C.	3,185	4,554	6,826	7,921	8,276	8,960	9,914
New South	1,510	10,943	16,064	26,827	38,466	31,550	33,986
Ga.	1,019	1,801	1,763	2,486	2,753	2,931	3,500
Fla.	–	–	–	844	817	932	932
Ala.	–	–	571	1,572	2,039	2,265	2,690
Miss.	182	240	458	519	1,366	930	773
Tenn.	309	1,317	2,737	4,555	5,524	6,422	7,300
Ark.	–	–	59	141	465	608	144
La.	–	7,585	10,476	16,710	25,502	17,462	18,647
Far West(d)	–	–	–	–	–	1,612	5,497

Notes:

(a)Eastern New York defined to include all counties east of the line formed by the following counties: St. Lawrence, Lewis, Oneida, Madison, Cortland, Tioga.

(b)Eastern Pennsylvania defined to include all counties east of the line formed by the following counties: Bradford, Tioga, Potter, Clinton, Clearfield, Cambria, Somerset.

(c)Western section of West Virginia defined to include all counties west of the line formed by the following counties: Tucker, Randolph, Pocahontas.

(d)All states and territories not noted above.

Sources: State totals from U.S. Bureau of the Census, *Negro Population in the United States, 1790-1915* (Washington, 1918), p. 57; county totals from U.S. Bureau of the Census, *Ninth Census of the United States, 1870, Population*, I, pp. 51, 58-9, 69-70, 72.

Table B-3. United States slave population by regions 1800-60

	1800	1810	1820	1830	1840	1850	1860
United States	893,602	1,191,362	1,538,022	2,009,043	2,487,355	3,204,313	3,953,760
New England	1,339	418	145	48	23	-	-
Me.	8	-	-	2	-	-	-
N.H.	-	-	-	3	1	-	-
Vt.	-	-	-	-	-	-	-
Mass.	-	-	-	1	-	-	-
R.I.	380	108	48	17	5	-	-
Conn.	951	310	97	25	17	-	-
Mid-Atlantic (coastal)	34,390	25,744	17,337	2,547	737	236	18
N.Y.-east(a)	20,691	14,266	9,634	60	4	-	-
N.J.(b)	12,422	10,851	7,557	2,254	674	236	18
Pa.-east(b)	1,277	627	146	233	59	-	-
North-West	42,850	88,644	144,866	199,400	249,714	309,000	350,116
N.Y.-west(a)	212	751	454	15	5	-	-
Pa.-west(b)	429	168	65	170	3	-	-
Ohio	-	-	-	6	3	-	-
Ind.	135	237	190	3	-	-	-
Ill.	-	168	917	747	331	-	-
Mich.	-	24	-	32	-	-	-
Wis.	-	-	-	-	11	-	-
Minn.	-	-	-	-	-	-	-
Iowa	-	-	-	-	16	-	-
Mo.	-	3,011	10,222	25,091	58,240	87,422	114,931
Ky.	40,343	80,561	126,732	165,213	182,258	210,981	225,483
W.Va.-west(c)	1,731	3,724	6,286	8,123	8,847	10,597	9,702

Table B-3 (contd.)

	1800	1810	1820	1830	1840	1850	1860
Old South	738,544	875,055	1,000,537	1,135,041	1,110,031	1,231,803	1,306,800
Del.	6,153	4,177	4,509	3,292	2,605	2,290	1,798
Md.	105,635	111,502	107,397	102,994	89,737	90,368	87,189
D.C.	3,244	5,395	6,377	6,119	4,694	3,687	3,185
Va.	338,624	381,680	410,029	452,084	430,499	452,028	472,494
W.Va.-east(c)	5,441	7,112	8,833	9,550	9,641	9,903	8,669
N.C.	133,296	168,824	204,917	245,601	245,817	288,548	331,059
S.C.	146,151	196,365	258,475	315,401	327,038	384,984	402,406
New South	76,479	201,501	375,137	672,007	1,126,850	1,605,082	2,114,214
Ga.	59,406	105,218	149,656	217,531	280,944	381,682	462,198
Fla.	-	-	-	15,501	25,717	39,310	61,745
Ala.	-	-	41,879	117,549	253,532	342,844	435,080
Miss.	3,489	17,088	32,814	65,659	195,211	309,878	436,631
Tenn.	13,584	44,535	80,107	141,603	183,059	239,459	275,719
Ark.	-	-	1,617	4,576	19,935	47,100	111,115
La.	-	34,660	69,064	109,588	168,452	244,809	331,726
Far West(d)	-	-	-	-	-	58,137	182,612

Notes:

(a)Eastern New York defined to include all counties east of the line formed by the following counties: St. Lawrence, Lewis, Oneida, Madison, Cortland, Tioga.

(b)Eastern Pennsylvania defined to include all counties east of the line formed by the following counties: Bradford, Tioga, Potter, Clinton, Clearfield, Cambria, Somerset.

(c)Western section of West Virginia defined to include all counties west of the line formed by the following counties: Tucker, Randolph, Pocahontas.

(d)All states and territories not noted above.

Sources: State totals from U.S. Bureau of the Census, *Negro Population in the United States, 1790-1915* (Washington, 1918), p. 57; county totals from U.S. Bureau of the Census, *Ninth Census of the United States, 1870, Population*, I, pp.51-2, 59, 70, 72.

Table B-4. *United States Negro population: estimated population in territories not enumerated 1800-50*

	1800	1810	1820	1830	1840	1850
Recorded population	1,002,037	1,377,808	1,771,656	2,328,642	2,873,648	3,638,808
Estimated population in territories not enumerated(a)						
Miss.(b)	1,579					
Mo.(c)	1,552					
La.(d)	12,800					
Fla.(e)	841	2,803	9,344			
Iowa(f)	3	10	34	114		
Tex.(g)	351	1,169	3,897	12,992	43,305	
New Mex.(h)		-	1	4	12	
Utah(i)		-	3	8	28	
Oreg.(j)		2	5	17	57	
Cal.(k)	2	7	24	80	267	
Minn.(l)		-	1	4	13	42
Dak.(m)		-	-	-	-	-
Kans.(n)	}1					
Neb.	}1	4	14	48	168	536
Col.(o)		-	1	2	7	23
Nev.(p)		-	1	3	11	38
Estimated gross population	1,019,166	1,381,803	1,784,981	2,341,914	2,917,516	3,639,447

Notes to Table B-4.

(a) The procedures used to estimate the population of a given state for the census year immediately preceding the first census enumeration of that state are noted in subsequent footnotes. Thus, the method used to calculate the Florida population of 1820 is described in note *(e)*. All other estimates for the beginning of a decade are 30 per cent of the estimated population at the end of that decade. See note *(a)*, **Table A-2.**

(b) Calculated by assuming that the growth of Mississippi population between 1800 and 1810 was the same as that for Tennessee between 1800 and 1010. Part of Mississippi was enumerated in 1800. The estimate of 1,579 is therefore the difference between estimated total population of 5,250 and reported population of 3,671.

(c) Calculated by assuming that the growth of Missouri population between 1800 and 1810 was the same as that for the combined populations of Kentucky and Tennessee between 1800 and 1810.

(d) Calculated by assuming that the growth of Louisiana population between 1800 and 1810 was the same as that for Tennessee between 1800 and 1810.

(e) Calculated by assuming that the growth of Florida population between 1820 and 1830 was the same as that for the combined populations of Alabama and Georgia between 1820 and 1830.

(f) Calculated by assuming that the growth of Iowa population between 1830 and 1840 was the same as that for Illinois between 1830 and 1840.

(g) Calculated by assuming that the growth of Texas population between 1840 and 1850 was the same as that for Louisiana between 1840 and 1850.

(h) Calculated by assuming that the growth of New Mexico population between 1840 and 1850 was the same as that for Iowa between 1840 and 1850.

(i) Calculated under the same assumptions as *(h)*.

(j) Calculated by assuming that the growth of Oregon population between 1840 and 1850 was the same as that for the combined populations of California and Oregon between 1850 and 1860.

(k) Calculated under the same assumptions as *(j)*.

(l) Calculated by assuming that the growth of Minnesota population between 1850 and 1860 was the same as that for Iowa between 1850 and 1860. Part of Minnesota was enumerated in 1850. The estimate of 42 is therefore the difference between estimated total population of 81 and reported population of 39.

(m) No Negroes were recorded in Dakota territory when it was first enumerated in 1860.

(n) Calculated by assuming that the growth of the combined populations of Kansas and Nebraska between 1850 and 1860 was the same as that for the combined populations of Iowa and Missouri between 1850 and 1860.

(o) Calculated by assuming that the growth of Colorado population between 1850 and 1860 was the same as that for the combined populations of Utah and New Mexico between 1850 and 1860.

(p) Calculated by assuming that the growth of Nevada population between 1850 and 1860 was the same as that for Utah between 1850 and 1860.

Source: of recorded population, U.S. Bureau of the Census, *Negro Population, 1790-1915* (Washington, 1918), pp.44-5.

Table B-5. *United States Negro population: recorded slave imports 1804-07*

	1804	1805	1806	1807	Total 1804-07
Compiled from: *Charleston Courier*[a]	4,565	5,079	8,323	6,080	24,047
Virginia Argus[b]	5,386	6,790	11,458	15,676	39,310
Charleston customs house records[c]					39,075

Notes:

[a] Elizabeth Donnan, *Documents Illustrative of the History of the Slave Trade to America* (Washington: Carnegie Institution, 1935), Vol. IV, pp.504-22.

[b] *Virginia Argus*, Tuesday, January 19, 1808, p.3.

[c] Evidence from the customs house officer of Charleston, compiled from the customs house books, submitted by William Smith of South Carolina to the Senate; U.S., Congress, Senate, *Annals of Congress*, 16th Cong., 2nd Sess., 1820-21, pp.75-6.

Table B-6. *United States Negro population: estimates of net slave imports 1800-60*

Author	1800-10	1810-20	1820-30	1830-40	1840-50	1850-60
Gray [a]	60,000	50,000	40,000	40,000	55,000	75,000
Collins [b]		60,000 [c]	50,000	40,000	50,000	70,000
Curtin [d]	10,000	10,000	10,000	10,000	10,000	10,000
Deerr [e]	155,000	175,000	175,000	175,000	175,000	175,000

Notes:

[a] Lewis C. Gray, *History of Agriculture in the Southern United States to 1860* (Washington, 1933), II, p.650.

[b] Winfield H. Collins, *The Domestic Slave Trade of the Southern States* (New York, 1904), p.20.

[c] Estimate for the period 1808-20.

[d] Philip D. Curtin, *The Atlantic Slave Trade* (Madison, 1969), p.74.

[e] Noel Deerr, *The History of Sugar* (London, 1949-50), II, p.282. For the period 1786-1808 Deerr estimated an annual average of 15,000; for the period 1808-64 'a total introduction of 1,000,000 does not seem too large an estimate', or roughly 17,500 per year. The estimate for the decade 1800-10 was therefore calculated as (15,000 x 8) + (17,500 x 2) = 155,000.

Table B-7. *United States Negro population: implied rates of natural increase for various estimates of net slave imports 1800–60*

	1800–10	1810–20	1820–30	1830–40	1840–50	1850–60
Total decade net immigration	0	0	0	0	0	0
implied r.	3.09	2.59	2.75	2.22	2.34	2.01
Total decade net immigration	10,000	10,000	10,000	10,000	10,000	10,000
implied r.	3.0	2.53	2.70	2.18	2.20	1.99
Total decade net immigration	60,000	50,000	40,000	40,000	55,000	75,000
implied r.	2.57	2.27	2.55	2.07	2.06	1.82
Total decade net immigration	155,000	175,000	175,000	175,000	175,000	175,000
implied r.	1.75	1.46	1.88	1.54	1.69	1.57

Source: Calculated using the immigration estimates of Table B-6, the population totals of Table B-1, and the assumption that annual immigration was at a uniform rate throughout the year, totalling one tenth of the decade estimate shown.

Table B-8. Tonnage entering selected southern seaports 1821-60

Year ending(a)	Gulf ports(b)	South Atlantic ports(c)	Total	Year ending(a)	Gulf ports(b)	South Atlantic ports(c)	Total
1821	88,204	85,033	173,237	1841	335,185	102,784	437,969
1822	56,563	66,547	123,110	1842	323,044	104,233	427,277
1823	75,547	77,786	153,333	1843	471,881	142,061	613,942
1824	100,728	87,439	188,167	1844	410,179	122,121	532,300
1825	80,388	62,581	142,969	1845	507,131	121,105	628,236
1826	87,974	79,695	167,669	1846	402,126	116,678	518,804
1827	130,632	94,491	225,123	1847	485,116	123,837	608,953
1828	143,777	72,323	216,100	1848	450,313	99,749	550,062
1829	124,541	72,904	197,445	1849	532,296	162,560	694,856
1830	135,412	100,300	235,712	1850	464,785	154,001	618,786
1831	158,669	82,424	241,093	1851	409,841	140,160	550,001
1832	155,735	82,927	238,662	1852	556,429	151,971	708,400
1833	158,192	82,364	240,556	1853	640,179	147,305	787,484
1834	163,555	82,079	245,634	1854	616,598	146,313	762,911
1835	195,512	90,672	286,184	1855	567,624	141,516	705,140
1836	185,169	89,359	274,528	1856	903,194	195,601	1,098,795
1837	174,771	92,934	267,705	1857	778,222	250,925	1,029,147
1838	231,339	112,204	343,543	1858	764,694	208,911	973,605
1839	233,998	86,145	320,143	1859	880,348	230,463	1,110,811
1840	333,623	125,570	459,193	1860	885,986	241,188	1,127,174

Notes to Table B-8.

(a) 1821 to 1842 for year ending September 30; 1843 for 9 months ending June 30; 1844 to 1860 for year ending June 30.

(b) Gulf ports include those of Louisiana (New Orleans and Teche), Alabama (Mobile), and western Florida (Key West, St. Mark's, Apalachicola, and Pensacola). From 1821 to 1826, inclusive, data are available by state but not by individual port. During that period, tonnage entering eastern and western Florida was distinguished only for 1821. The assumption was made that for the years 1822 to 1826 all tonnage entering Florida entered western Florida ports. (For the years 1827 to 1830, inclusive, the tonnage entering western Florida ports averaged 95 percent of the tonnage entering all Florida ports.)

(c) South Atlantic ports include those of South Carolina (Charleston, and Georgetown), Georgia (Savannah, Brunswick, and St. Mary's), and eastern Florida (Fernandina, St. John's, and St. Augustine).

Source: calculated from United States, Secretary of the Treasury, *Annual Statement of the Commerce and Navigation of the United States.*

Table B-9. *United States Negro population: regional emigration to Africa 1820-60*[a]

	New England	Mid-Atlantic	Old South	New South	North-west	Other	Total
1820	-	73	13	-	-	-	86
1	-	-	33	-	-	-	33
?	=	1?	?5	-	-	-	37
3	-	20	45	-	-	-	65
4	-	-	103	-	-	-	103
1825	-	-	66	-	-	-	66
6	32	-	150	-	-	-	182
7	-	14	180	27	1	-	222
8	-	-	163	-	-	-	163
9	-	-	189	15	1	-	205
1830	1	-	210	48	-	-	259
1	-	-	403	18	-	-	421
2	-	11	697	88	-	-	796
3	3	8	111	7	141	-	270
4	-	-	126	1	-	-	127
1835	-	5	2	139	-	-	146
6	2	-	176	56	-	-	234
7	-	8	95	34	1	-	138
8	-	-	72	37	-	-	109
9	-	2	43	2	-	-	47
1840	-	-	95	3	17	-	115
1	1	-	34	30	20	-	85
2	-	1	58	170	19	-	248
3	-	-	8	77	-	-	85
4	-	-	40	91	39	-	170
1845	-	7	180	-	-	-	187
6	-	2	25	25	37	-	89
7	-	2	38	5	8	-	53
8	-	14	237	155	35	-	441
9	-	6	113	284	19	-	422
1850	4	24	229	211	37	-	505
1	29	38	279	268	62	-	676
2	5	51	378	124	53	19	630
3	10	53	312	295	111	5	786
4	6	30	288	131	98	-	553
1855	12	31	63	49	52	-	207
6	8	1	219	216	93	1	538
7	3	6	285	24	52	-	370
8	20	11	105	7	24	-	167
9	-	80	71	93	4	-	248
1860	7	79	90	109	31	-	316

Note to Table B-9.

[a]For a definition of states included in each region, see Table B-2. Excluded from these emigration data are the 1,227 Negroes that the Maryland State Colonization Scoiety settled in 'Maryland in Liberia'. (American Colonization Society, *The African Repository*, XLIII (1867), p.117.) Also excluded are the 5,722 recaptured Africans sent to Liberia by the United States Government. (*Ibid.* LXII (1886), p.63.) Emigration of American Negroes to the British West Indies was insignificant. Between 1843 and 1862, for example, only 70 'Immigrants and Liberated Africans' were recorded as entering the British West India Colonies and Mauritius from the United States. (Great Britain, *Parliamentary Papers*, Vol. XXXVIII (*Accounts and Papers*, Vol. X), 183, April 20, 1863, 'Colonies and Certain Places Abroad' p.5.)

Source: American Colonization Society, *The African Repository*, XLIII (1867), pp.109-16.

Table B-10. *United States Negro population:*
percentage distribution by age 1830

		Free Negro population					
		Males			Females		
		0-10	10-36	36+	0-10	10-36	36+
		%	%	%	%	%	%
A	New England	25	49	26	23	49	28
B	Mid-Atlantic	28	50	21	26	53	21
C	Northwest	32	44	24	32	47	22
D	Old South	35	43	22	30	46	23
E	New South	34	46	20	29	48	23
F	North (A+B+C)	28	49	23	26	51	23
G	South (D+E)	35	43	22	30	47	23
	United States	32	46	22	28	49	23

		Slave population					
		Males			Females		
		0-10	10-36	36+	0-10	10-36	36+
		%	%	%	%	%	%
A	New England	9	36	55	3	30	68
B	Mid-Atlantic	3	43	54	4	40	55
C	Northwest	38	50	12	37	50	13
D	Old South	35	47	18	35	48	17
E	New South	34	52	14	34	53	13
F	North (A+B+C)	38	50	12	37	50	13
G	South (D+E)	35	49	16	35	50	16
	United States	35	49	16	35	50	15

Source: Calculated from age data in original census reports. For defini-
tions of regions cited, see Table B-2.

Table B-11. *United States Negro population:*
percentage distribution by age 1840

		Free Negro population					
		Males			Females		
		0-10	10-36	36+	0-10	10-36	36+
		%	%	%	%	%	%
A	New England	22	51	27	22	49	29
B	Mid-Atlantic	27	50	23	25	53	23
C	Northwest	29	47	24	30	48	22
D	Old South	33	45	22	29	48	23
E	New South	34	45	22	30	47	24
F	North (A+B+C)	27	50	24	25	51	23
G	South (D+E)	33	45	22	30	47	23
United States		30	47	23	28	49	23

		Slave population					
		Males			Females		
		0-10	10-36	36+	0-10	10-36	36+
		%	%	%	%	%	%
A	New England	–	–	100	–	7	93
B	Mid-Atlantic	4	8	88	2	5	93
C	Northwest	36	52	12	36	51	13
D	Old South	34	48	18	34	48	18
E	New South	33	52	14	34	53	13
F	North (A+B+C)	36	51	12	36	51	13
G	South (D+E)	34	50	16	34	51	15
United States		34	50	16	34	51	15

Source: See Table B-10.

Table B-12. *United States Negro population:*
percentage distribution by age 1850

		Free Negro population					
		Males			Females		
		0-10	10-40	40+	0-10	10-40	40+
		%	%	%	%	%	%
A	New England	22	55	22	22	53	25
B	Mid-Atlantic	26	54	21	25	55	20
C	Northwest	29	51	20	29	53	18
D	Old South	31	51	18	28	53	19
E	New South	31	49	20	25	52	23
F	North (A+B+C)	26	53	21	25	54	20
G	South (D+E)	31	51	19	27	53	20
United States		28	52	20	26	53	20

		Slave population					
		Males			Females		
		0-10	10-40	40+	0-10	10-40	40+
		%	%	%	%	%	%
A	New England	-	-	-	-	-	-
B	Mid-Atlantic	1	18	81	1	4	95
C	Northwest	33	55	12	34	53	13
D	Old South	32	52	16	32	52	16
E	New South	31	55	14	32	55	13
F	North (A+B+C)	33	55	12	34	53	13
G	South (D+E)	31	54	15	32	54	15
United States		32	54	14	32	54	14

Source: See Table B-10.

132

Table B-13. *United States Negro population:*
percentage distribution by age 1860

		Free Negro population					
		Males			Females		
		0-10	10-40	40+	0-10	10-40	40+
		%	%	%	%	%	%
A	New England	21	54	25	21	53	26
B	Mid-Atlantic	24	53	22	23	55	22
C	Northwest	28	53	20	28	54	18
D	Old South	29	52	18	27	53	20
E	New South	29	51	19	24	53	23
F	North (A+B+C)	25	53	22	24	55	21
G	South (D+E)	29	52	19	26	53	20
	United States	27	53	20	25	54	21

		Slave population					
		Males			Females		
		0-10	10-40	40+	0-10	10-40	40+
		%	%	%	%	%	%
A	New England	–	–	–	–	–	–
B	Mid-Atlantic	–	–	100	–	8	92
C	Northwest	33	54	12	34	53	13
D	Old South	31	53	16	32	52	16
E	New South	30	55	14	31	55	14
F	North (A+B+C)	33	54	12	34	53	13
G	South (D+E)	31	54	15	31	54	15
	United States	31	54	15	32	54	14

Source: See Table B-10.

Table B-14. *United States population in nineteen major cities*[a] *1800-60*

		1800	1810	1820	1830	1840	1850	1860
Population in 19 major cities								
Negro:	free	23,726	47,930	65,475	90,777	116,402	122,344	129,99
	slave	91,673	116,158	136,574	149,025	158,990	164,190	145,02
White		404,857	539,957	696,372	956,361	1,384,406	2,335,905	3,515,19
Percentage of total population								
Negro:	free	21.4	25.7	30.0	28.4	30.1	28.1	26.6
	slave	10.1	9.7	8.8	7.4	6.3	5.1	3.7
White		9.3	9.2	8.8	9.0	9.6	11.9	13.1

[a] Population in the counties embracing the following cities:

Baltimore, Md. (Baltimore)
Boston, Mass. (Suffolk)
Charleston, S.C. (Charleston)
Cincinnati, Ohio (Hamilton)
Louisville, Ky. (Jefferson)
Mobile, Ala. (Mobile)
Nashville, Tenn. (Davidson)
New Haven, Conn. (New Haven)
New Orleans, La. (Orleans)
New York, N.Y. (New York, Kings, Queens, Westchester)
Newark, N.J. (Essex)
Norfolk, Va. (Norfolk)
Philadelphia, Pa. (Philadelphia)
Pittsburgh, Pa. (Allegheny)
Providence, R.I. (Providence)
Richmond, Va. (Henrico)
St. Louis, Mo. (St. Louis)
Savannah, Ga. (Chatham)
Washington, D.C. (District of Columbia)

Source: See Table B-2.

Table B-15. *United States population in cities of 5,000 or over 1860*

Region	White			Free Negro			Slave		
	Male	Female	Total	Male	Female	Total	Male	Female	Total
North (a)	2,570,913	2,677,150	5,248,063	46,784	57,199	103,983	5,487	7,274	12,761
South (b)	336,995	330,337	667,332	30,188	42,275	72,463	55,829	61,602	117,431
United States	2,977,915	3,043,994	6,021,909	78,028	100,014	178,042	62,111	69,830	131,941

Percentage of total regional population in cities of 5,000 or over

Region	White			Free Negro			Slave		
	%	%	%	%	%	%	%	%	%
North	25	27	26	41	47	44	3	4	4
South	12	12	12	26	32	29	3	4	3
United States	22	23	22	33	39	36	3	4	3

Notes:

(a) Me., N.H., Vt., Mass., R.I., Conn., N.Y., N.J., Pa., Ohio, Ind., Ill., Mich., Wis., Minn., Iowa, Mo., Ky.

(b) Del., Md., D.C., Va., N.C., S.C., Ga., Fla., Ala., Miss., Tenn., Ark., La.

Source: Calculated from 'Population of Cities, Towns, Etc.' data in U.S. Bureau of the Census, *Eighth Census of the United States. I. Population.*

Table B-16. *United States Negro population:*
percentage increase by regions 1800-60

Regions	1800-10 %	1810-20 %	1820-30 %	1830-40 %	1840-50 %	1850-60 %
New England	7	5	2	6	2	7
Mid-Atlantic (coastal)	25	7	13	13	3	4
Northwest	107	65	43	31	28	16
Old South	21	15	15	-1	12	7
New South	131	86	74	67	40	31
United States	36	29	31	25	25	22

Source: See Tables B-2 and B-3.

Table B-17. *United States slave population:*
percentage increase by regions 1800-60

Regions	1800-10 %	1810-20 %	1820-30 %	1830-40 %	1840-50 %	1850-60 %
New England	-69	-65	-67	-52	–	–
Mid-Atlantic (coastal)	-25	-33	-85	-71	-68	-92
Northwest	101	63	38	25	24	13
Old South	18	14	13	-2	11	6
New South	129	64	75	68	40	30
United States	32	30	30	25	28	23

Source: See Tables B-2 and B-3.

Table B-18. *United States free Negro population:*
percentage increase by regions 1800-60

Regions	1800-10 %	1810-20 %	1820-30 %	1830-40 %	1840-50 %	1850-60 %
A New England	13	7	3	6	2	7
B Mid-Atlantic	88	26	39	15	3	4
C Northwest	198	82	91	71	46	27
D Old South	61	21	30	12	15	10
E New South	186	49	62	43	-18	8
'North' (A+B+C)	68	27	40	26	16	13
'South' (D+E)	68	24	34	17	9	10
United States	68	26	37	21	12	12

Source: See Tables B-2 and B-3.

Table B-19. *United States Negro*
population: estimated annual
net immigration 1800-19

Year	Net immigration
1800	5,000
1	5,000
2	5,000
3	5,000
4	6,463
1805	7,148
6	13,750
7	18,811
8	8,000
9	15,440
1810	5,000
1	5,000
2	5,000
3	5,000
4	5,000
1815	5,000
6	5,000
7	5,000
8	5,000
9	5,000

Source: See section 3.6.

Table B-20. *United States Negro population: estimated*
contribution of immigration to total population
increase 1800-60

Time period	Population increase	Immigration contribution	
		Number	% Total increase
1800-10	362,637	100,739	27.8
1800-20	765,815	150,933	19.7
1800-30	1,322,748	206,471	15.6
1800-40	1,898,350	261,643	13.8
1800-50	2,620,281	316,949	12.1
1800-60	3,422,664	371,745	10.9

Source: Population totals from Table B-4; immigration
estimates from Table B-19; rates of natural increase from
Table 6.5.1.

Table B-21. *Age and sex classification of slaves captured by the British 1808-41*

Time period	Male	Female	Total	Percentage	
				Male	Female
1808-19	4,639	1,929	6,568	70.6	29.4
1820-29	11,713	6,916	18,629	62.9	37.1
1830-39	18,809	8,515	27,324	68.8	31.2
1840-41	776	231	1,007	77.1	22.9
1808-41	35,937	17,591	53,528	67.1	32.9

	Adults	Children	Total	Percentage	
				Adults	Children
1808-19	3,763	1,513	5,276	71.3	28.7
1820-29	12,663	6,740	19,403	65.3	34.7
1830-39	15,607	11,717	27,324	57.1	42.9
1840-41	616	391	1,007	61.2	38.8
1808-41	32,649	20,361	53,010	61.6	38.4

Source: Calculated from Great Britain, *Parliamentary Papers (Accounts and Papers)* as follows: 1808-14, *A&P,* 1813-14, XII, 289
A&P, 1813-14, XII, 342
1815-18, *A&P,* 1818, XVII, 20
1819-29, *A&P,* 1830, X, 661
1830-41, *A&P,* 1842, XLIV, 385.

Table C-1. *Estimated interregional migrations of the white population*
1800–60

Underenumeration in previous decade = 0 percent
1800-10

Both sexes	Death rates				
Age	10-20	20-30	30-40	40-50	50 & up
Abs.	80,324	135,972	111,213	82,858	144,979
Rate per thousand	53.81	128.754	161.708	182.911	213.372
	Net in-migrations				
New England	-20,538	-18,644	-10,354	-9,391	-5,505
Mid-Atlantic	-9,893	-20,783	-13,023	-10,520	-6,677
Northwest	97,440	74,589	47,795	30,245	32,121
Old South	-87,305	-53,865	-36,106	-18,607	-25,786
New South	19,658	17,696	11,247	8,081	5,719
Far West	638	1,008	439	193	128
Total immigration	9,270	26,505	25,073	10,010	6,417

Male	Death rates				
Age	10-20	20-30	30-40	40-50	50 & up
Abs.	55,568	95,794	50,295	39,569	77,310
Rate per thousand	72.051	175.024	146.678	169.309	219.748
	Net in-migrations				
New England	-8,583	-10,020	-6,220	-4,494	-3,264
Mid-Atlantic	-6,278	-14,817	-10,857	-7,375	-4,882
Northwest	50,052	38,509	27,356	17,020	19,506
Old South	-46,097	-24,571	-17,125	-9,712	-14,600
New South	10,566	10,137	6,534	4,443	3,162
Far West	340	764	311	117	77
Total immigration	5,149	19,358	19,496	7,669	4,743

Female	Death rates				
Age	10-20	20-30	30-40	40-50	50 & up
Abs.	24,755	40,178	60,918	43,289	67,669
Rate per thousand	34.311	78.975	176.653	197.409	206.527
	Net in-migrations				
New England	-12,044	-8,848	-4,042	-4,802	-2,331
Mid-Atlantic	-3,501	-5,405	-2,252	-3,170	-1,774
Northwest	47,380	36,081	20,421	13,177	12,658
Old South	-41,221	-29,620	-18,942	-8,891	-11,177
New South	9,087	7,548	4,687	3,611	2,573
Far West	299	244	126	74	51
Total immigration	4,121	7,147	5,577	2,341	1,674

Table C-1 (contd.)

Underenumeration in previous decade = 0 percent
1810-20

Both sexes	Death rates				
Age	10-20	20-30	30-40	40-50	50 & up
Abs.	123,935	143,409	170,861	112,452	175,382
Rate per thousand	61.206	100.063	180.869	189.444	191.517
	Net in-migrations				
New England	-28,178	-38,933	-20,300	-15,621	-8,959
Mid-Atlantic	-43,603	-38,580	-21,037	-11,794	-18,620
Northwest	121,569	101,357	60,816	38,341	42,991
Old South	-82,368	-55,349	-36,035	-20,957	-28,068
New South	30,442	28,175	15,066	9,384	12,242
Far West	2,138	3,329	1,489	648	413
Total immigration	14,944	45,550	31,870	12,664	8,152

Male	Death rates				
Age	10-20	20-30	30-40	40-50	50 & up
Abs.	86,249	92,158	79,810	57,978	96,262
Rate per thousand	82.961	126.186	169.808	189.592	201.807
	Net in-migrations				
New England	-14,110	-23,322	-11,762	-7,573	-6,285
Mid-Atlantic	-21,383	-24,159	-15,931	-7,907	-12,039
Northwest	63,190	54,886	34,560	20,716	25,635
Old South	-44,486	-26,663	-17,244	-10,885	-14,522
New South	15,648	16,739	9,321	5,247	6,961
Far West	1,140	2,519	1,056	401	250
Total immigration	8,576	34,137	24,766	9,664	6,003

Female	Death rates				
Age	10-20	20-30	30-40	40-50	50 & up
Abs.	37,685	51,251	91,050	54,474	79,120
Rate per thousand	38.25	72.919	191.821	189.288	180.329
	Net in-migrations				
New England	-14,126	-15,660	-8,457	-8,050	-2,861
Mid-Atlantic	-22,222	-14,270	-5,161	-3,887	-6,590
Northwest	58,389	46,490	26,228	17,626	17,525
Old South	-37,849	-28,831	-18,752	-10,073	-13,571
New South	14,810	11,461	5,715	4,138	5,331
Far West	998	811	427	246	165
Total immigration	6,368	11,413	7,104	3,000	2,149

Table C-1 (contd.)

Underenumeration in previous decade = 0.5 percent
1820-30

Both sexes	Death rates				
Age	10-20	20-30	30-40	40-50	50 & up
Abs.	180,496	99,917	225,929	92,654	378,591
Rate per thousand	67.878	51.237	167.354	114.669	303.522
	Net in-migrations				
New England	1,972	-30,349	-12,940	-2,329	6,081
Mid-Atlantic	-24,942	-28,567	-17,163	-12,709	-14,621
Northwest	72,031	69,159	41,284	24,308	24,650
Old South	-78,768	-52,803	-35,730	-19,834	-25,516
New South	22,571	31,646	19,660	8,606	7,788
Far West	7,136	10,914	4,889	1,958	1,618
Total immigration	24,747	73,122	59,095	23,554	15,129

Male	Death rates				
Age	10-20	20-30	30-40	40-50	50 & up
Abs.	120,291	48,883	109,391	54,893	210,263
Rate per thousand	88.263	49.581	160.314	132.08	325.259
	Net in-migrations				
New England	4,575	-20,504	-7,809	-526	2,582
Mid-Atlantic	-9,492	-20,863	-14,194	-6,746	-8,383
Northwest	33,973	38,611	23,731	12,198	12,555
Old South	-42,952	-26,855	-17,908	-10,523	-12,822
New South	10,096	21,359	12,701	4,371	5,062
Far West	3,800	8,252	3,480	1,226	1,005
Total immigration	14,002	54,188	45,935	18,011	11,162

Female	Death rates				
Age	10-20	20-30	30-40	40-50	50 & up
Abs.	60,205	51,034	116,538	37,761	168,327
Rate per thousand	46.445	52.93	174.548	96.229	280.136
	Net in-migrations				
New England	-2,685	-9,838	-5,037	-2,003	2,940
Mid-Atlantic	-15,503	-7,711	-2,982	-6,000	-6,391
Northwest	38,098	30,537	17,479	12,282	12,694
Old South	-35,782	-25,936	-17,777	-9,358	-12,781
New South	12,537	10,286	6,920	4,330	2,913
Far West	3,336	2,663	1,397	749	625
Total immigration	10,745	18,934	13,160	5,543	3,967

Table C-1 (contd.)

Underenumeration in previous decade = 0 percent
1830-40

Both sexes	Death rates				
Age	10-20	20-30	30-40	40-50	50 & up
Abs.	254,775	74,676	403,117	184,856	460,609
Rate per thousand	72.716	28.77	203.069	154.259	202.752
	Net in-migrations				
New England	-4,615	-47,353	-12,723	-4,382	-5,265
Mid-Atlantic	-52,082	-105,546	-80,478	-40,842	-21,184
Northwest	157,727	190,096	122,458	64,555	54,527
Old South	-118,297	-97,871	-61,900	-30,545	-35,119
New South	-6,663	24,495	15,782	4,316	1,775
Far West	23,930	36,179	16,860	6,897	5,266
Total immigration	109,899	206,962	185,526	79,595	44,646

Male	Death rates				
Age	10-20	20-30	30-40	40-50	50 & up
Abs.	172,025	29,506	214,285	109,503	243,363
Rate per thousand	95.732	22.388	207.08	174.443	293.621
	Net in-migrations				
New England	841	-31,998	-5,351	-1,140	-3,034
Mid-Atlantic	-26,373	-81,397	-60,526	-26,383	-14,896
Northwest	79,552	119,895	75,248	35,893	31,106
Old South	-61,648	-55,142	-32,955	-15,388	-17,816
New South	-5,133	21,269	11,478	2,651	1,423
Far West	12,760	27,373	12,106	4,368	3,216
Total immigration	62,314	135,586	132,927	55,886	29,738

Female	Death rates				
Age	10-20	20-30	30-40	40-50	50 & up
Abs.	82,750	45,171	188,833	75,352	217,247
Rate per thousand	48.484	35.353	198.701	132.054	271.493
	Net in-migrations				
New England	-5,529	-15,359	-7,456	-3,605	-2,551
Mid-Atlantic	-25,723	-24,243	-19,923	-14,484	-6,340
Northwest	78,200	70,243	47,255	28,963	23,723
Old South	-56,644	-42,678	-28,992	-15,311	-17,387
New South	-1,473	3,233	4,340	1,841	483
Far West	11,169	8,805	4,776	2,597	2,072
Total immigration	47,585	71,376	52,599	23,709	14,908

Table C-1 (contd.)

Underenumeration in previous decade = 0 percent
1840-50

Both sexes	Death rates				
Age	10-20	20-30	30-40	40-50	50 & up
Abs.	258,510	196,486	563,563	226,973	550,122
Rate per thousand	55.626	55.743	203.025	130.819	241.256
	Net in-migrations				
New England	18,378	-6,175	-580	-1,917	-5,998
Mid-Atlantic	-108,119	-226,104	-161,312	-62,966	-30,104
Northwest	161,088	225,916	169,958	82,128	63,806
Old South	-57,656	-48,914	-25,390	-12,517	-23,314
New South	-40,865	-26,662	-12,322	-11,055	-6,846
Far West	27,175	81,939	29,646	6,328	2,456
Total immigration	269,959	554,143	377,822	148,959	89,401

Male	Death rates				
Age	10-20	20-30	30-40	40-50	50 & up
Abs.	188,075	91,973	297,943	136,882	287,737
Rate per thousand	79.037	51.457	204.786	147.88	246.214
	Net in-migrations				
New England	7,639	-13,461	-1,755	-342	-2,359
Mid-Atlantic	-56,707	-154,128	-109,215	-38,843	-20,106
Northwest	83,271	135,758	105,139	48,579	38,447
Old South	-28,565	-27,619	-11,589	-5,518	-12,417
New South	-21,847	-12,148	-7,573	-8,609	-5,217
Far West	16,209	71,598	24,994	4,732	1,652
Total immigration	142,563	329,170	246,277	95,413	54,513

Female	Death rates				
Age	10-20	20-30	30-40	40-50	50 & up
Abs.	70,435	104,513	265,620	90,090	262,386
Rate per thousand	31.06	60.151	201.085	111.308	236.043
	Net in-migrations				
New England	10,671	7,278	1,141	-1,891	-3,828
Mid-Atlantic	-51,460	-72,065	-52,119	-24,361	-10,064
Northwest	77,837	90,214	64,857	33,934	25,560
Old South	-29,111	-21,261	-13,840	-7,228	-10,962
New South	-18,903	-14,501	-4,722	-2,232	-1,544
Far West	10,966	10,336	4,684	1,778	838
Total immigration	127,396	224,973	131,545	53,546	34,888

Table C-1 (contd.)

Underenumeration in previous decade = 0 percent
1850-60

Both sexes	Death rates				
Age	10-20	20-30	30-40	40-50	50 & up
Abs.	70,897	428,086	890,160	460,531	1,000,531
Rate per thousand	12.003	05.320	217.070	170.024	206.040
	Net in-migrations				
New England	-11,619	-15,017	-31,167	-6,185	-257
Mid-Atlantic	-191,578	-393,469	-357,907	-135,128	-77,449
Northwest	243,683	378,484	379,249	160,980	122,972
Old South	-47,552	-57,856	-21,836	-8,485	-25,067
New South	-79,845	-96,832	-60,689	-35,529	-37,703
Far West	86,911	184,691	92,350	24,348	17,503
Total immigration	406,054	809,879	742,891	306,916	201,868

Male	Death rates				
Age	10-20	20-30	30-40	40-50	50 & up
Abs.	84,563	232,553	509,538	285,058	545,677
Rate per thousand	28.321	91.337	233.965	200.085	297.982
	Net in-migrations				
New England	-6,919	-23,260	-20,062	-2,228	-2,194
Mid-Atlantic	-106,936	-262,360	-251,192	-93,634	-53,099
Northwest	132,012	221,976	244,097	104,328	76,037
Old South	-23,259	-34,488	-10,131	-2,531	-11,321
New South	-41,286	-43,709	-31,114	-20,592	-19,727
Far West	46,388	141,840	68,402	14,657	10,303
Total immigration	216,322	467,305	494,230	207,654	123,976

Female	Death rates				
Age	10-20	20-30	30-40	40-50	50 & up
Abs.	-13,666	195,533	380,621	175,473	454,854
Rate per thousand	-4.743	79.132	199.123	147.257	272.93
	Net in-migrations				
New England	-4,753	8,186	-11,588	-4,561	1,371
Mid-Atlantic	-84,545	-130,905	-106,213	-41,652	-24,558
Northwest	111,548	156,360	134,531	56,881	47,605
Old South	-24,288	-23,403	-12,105	-6,468	-14,031
New South	-38,501	-53,126	-29,603	-14,713	-17,802
Far West	40,538	42,888	24,977	10,514	7,416
Total immigration	189,732	342,574	248,661	99,262	77,892

Table C-2. *Estimated death rates for white population 1800-60 (both sexes)*

Relative underenumeration of each starting census - 0%
Except U(1820) = 0.5%
Relative underenumeration of children each census year - 0%

Decade starting	Ages at end of decade	Deaths per decade per thousand	Death rate per thousand	Crude death rate per thousand
1800				13.52
	10 - 20	53.8	5.5	
	20 - 30	128.8	13.7	
	30 - 40	161.7	17.5	
	40 - 50	182.9	20	
	50 & up	213.4	23.7	
1810				13.04
	10 - 20	61.2	6.3	
	20 - 30	100.1	10.5	
	30 - 40	180.9	19.7	
	40 - 50	189.4	20.8	
	50 & up	191.5	21	
1820				13.23
	10 - 20	67.9	7.1	
	20 - 30	51.2	5.3	
	30 - 40	167.4	18.5	
	40 - 50	114.7	12.3	
	50 & up	303.5	36.2	
1830				13.48
	10 - 20	72.7	7.5	
	20 - 30	28.8	2.9	
	30 - 40	203.1	22.4	
	40 - 50	154.3	16.6	
	50 & up	282.8	32.7	
1840				12.75
	10 - 20	55.6	5.7	
	20 - 30	55.7	5.7	
	30 - 40	203	22.4	
	40 - 50	130.8	13.9	
	50 & up	241.3	27.2	
1850				14.38
	10 - 20	12.1	1.2	
	20 - 30	85.3	8.9	
	30 - 40	217.7	24.3	
	40 - 50	176	19.2	
	50 & up	286	33.1	

Table C-3. *Estimated death rates for the white population 1800-60*
(both sexes)
Relative underenumeration of each census year - 0%
Except U(1820) = 0.5%
Relative underenumeration of children each census year - 0%
Children's one-year death rate multiplied by 3

Decade starting	Ages at end of decade	Deaths per decade per thousand	Death rate per thousand	Crude death rate per thousand
1800				17.41
	10 - 20	153.7	16.5	
	20 - 30	128.8	13.7	
	30 - 40	161.7	17.5	
	40 - 50	182.9	20	
	50 & up	213.4	23.7	
1810				17.47
	10 - 20	173.6	18.9	
	20 - 30	100.1	10.5	
	30 - 40	180.9	19.7	
	40 - 50	189.4	20.8	
	50 & up	191.5	21	
1820				18.08
	10 - 20	191.4	21.4	
	20 - 30	51.2	5.3	
	30 - 40	167.4	18.5	
	40 - 50	114.7	12.3	
	50 & up	303.5	36.2	
1830				18.43
	10 - 20	204.1	22.6	
	20 - 30	28.8	2.9	
	30 - 40	203.1	22.4	
	40 - 50	154.3	16.6	
	50 & up	282.8	32.7	
1840				16.39
	10 - 20	158.6	17.1	
	20 - 30	55.7	5.7	
	30 - 40	203	22.4	
	40 - 50	130.8	13.9	
	50 & up	241.3	27.2	
1850				15.2
	10 - 20	35.9	3.6	
	20 - 30	85.3	8.9	
	30 - 40	217.7	24.3	
	40 - 50	176	19.2	
	50 & up	286	33.1	

Table C-4. *Estimated death rates for the white population 1800-60*
(both sexes)
Relative underenumeration of each starting census - 0%
Except U(1820) = 0.5%

Relative underenumeration of children each census year - C(t)
Calculated using Massachussetts-Maryland life tables

Decade starting	Ages at end of decade	Deaths per decade per thousand	Death rate per thousand	Crude death rate per thousand
1800				16.15
	10 - 20	123.7	13.1	
	20 - 30	128.8	13.7	
	30 - 40	161.7	17.5	
	40 - 50	182.9	20	
	50 & up	213.4	23.7	
1810				15.68
	10 - 20	130.6	13.9	
	20 - 30	100.1	10.5	
	30 - 40	180.9	19.7	
	40 - 50	189.4	20.8	
	50 & up	191.5	21	
1820				15.2
	10 - 20	120.4	13	
	20 - 30	51.2	5.3	
	30 - 40	167.4	18.5	
	40 - 50	114.7	12.3	
	50 & up	303.5	36.2	
1830				15.33
	10 - 20	124.4	13.2	
	20 - 30	28.8	2.9	
	30 - 40	203.1	22.4	
	40 - 50	154.3	16.6	
	50 & up	282.8	32.7	
1840				15.1
	10 - 20	124.1	13.2	
	20 - 30	55.7	5.7	
	30 - 40	203	22.4	
	40 - 50	130.8	13.9	
	50 & up	241.3	27.2	
1850				17.77
	10 - 20	121.7	12.9	
	20 - 30	85.3	8.9	
	30 - 40	217.7	24.3	
	40 - 50	176	19.2	
	50 & up	286	33.1	

Table C-5. *Estimated death rates for the white population 1800-60*
(both sexes)

Relative underenumeration of each census year - 0%
Except U(1820) = 0.5%
Relative underenumeration of children each census year - C(t)'s
Calculated using Massachussets-Maryland life tables
Children's one-year death rate multiplied by 3

Decade starting	Ages at end of decade	Deaths per decade per thousand	Death rate per thousand	Crude death rate per thousand
1800				25.69
	10 - 20	330.7	39.3	
	20 - 30	128.8	13.7	
	30 - 40	161.7	17.5	
	40 - 50	182.9	20	
	50 & up	213.4	23.7	
1810				25.74
	10 - 20	346.7	41.7	
	20 - 30	100.1	10.5	
	30 - 40	180.9	19.7	
	40 - 50	189.4	20.8	
	50 & up	191.5	21	
1820				24.23
	10 - 20	323.1	39	
	20 - 30	51.2	5.3	
	30 - 40	167.4	18.5	
	40 - 50	114.7	12.3	
	50 & up	303.5	36.2	
1830				24.23
	10 - 20	332.4	39.6	
	20 - 30	28.8	2.9	
	30 - 40	203.1	22.4	
	40 - 50	154.3	16.6	
	50 & up	282.8	32.7	
1840				23.76
	10 - 20	331.6	39.5	
	20 - 30	55.7	5.7	
	30 - 40	203	22.4	
	40 - 50	130.8	13.9	
	50 & up	241.3	27.2	
1850				25.86
	10 - 20	326	38.7	
	20 - 30	85.3	8.9	
	30 - 40	217.7	24.3	
	40 - 50	176	19.2	
	50 & up	286	33.1	

Table C-6. *Estimated death rates for white males 1800-60*

Relative underenumeration of each starting census - 0%
Except U(1820) = 0.5%
Relative underenumeration of children each census year - 0%

Decade starting	Ages at end of decade	Deaths per decade per thousand	Death rate per thousand	Crude death rate per thousand
1800				15.18
	10 - 20	72.1	7.4	
	20 - 30	175	19	
	30 - 40	146.7	15.7	
	40 - 50	169.3	18.4	
	50 & up	219.7	24.5	
1810				14.58
	10 - 20	83	8.6	
	20 - 30	126.2	13.4	
	30 - 40	169.8	18.4	
	40 - 50	189.6	20.8	
	50 & up	201.8	22.3	
1820				14.5
	10 - 20	88.3	9.4	
	20 - 30	49.6	5.2	
	30 - 40	160.3	17.6	
	40 - 50	132.1	14.3	
	50 & up	325.3	39.3	
1830				14.72
	10 - 20	95.7	10	
	20 - 30	22.4	2.3	
	30 - 40	207.1	22.9	
	40 - 50	174.4	19	
	50 & up	293.6	34.2	
1840				13.87
	10 - 20	79	8.2	
	20 - 30	51.5	5.3	
	30 - 40	204.8	22.7	
	40 - 50	147.9	15.9	
	50 & up	246.2	27.9	
1850				16.32
	10 - 20	28.3	2.9	
	20 - 30	91.3	9.5	
	30 - 40	234	26.3	
	40 - 50	200.1	22.1	
	50 & up	298	34.8	

Table C-7. *Estimated death rates for white males 1800-60*

Relative underenumeration of each census year - 0%
Except U(1820) = 0.5%
Relative underenumeration of children each census year - 0%
Children's one-year death rate multiplied by 3

Decade starting	Ages at end of decade	Deaths per decade per thousand	Death rate per thousand	Crude death rate per thousand
1800				20.46
	10 - 20	202.3	22.3	
	20 - 30	175	19	
	30 - 40	146.7	15.7	
	40 - 50	169.3	18.4	
	50 & up	219.7	24.5	
1810				20.64
	10 - 20	230.6	25.9	
	20 - 30	126.2	13.4	
	30 - 40	169.8	18.4	
	40 - 50	189.6	20.8	
	50 & up	201.8	22.3	
1820				20.86
	10 - 20	244.1	28.1	
	20 - 30	49.6	5.2	
	30 - 40	160.3	17.6	
	40 - 50	132.1	14.3	
	50 & up	325.3	39.3	
1830				21.27
	10 - 20	262.9	30	
	20 - 30	22.4	2.3	
	30 - 40	207.1	22.9	
	40 - 50	174.4	19	
	50 & up	293.6	34.2	
1840				19.03
	10 - 20	220.5	24.6	
	20 - 30	51.5	5.3	
	30 - 40	204.8	22.7	
	40 - 50	147.9	15.9	
	50 & up	246.2	27.9	
1850				17.98
	10 - 20	82.8	8.6	
	20 - 30	91.3	9.5	
	30 - 40	234	26.3	
	40 - 50	200.1	22.1	
	50 & up	298	34.8	

Table C-8. *Estimated death rates for white males 1800-60*

Relative underenumeration of each starting census - 0%
Except U(1820) = 0.5%

Relative underenumeration of children each census year - C(t)
Generated using Massachussetts-Maryland life tables

Decade starting	Ages at end of decade	Deaths per decade per thousand	Death rate per thousand	Crude death rate per thousand
1800				17.82
	10 - 20	140.6	15	
	20 - 30	175	19	
	30 - 40	146.7	15.7	
	40 - 50	169.3	18.4	
	50 & up	219.7	24.5	
1810				17.23
	10 - 20	150.7	16.2	
	20 - 30	126.2	13.4	
	30 - 40	169.8	18.4	
	40 - 50	189.6	20.8	
	50 & up	201.8	22.3	
1820				16.46
	10 - 20	139.7	15.2	
	20 - 30	49.6	5.2	
	30 - 40	160.3	17.6	
	40 - 50	132.1	14.3	
	50 & up	325.3	39.3	
1830				16.56
	10 - 20	146.1	15.7	
	20 - 30	22.4	2.3	
	30 - 40	207.1	22.9	
	40 - 50	174.4	19	
	50 & up	293.6	34.2	
1840				16.2
	10 - 20	145.7	15.6	
	20 - 30	51.5	5.3	
	30 - 40	204.8	22.7	
	40 - 50	147.9	15.9	
	50 & up	246.2	27.9	
1850				19.59
	10 - 20	136	14.5	
	20 - 30	91.3	9.5	
	30 - 40	234	26.3	
	40 - 50	200.1	22.1	
	50 & up	298	34.8	

Table C-9. *Estimated death rates for white males 1800-60*

Relative underenumeration of each census year - 0%
Except U(1820) = 0.5%
Relative underenumeration of children each census year - C(t)'s
Calculated using Massachussets-Maryland life tables
Children's one-year death rate multiplied by 3

Decade starting	Ages at end of decade	Deaths per decade per thousand	Death rate per thousand	Crude death rate per thousand
1800				28.8
	10 - 20	369.7	45.1	
	20 - 30	175	19	
	30 - 40	146.7	15.7	
	40 - 50	169.3	18.4	
	50 & up	219.7	24.5	
1810				28.97
	10 - 20	392.4	48.6	
	20 - 30	126.2	13.4	
	30 - 40	169.8	18.4	
	40 - 50	189.6	20.8	
	50 & up	201.8	22.3	
1820				27.03
	10 - 20	367.7	45.6	
	20 - 30	49.6	5.2	
	30 - 40	160.3	17.6	
	40 - 50	132.1	14.3	
	50 & up	325.3	39.3	
1830				27.06
	10 - 20	382.1	47	
	20 - 30	22.4	2.3	
	30 - 40	207.1	22.9	
	40 - 50	174.4	19	
	50 & up	293.6	34.2	
1840				26.36
	10 - 20	381.4	46.9	
	20 - 30	51.5	5.3	
	30 - 40	204.8	22.7	
	40 - 50	147.9	15.9	
	50 & up	246.2	27.9	
1850				28.46
	10 - 20	359.2	43.5	
	20 - 30	91.3	9.5	
	30 - 40	234	26.3	
	40 - 50	200.1	22.1	
	50 & up	298	34.8	

Table C-10. *Estimated death rates for white females 1800-60*

Relative underenumeration of each starting census - 0%
Except U(1820) = 0.5%

Relative underenumeration of children each census year - 0%

Decade starting	Ages at end of decade	Deaths per decade per thousand	Death rate per thousand	Crude death rate per thousand
1800				11.79
	10 - 20	34.3	3.5	
	20 - 30	79	8.2	
	30 - 40	176.7	19.2	
	40 - 50	197.4	21.7	
	50 & up	206.5	22.9	
1810				11.45
	10 - 20	38.3	3.9	
	20 - 30	72.9	7.5	
	30 - 40	191.8	21.1	
	40 - 50	189.3	20.8	
	50 & up	180.3	19.7	
1820				11.93
	10 - 20	46.4	4.8	
	20 - 30	52.9	5.5	
	30 - 40	174.5	19.4	
	40 - 50	96.2	10.3	
	50 & up	280.1	32.9	
1830				12.19
	10 - 20	48.5	5	
	20 - 30	35.4	3.6	
	30 - 40	198.7	21.9	
	40 - 50	132.1	14.1	
	50 & up	271.5	31.2	
1840				11.57
	10 - 20	31.1	3.2	
	20 - 30	60.2	6.2	
	30 - 40	201.1	22.2	
	40 - 50	111.3	11.7	
	50 & up	236	26.6	
1850				12.43
	10 - 20	-4.7	-0.5	
	20 - 30	79.1	8.2	
	30 - 40	199.1	22	
	40 - 50	147.3	15.8	
	50 & up	272.9	31.4	

Table C-11. *Estimated death rates for white females 1800-60*

Relative underenumeration of each census year - 0%
Except U(1820) = 0.5%

Relative underenumeration of children each census year - 0%
Children's one-year death rate multiplied by 3

Decade starting	Ages at end of decade	Deaths per decade per thousand	Death rate per thousand	Crude death rate per thousand
1800				14.24
	10 - 20	99.8	10.4	
	20 - 30	79	8.2	
	30 - 40	176.7	19.2	
	40 - 50	197.4	21.7	
	50 & up	206.5	22.9	
1810				14.19
	10 - 20	110.8	11.7	
	20 - 30	72.9	7.5	
	30 - 40	191.8	21.1	
	40 - 50	189.3	20.8	
	50 & up	180.3	19.7	
1820				15.22
	10 - 20	133.6	14.5	
	20 - 30	52.9	5.5	
	30 - 40	174.5	19.4	
	40 - 50	96.2	10.3	
	50 & up	280.1	32.9	
1830				15.48
	10 - 20	139.2	14.9	
	20 - 30	35.4	3.6	
	30 - 40	198.7	21.9	
	40 - 50	132.1	14.1	
	50 & up	271.5	31.2	
1840				13.61
	10 - 20	90.6	9.5	
	20 - 30	60.2	6.2	
	30 - 40	201.1	22.2	
	40 - 50	111.3	11.7	
	50 & up	236	26.6	
1850				12.25
	10 - 20	-14.3	-1.4	
	20 - 30	79.1	8.2	
	30 - 40	199.1	22	
	40 - 50	147.3	15.8	
	50 & up	272.9	31.4	

Table C-12. *Estimated death rates for white females 1800-60*

Relative underenumeration of each census year - 0%
Except U(1820) = 0.5%
Relative underenumeration of children each census year - C(t)'s
Calculated using Massachusetts-Maryland life tables

Decade starting	Ages at end of decade	Deaths per decade per thousand	Death rate per thousand	Crude death rate per thousand
1800				14.42
	10 - 20	105.7	11.1	
	20 - 30	79	8.2	
	30 - 40	176.7	19.2	
	40 - 50	197.4	21.7	
	50 & up	206.5	22.9	
1810				14.09
	10 - 20	109.3	11.5	
	20 - 30	72.9	7.5	
	30 - 40	191.8	21.1	
	40 - 50	189.3	20.8	
	50 & up	180.3	19.7	
1820				13.89
	10 - 20	100.2	10.7	
	20 - 30	52.9	5.5	
	30 - 40	174.5	19.4	
	40 - 50	96.2	10.3	
	50 & up	280.1	32.9	
1830				14.04
	10 - 20	101.6	10.7	
	20 - 30	35.4	3.6	
	30 - 40	198.7	21.9	
	40 - 50	132.1	14.1	
	50 & up	271.5	31.2	
1840				13.94
	10 - 20	101.3	10.6	
	20 - 30	60.2	6.2	
	30 - 40	201.1	22.2	
	40 - 50	111.3	11.7	
	50 & up	236	26.6	
1850				15.97
	10 - 20	107	11.2	
	20 - 30	79.1	8.2	
	30 - 40	199.1	22	
	40 - 50	147.3	15.8	
	50 & up	272.9	31.4	

Table C-13. *Estimated death rates for white females 1800-60*

Relative underenumeration of each census year - 0%
Except U(1820) = 0.5%
Relative underenumeration of children each census year - C(t)'s
Calculated using Massachusetts-Maryland life tables
Children's one-year death rate multiplied by 3

Decade starting	Ages at end of decade	Deaths per decade per thousand	Death rate per thousand	Crude death rate per thousand
1800				22.46
	10 - 20	287.4	33.3	
	20 - 30	79	8.2	
	30 - 40	176.7	19.2	
	40 - 50	197.4	21.7	
	50 & up	206.5	22.9	
1810				22.42
	10 - 20	296.4	34.5	
	20 - 30	72.9	7.5	
	30 - 40	191.8	21.1	
	40 - 50	189.3	20.8	
	50 & up	180.3	19.7	
1820				21.34
	10 - 20	274.1	32.1	
	20 - 30	52.9	5.5	
	30 - 40	174.5	19.4	
	40 - 50	96.2	10.3	
	50 & up	280.1	32.9	
1830				21.28
	10 - 20	277.5	32	
	20 - 30	35.4	3.6	
	30 - 40	198.7	21.9	
	40 - 50	132.1	14.1	
	50 & up	271.5	31.2	
1840				21.03
	10 - 20	276.8	31.9	
	20 - 30	60.2	6.2	
	30 - 40	201.1	22.2	
	40 - 50	111.3	11.7	
	50 & up	236	26.6	
1850				23.1
	10 - 20	290.6	33.7	
	20 - 30	79.1	8.2	
	30 - 40	199.1	22	
	40 - 50	147.3	15.8	
	50 & up	272.9	31.4	

Table C-14. Estimated birth rates for the white population 1800-60

Correction factor for children, A = 0

Underenumeration of children in each census year = 0%

Year	INC[a]	DIFF[a]	Male births	Female births	Total births	Crude births	Refined births	Sex ratios at birth (M/F)
1800	1.031	1	113,375	102,356	215,731	49.8	248.8	1.108
1810	1.031	1	152,893	139,849	292,742	49.9	248.9	1.093
1820	1.027	1	196,112	180,045	376,157	47.6	232.6	1.089
1830	1.027	1	250,726	230,791	481,517	45.4	210.8	1.086
1840	1.028	1	326,372	300,257	626,629	43.5	199.5	1.087
1850	1.022	1	373,911	351,423	725,334	36.9	164.4	1.064
1860	1.031	1	536,163	504,535	1,040,699	38.6	170.6	1.063

Note:

(a) See pp. 69-71.

Table C-15. Estimated birth rates for the white population 1800-60

Underenumeration of children in each census year = C(t)'s

Calculated using Massachusetts-Maryland life tables

Year	INC[a]	DIFF[a]	Male births	Female births	Total births	Crude births	Refined births	Sex ratios at birth (M/F)
1800	1.031	1	122,445	110,544	232,989	53.8	268.7	1.108
1810	1.031	1	165,125	151,037	316,161	53.8	268.8	1.093
1820	1.027	1	207,879	190,848	398,726	50.5	246.6	1.089
1830	1.027	1	265,770	244,639	510,408	48.1	223.5	1.086
1840	1.028	1	352,482	324,278	676,760	47	215.4	1.087
1850	1.022	1	422,519	397,109	819,628	41.7	185.7	1.064
1860	1.031	1	643,396	605,443	1,248,839	46.4	204.7	1.063

Note:

(a) See pp. 69-71.

Table C-16. *Estimated birth rates for the white population 1800-60*

Correction factor for children, A = 0.03

Underenumeration of children in each census year = 0%

Year	INC[a]	DIFF[a]	Male births	Female births	Total births	Crude births	Refined births	Sex ratio at birth (M/F)
1800	1.031	1	114,115	102,918	217,033	50.1	250.3	1.109
1810	1.031	1	153,891	140,616	294,507	50.2	250.4	1.094
1820	1.027	1	197,397	181,037	378,434	47.9	234	1.09
1830	1.027	1	252,001	231,767	483,769	45.6	211.8	1.087
1840	1.028	1	328,031	301,526	629,557	43.7	200.4	1.088
1850	1.022	1	375,820	352,915	728,735	37.1	165.1	1.065
1860	1.031	1	538,882	506,662	1,045,544	38.8	171.4	1.064

Note:

(a) See pp.69-71.

Table C-17. *Estimated birth rates for the white population 1800-60*

Underenumeration of children in each census year = C(t)'s

Calculated using Massachusetts-Maryland life tables

Year	INC[a]	DIFF[a]	Male births	Female births	Total births	Crude births	Refined births	Sex ratio at birth (M/F)
1800	1.031	1	123,244	111,151	234,395	54.1	270.4	1.109
1810	1.031	1	166,202	151,865	318,068	54.2	270.4	1.094
1820	1.027	1	209,241	191,899	401,140	50.8	248	1.09
1830	1.027	1	267,121	245,673	512,795	48.4	224.5	1.087
1840	1.028	1	354,273	325,648	679,921	47.2	216.4	1.088
1850	1.022	1	424,676	398,794	823,471	41.9	186.6	1.065
1860	1.031	1	646,659	607,995	1,254,653	46.6	205.7	1.064

Note:

(a) See pp.69-71.

Table C-18. *Estimated birth rates for the white population 1800-60*

Correction factor for children, A = 0.1

Underenumeration of children in each census year = 0%

Year	INC[a]	DIFF[a]	Male births	Female births	Total births	Crude births	Refined births	Sex ratios at birth (M/F)
1800	1.031	1	115,868	104,245	220,113	50.8	253.9	1.112
1810	1.031	1	156,255	142,429	298,684	50.9	253.9	1.097
1820	1.027	1	200,441	183,381	383,823	48.6	237.3	1.093
1830	1.027	1	255,014	234,067	489,081	46.1	214.1	1.089
1840	1.028	1	331,949	304,516	636,465	44.2	202.6	1.09
1850	1.022	1	380,331	356,431	736,762	37.5	166.9	1.067
1860	1.031	1	545,305	511,674	1,056,979	39.2	173.3	1.066

Note:

(a) See pp. 69-71.

Table C-19. *Estimated birth rates for the white population 1800-60*

Underenumeration of children in each census year = C(t)'s

Calculated using Massachusetts-Maryland life tables

Year	INC[a]	DIFF[a]	Male births	Female births	Total births	Crude births	Refined births	Sex ratios at birth (M/F)
1800	1.031	1	125,137	112,584	237,722	54.9	274.2	1.112
1810	1.031	1	168,755	153,824	322,579	54.9	274.3	1.097
1820	1.027	1	212,468	194,384	406,852	51.5	251.6	1.093
1830	1.027	1	270,315	248,111	518,426	48.9	227	1.089
1840	1.028	1	358,505	328,877	687,383	47.8	218.8	1.09
1850	1.022	1	429,774	402,767	832,541	42.3	188.7	1.067
1860	1.031	1	654,366	614,009	1,268,375	47.1	207.9	1.066

Note:

(a) See pp. 69-71.

Table D-1. *Estimated interregional migrations of the Negro population*
1800-60

Underenumeration in previous decade = 0 percent
1800-10

Both sexes	Death rates				
Age	10-20	20-30	30-40	40-50	50 & up
Abs.	-14,164	46,044	49,062	30,124	47,099
Rate per thousand	-43.076	173.122	266.857	259.221	313.946
	Net in-migrations				
New England	-501	327	308	76	-384
Mid-Atlantic	2,461	1,748	917	1,058	-278
Northwest	8,905	5,957	3,606	2,658	1,414
Old South	-28,363	-2,825	6,909	2,691	-2,451
New South	18,159	-2,942	-9,474	-5,130	1,808
Far West	-662	-2,265	-2,267	-1,353	-109
Total immigration	8,451	25,718	26,171	15,595	1,555

Males	Death rates				
Age	10-20	20-30	30-40	40-50	50 & up
Abs.	-482	25,534	26,202	16,036	25,115
Rate per thousand	-2.83	190.096	280.032	264.894	320.559
	Net in-migrations				
New England	-349	171	177	57	-156
Mid-Atlantic	728	623	381	592	-32
Northwest	4,486	2,978	1,780	1,384	790
Old South	-12,703	773	5,159	2,220	-1,550
New South	8,248	-3,183	-6,139	-3,441	1,013
Far West	-410	-1,362	-1,358	-813	-67
Total immigration	5,071	15,431	15,703	9,357	933

Females	Death rates				
Age	10-20	20-30	30-40	40-50	50 & up
Abs.	-13,680	20,510	22,861	14,388	22,785
Rate per thousand	-86.313	155.801	253.213	253.185	306.973
	Net in-migrations				
New England	-152	152	127	17	-233
Mid-Atlantic	1,756	1,124	529	462	-252
Northwest	4,423	2,978	1,824	1,273	623
Old South	-15,697	-3,614	1,743	471	-895
New South	9,922	260	-3,317	-1,684	800
Far West	-250	-900	-907	-539	-43
Total immigration	3,381	10,287	10,469	6,238	622

Table D-1   (contd.)

Underenumeration in previous decade = 0 percent
1810-20

Both sexes	Death rates				
Age	10-20	20-30	30-40	40-50	50 & up
Abs.	394	64,824	53,616	31,467	72,592
Rate per thousand	0.878	180.331	221.366	204.912	358.328
Net in-migrations					
New England	-577	193	65	-100	-32
Mid-Atlantic	-1,577	-254	-702	-413	-1,339
Northwest	9,013	5,712	2,800	2,457	1,256
Old South	-36,545	-11,874	-5,623	-6,722	-2,433
New South	29,868	7,811	4,311	5,059	2,500
Far West	-181	-1,587	-851	-282	49
Total immigration	8,510	22,495	12,650	5,065	660

Males	Death rates				
Age	10-20	20-30	30-40	40-50	50 & up
Abs.	9,053	34,123	26,313	15,171	37,719
Rate per thousand	38.988	188.836	215.4	192.935	361.578
Net in-migrations					
New England	-390	93	33	-46	-31
Mid-Atlantic	-1,362	-305	-387	-181	-561
Northwest	4,542	2,786	1,247	1,263	743
Old South	-16,675	-4,282	-2,359	-3,341	-1,687
New South	14,056	2,699	1,998	2,488	1,512
Far West	-170	-991	-532	-182	24
Total immigration	5,106	13,497	7,590	3,039	396

Females	Death rates				
Age	10-20	20-30	30-40	40-50	50 & up
Abs.	-8,659	30,700	27,303	16,296	34,873
Rate per thousand	-40.001	171.729	227.438	217.477	354.874
Net in-migrations					
New England	-187	98	34	-51	-3
Mid-Atlantic	-202	45	-310	-222	-781
Northwest	4,480	2,926	1,554	1,200	512
Old South	-19,903	-7,596	-3,266	-3,387	-746
New South	15,820	5,121	2,308	2,560	992
Far West	-8	-594	-320	-100	26
Total immigration	3,404	8,998	5,060	2,026	264

Table D-1   (contd.)

Underenumeration in previous decade = 0.5 percent
1820-30

Both sexes	Death rates				
Age	10-20	20-30	30-40	40-50	50 & up
Abs.	49,517	42,973	54,518	55,571	100,702
Rate per thousand	84.79	92.208	173.764	280.064	392.511
	Net in-migrations				
New England	-305	100	-11	-30	-214
Mid-Atlantic	-684	1,242	661	38	-225
Northwest	4,629	2,211	635	794	1,029
Old South	-49,061	-24,181	-10,002	-3,312	-5,474
New South	44,208	21,143	8,962	2,531	4,578
Far West	1,213	-515	-245	-21	306
Total immigration	8,510	22,495	12,650	5,065	660

Males	Death rates				
Age	10-20	20-30	30-40	40-50	50 & up
Abs.	35,245	25,826	29,039	29,066	54,848
Rate per thousand	116.719	110.57	183.918	285.919	413.528
	Net in-migrations				
New England	-258	56	14	-8	-134
Mid-Atlantic	-764	748	567	194	-15
Northwest	2,086	1,177	419	443	501
Old South	-23,674	-11,430	-4,951	-1,519	-2,702
New South	22,069	9,899	4,173	935	2,195
Far West	541	-450	-222	-46	154
Total immigration	5,106	13,497	7,590	3,039	396

Females	Death rates				
Age	10-20	20-30	30-40	40-50	50 & up
Abs.	14,273	17,146	25,480	26,504	45,854
Rate per thousand	50.605	73.759	163.477	273.912	370.016
	Net in-migrations				
New England	-47	39	-27	-23	-93
Mid-Atlantic	85	476	83	-161	-230
Northwest	2,557	1,034	211	346	522
Old South	-25,407	-12,745	-5,042	-1,791	-2,782
New South	22,139	11,256	4,797	1,604	2,431
Far West	673	-61	-22	24	153
Total immigration	3,404	8,998	5,060	2,026	264

Table D-1 (contd.)

Underenumeration in previous decade = O percent
1830-40

Both sexes	Death rates				
Age	10-20	20-30	30-40	40-50	50 & up
Abs.	131,632	4,139	107,606	89,064	111,999
Rate per thousand	163.326	7.526	244.205	332.217	370.982
	Net in-migrations				
New England	343	87	353	253	-101
Mid-Atlantic	1,188	1,399	1,355	436	-38
Northwest	6,097	-554	-229	1,459	1,614
Old South	-84,722	-51,562	-28,962	-12,020	-13,426
New South	71,179	47,167	25,307	8,812	10,715
Far West	5,915	3,462	2,175	1,058	1,236
Total immigration	8,510	22,495	12,650	5,065	660

Males	Death rates				
Age	10-20	20-30	30-40	40-50	50 & up
Abs.	71,027	8,100	53,990	43,744	57,129
Rate per thousand	174.511	29.346	247.329	326.048	375.123
	Net in-migrations				
New England	200	258	358	184	-48
Mid-Atlantic	207	482	654	294	-116
Northwest	3,332	384	-3	654	813
Old South	-41,205	-25,128	-14,453	-6,314	-7,299
New South	34,606	22,484	12,444	4,662	6,001
Far West	2,861	1,520	998	520	650
Total immigration	5,106	13,497	7,590	3,039	396

Females	Death rates				
Age	10-20	20-30	30-40	40-50	50 & up
Abs.	60,605	-3,961	53,616	45,320	54,870
Rate per thousand	151.916	-14.458	241.138	338.398	366.766
	Net in-migrations				
New England	143	-176	-6	70	-55
Mid-Atlantic	982	899	699	145	76
Northwest	2,766	-947	-227	807	798
Old South	-43,522	-26,445	-14,511	-5,704	-6,127
New South	36,576	24,723	12,868	4,143	4,722
Far West	3,055	1,947	1,177	538	586
Total immigration	3,404	8,998	5,060	2,026	264

Table D-1   (contd.)

Underenumeration in previous decade = O percent
1840-50

Both sexes	Death rates				
Age	10-20	20-30	30-40	40-50	50 & up
Abs.	87,732	50,100	159,915	85,920	81,403
Rate per thousand	90.04	72.628	283.829	251.309	218.756
	Net in-migrations				
New England	-81	352	142	-225	-892
Mid-Atlantic	-1,833	560	-276	-1,073	-3,292
Northwest	3,871	-2,005	-327	2,594	1,169
Old South	-41,988	-29,462	-13,202	-6,555	-10,188
New South	39,052	30,399	14,036	5,774	14,032
Far West	979	157	-373	-514	-829
Total immigration	8,510	22,495	12,650	5,065	660

Males	Death rates				
Age	10-20	20-30	30-40	40-50	50 & up
Abs.	46,685	26,085	80,379	32,501	41,861
Rate per thousand	95.507	75.547	288.654	256.467	223.257
	Net in-migrations				
New England	-108	259	63	-179	-484
Mid-Atlantic	-1,457	-160	278	-228	-1,650
Northwest	1,860	-276	-134	1,017	431
Old South	-19,637	-15,306	-6,485	-2,906	-4,515
New South	19,027	15,364	6,509	2,582	6,608
Far West	324	119	-231	-286	-389
Total immigration	5,106	13,497	7,590	3,039	396

Females	Death rates				
Age	10-20	20-30	30-40	40-50	50 & up
Abs.	41,047	24,015	79,536	42,419	39,542
Rate per thousand	84.536	69.703	279.113	246.231	214.184
	Net in-migrations				
New England	27	93	79	-45	-410
Mid-Atlantic	-376	718	-560	-848	-1,645
Northwest	2,022	-1,728	-190	1,577	734
Old South	-22,353	-14,156	-6,725	-3,658	-5,682
New South	20,025	15,034	7,537	3,203	7,442
Far West	655	39	-141	-228	-439
Total immigration	3,404	8,998	5,060	2,026	264

Table D-1   (contd.)

Underenumeration in previous decade = 0 percent
1850-60

All sexes	Death rates				
Age	10-20	20-30	30-40	40-50	50 & up
Abs.	39,290	125,134	160,117	88,563	201,807
Rate per thousand	34.333	138.709	243.603	214.769	367.004
	Net in-migrations				
New England	388	555	118	91	38
Mid-Atlantic	-943	1,430	-252	-476	-967
Northwest	-4,171	-9,714	-4,169	116	-336
Old South	-47,005	-50,447	-14,624	-7,730	-9,656
New South	23,465	36,934	7,880	1,953	6,031
Far West	28,266	21,242	11,047	6,045	4,890
Total immigration	8,510	22,495	12,650	5,065	660

Males	Death rates				
Age	10-20	20-30	30-40	40-50	50 & up
Abs.	15,638	61,518	84,628	41,724	99,246
Rate per thousand	27.495	136.274	256.651	205.136	362.647
	Net in-migrations				
New England	120	182	-67	-37	-68
Mid-Atlantic	-816	9	111	331	-744
Northwest	-2,046	-4,020	-2,571	-271	-76
Old South	-21,929	-26,308	-7,691	-4,034	-5,429
New South	10,742	19,190	4,626	1,674	3,717
Far West	13,929	10,947	5,592	2,998	2,599
Total immigration	5,106	13,497	7,590	3,039	396

Females	Death rates				
Age	10-20	20-30	30-40	40-50	50 & up
Abs.	23,652	63,616	75,489	46,839	102,561
Rate per thousand	41.089	141.147	230.467	224.145	371.321
	Net in-migrations				
New England	268	373	186	127	107
Mid-Atlantic	-124	1,423	-386	-143	-221
Northwest	-2,126	-5,693	-1,580	384	-253
Old South	-25,074	-24,142	-6,961	-3,677	-4,221
New South	12,719	17,743	3,279	264	2,298
Far West	14,337	10,295	5,463	3,045	2,290
Total immigration	3,404	8,998	5,060	2,026	264

Table D-2. *Estimated death rates for the Negro population (both sexes)*
1800-60

Relative underenumeration of each census year - 0%

Except U(1820) = 0.5%

Relative underenumeration of children each census year - 0%

Decade starting	Ages at end of decade	Deaths per decade per thousand	Death rate per thousand	Crude death rate per thousand
1800				16.51
	10 - 20	-43.1	-4.2	
	20 - 30	173.1	18.8	
	30 - 40	266.9	30.5	
	40 - 50	259.2	29.5	
	50 & up	313.9	37	
1810				17.22
	10 - 20	0.9	0.1	
	20 - 30	180.3	19.7	
	30 - 40	221.4	24.7	
	40 - 50	204.9	22.7	
	50 & up	358.3	43.4	
1820				18.56
	10 - 20	84.8	9	
	20 - 30	92.2	9.8	
	30 - 40	173.8	19.3	
	40 - 50	280.1	32.9	
	50 & up	392.5	49.5	
1830				20.72
	10 - 20	163.3	17.7	
	20 - 30	7.5	0.8	
	30 - 40	244.2	27.6	
	40 - 50	332.2	39.6	
	50 & up	371	45.3	
1840				17.12
	10 - 20	90	9.4	
	20 - 30	72.6	7.5	
	30 - 40	283.8	32.8	
	40 - 50	251.3	28.5	
	50 & up	218.8	24.4	
1850				18.29
	10 - 20	34.3	3.5	
	20 - 30	138.7	14.8	
	30 - 40	243.6	27.5	
	40 - 50	214.8	23.9	
	50 & up	367	44.7	

Table D-3. *Estimated death rates for the Negro population (both sexes)*
1800-60

Relative underenumeration of each census year - 0%

Except U(1820) = 0.5%

Relative underenumeration of children each census year - 0%

Children's one-year death rate multiplied by 3

Decade starting	Ages at end of decade	Deaths per decade per thousand	Death rate per thousand	Crude death rate per thousand
1800				13.64
	10 - 20	-134.3	-12.7	
	20 - 30	173.1	18.8	
	30 - 40	266.9	30.5	
	40 - 50	259.2	29.5	
	50 & up	313.9	37	
1810				17.28
	10 - 20	2.6	0.3	
	20 - 30	180.3	19.7	
	30 - 40	221.4	24.7	
	40 - 50	204.9	22.7	
	50 & up	358.3	43.4	
1820				24.56
	10 - 20	235.3	27	
	20 - 30	92.2	9.8	
	30 - 40	173.8	19.3	
	40 - 50	280.1	32.9	
	50 & up	392.5	49.5	
1830				32.91
	10 - 20	420	53	
	20 - 30	7.5	0.8	
	30 - 40	244.2	27.6	
	40 - 50	332.2	39.6	
	50 & up	371	45.3	
1840				23.55
	10 - 20	248.6	28.2	
	20 - 30	72.6	7.5	
	30 - 40	283.8	32.8	
	40 - 50	251.3	28.5	
	50 & up	218.8	24.4	
1850				20.61
	10 - 20	99.8	10.5	
	20 - 30	138.7	14.8	
	30 - 40	243.6	27.5	
	40 - 50	214.8	23.9	
	50 & up	367	44.7	

Table D-4. *Estimated death rates for the Negro population (both sexes)*
1800-60

Relative underenumeration of each census year - 0%

Except U(1820) = 0.5%

Relative underenumeration of children each census year - 10%

Decade starting	Ages at end of decade	Deaths per decade per thousand	Death rate per thousand	Crude death rate per thousand
1800				19.45
	10 - 20	50.9	5.2	
	20 - 30	173.1	18.8	
	30 - 40	266.9	30.5	
	40 - 50	259.2	29.5	
	50 & up	313.9	37	
1810				20.24
	10 - 20	90.9	9.5	
	20 - 30	180.3	19.7	
	30 - 40	221.4	24.7	
	40 - 50	204.9	22.7	
	50 & up	358.3	43.4	
1820				21.67
	10 - 20	167.4	18.5	
	20 - 30	92.2	9.8	
	30 - 40	173.8	19.3	
	40 - 50	280.1	32.9	
	50 & up	392.5	49.5	
1830				23.98
	10 - 20	239	26.9	
	20 - 30	7.5	0.8	
	30 - 40	244.2	27.6	
	40 - 50	332.2	39.6	
	50 & up	371	45.3	
1840				20.29
	10 - 20	172.4	18.7	
	20 - 30	72.6	7.5	
	30 - 40	283.8	32.8	
	40 - 50	251.3	28.5	
	50 & up	218.8	24.4	
1850				21.27
	10 - 20	121.8	12.9	
	20 - 30	138.7	14.8	
	30 - 40	243.6	27.5	
	40 - 50	214.8	23.9	
	50 & up	367	44.7	

Table D-5. *Estimated death rates for the Negro population (both sexes)*
1800-60

Relative underenumeration of each census year - 0%

Except U(1820) = 0.5%

Relative underenumeration of children each census year - 10%

Children's one-year death rate multiplied by 3

Decade starting	Ages at end of decade	Deaths per decade per thousand	Death rate per thousand	Crude death rate per thousand
1800				23.13
	10 - 20	145.8	15.6	
	20 - 30	173.1	18.8	
	30 - 40	266.9	30.5	
	40 - 50	259.2	29.5	
	50 & up	313.9	37	
1810				26.98
	10 - 20	250.8	28.5	
	20 - 30	180.3	19.7	
	30 - 40	221.4	24.7	
	40 - 50	204.9	22.7	
	50 & up	358.3	43.4	
1820				34.49
	10 - 20	429	55.5	
	20 - 30	92.2	9.8	
	30 - 40	173.8	19.3	
	40 - 50	280.1	32.9	
	50 & up	392.5	49.5	
1830				43.27
	10 - 20	569.5	80.8	
	20 - 30	7.5	0.8	
	30 - 40	244.2	27.6	
	40 - 50	332.2	39.6	
	50 & up	371	45.3	
1840				33.6
	10 - 20	439.5	56.2	
	20 - 30	72.6	7.5	
	30 - 40	283.8	32.8	
	40 - 50	251.3	28.5	
	50 & up	218.8	24.4	
1850				30.17
	10 - 20	326.3	38.7	
	20 - 30	138.7	14.8	
	30 - 40	243.6	27.5	
	40 - 50	214.8	23.9	
	50 & up	367	44.7	

Table D-6. *Estimated death rates for the Negro population (both sexes)*
1800-60

Relative underenumeration of each census year = 0%
Except U(1820) = 0.5%

Relative underenumeration of children = 10%

Except C(1800) = 15%; C(1810) = 15%

Children's one-year death rate multiplied by 3

Decade starting	Ages at end of decade	Deaths per decade per thousand	Death rate per thousand	Crude death rate per thousand
1800				27.77
	10 - 20	253.1	28.7	
	20 - 30	173.1	18.8	
	30 - 40	266.9	30.5	
	40 - 50	259.2	29.5	
	50 & up	313.9	37	
1810				31.71
	10 - 20	345.7	41.5	
	20 - 30	180.3	19.7	
	30 - 40	221.4	24.7	
	40 - 50	204.9	22.7	
	50 & up	358.3	43.4	
1820				34.49
	10 - 20	429	55.5	
	20 - 30	92.2	9.8	
	30 - 40	173.8	19.3	
	40 - 50	280.1	32.9	
	50 & up	392.5	49.5	
1830				43.27
	10 - 20	569.5	80.8	
	20 - 30	7.5	0.8	
	30 - 40	244.2	27.6	
	40 - 50	332.2	39.6	
	50 & up	371	45.3	
1840				33.6
	10 - 20	439.5	56.2	
	20 - 30	72.6	7.5	
	30 - 40	283.8	32.8	
	40 - 50	251.3	28.5	
	50 & up	218.8	24.4	
1850				30.17
	10 - 20	326.3	38.7	
	20 - 30	138.7	14.8	
	30 - 40	243.6	27.5	
	40 - 50	214.8	23.9	
	50 & up	367	44.7	

Table D-7. *Estimated death rates for the Negro population (both sexes)*
1800-60

(Increased annual immigration by 1,000 for 1800-03, 1808-60)

Relative underenumeration of each census year - 0%

Except U(1820) = 0.5%

Relative underenumeration of children each census year - 0%

Decade starting	Ages at end of decade	Deaths per decade per thousand	Death rate per thousand	Crude death rate per thousand
1800				16.98
	10 - 20	-37.7	-3.7	
	20 - 30	182	19.9	
	30 - 40	266.1	30.4	
	40 - 50	260.8	29.8	
	50 & up	314.7	37.1	
1810				17.98
	10 - 20	4.7	0.5	
	20 - 30	191.6	21	
	30 - 40	230.6	25.9	
	40 - 50	210.8	23.4	
	50 & up	358.9	43.5	
1820				19.16
	10 - 20	87.6	9.3	
	20 - 30	101.4	10.8	
	30 - 40	181.1	20.1	
	40 - 50	284.4	33.5	
	50 & up	392.9	49.6	
1830				21.18
	10 - 20	165.3	17.9	
	20 - 30	15.6	1.6	
	30 - 40	249.2	28.3	
	40 - 50	335.4	40	
	50 & up	371.3	45.4	
1840				17.48
	10 - 20	91.7	9.6	
	20 - 30	78.9	8.2	
	30 - 40	287.7	33.4	
	40 - 50	253.9	28.9	
	50 & up	219.1	24.4	
1850				18.58
	10 - 20	35.8	3.6	
	20 - 30	143.3	15.4	
	30 - 40	247	28	
	40 - 50	217	24.2	
	50 & up	367.2	44.7	

Table D-8. *Estimated death rates for the Negro population (both sexes)*
1800-60

(Increased annual immigration by 1,000 for 1800-03, 1808-60)

Relative underenumeration of each census year - 0%

Except U(1820) = 0.5%

Relative underenumeration of children each census year - 10%

Children's one-year death rate multiplied by 3

Decade starting	Ages at end of decade	Deaths per decade per thousand	Death rate per thousand	Crude death rate per thousand
1800				23.93
	10 - 20	158.6	17.1	
	20 - 30	182	19.9	
	30 - 40	266.1	30.4	
	40 - 50	260.8	29.8	
	50 & up	314.7	37.1	
1810				27.97
	10 - 20	259.1	29.5	
	20 - 30	191.6	21	
	30 - 40	230.6	25.9	
	40 - 50	210.8	23.4	
	50 & up	358.9	43.5	
1820				35.28
	10 - 20	434.2	56.4	
	20 - 30	101.4	10.8	
	30 - 40	181.1	20.1	
	40 - 50	284.4	33.5	
	50 & up	392.9	49.6	
1830				43.87
	10 - 20	572.6	81.5	
	20 - 30	15.6	1.6	
	30 - 40	249.2	28.3	
	40 - 50	335.4	40	
	50 & up	371.3	45.4	
1840				34.08
	10 - 20	442.5	56.8	
	20 - 30	78.9	8.2	
	30 - 40	287.7	33.4	
	40 - 50	253.9	28.9	
	50 & up	219.1	24.4	
1850				30.55
	10 - 20	329.2	39.1	
	20 - 30	143.3	15.4	
	30 - 40	247	28	
	40 - 50	217	24.2	
	50 & up	367.2	44.7	

Table D-9. *Estimated death rates for the Negro population (both sexes)*
1800-60

Relative underenumeration of each census year - 0%

Relative underenumeration of children each census year - 10%

Children's one-year death rate multiplied by 3

Increased slave import estimates for 1800-10, 1810-20 by 50%

Decade starting	Ages at end of decade	Deaths per decade per thousand	Death rate per thousand	Crude death rate per thousand
1800				28.05
	10 - 20	176.6	19.2	
	20 - 30	217.5	24.2	
	30 - 40	329.1	39.1	
	40 - 50	317.7	37.5	
	50 & up	318.4	37.6	
1810				29.47
	10 - 20	271.3	31.1	
	20 - 30	208.4	23.1	
	30 - 40	244.3	27.6	
	40 - 50	219.6	24.5	
	50 & up	359.7	43.6	
1820				34.49
	10 - 20	429	55.5	
	20 - 30	92.2	9.8	
	30 - 40	173.8	19.3	
	40 - 50	280.1	32.9	
	50 & up	392.5	49.5	
1830				43.27
	10 - 20	569.5	80.8	
	20 - 30	7.5	0.8	
	30 - 40	244.2	27.6	
	40 - 50	332.2	39.6	
	50 & up	371	45.3	
1840				33.6
	10 - 20	439.5	56.2	
	20 - 30	72.6	7.5	
	30 - 40	283.8	32.8	
	40 - 50	251.3	28.5	
	50 & up	218.8	24.4	
1850				30.17
	10 - 20	326.3	38.7	
	20 - 30	138.7	14.8	
	30 - 40	243.6	27.5	
	40 - 50	214.8	23.9	
	50 & up	367	44.7	

Table D-10. *Estimated death rates for Negro males 1800-60*

Relative underenumeration of each census year - 0%

Except U(1820) = 0.5%

Relative underenumeration of children each census year - 0%

Decade starting	Ages at end of decade	Deaths per decade per thousand	Death rate per thousand	Crude death rate per thousand
1800				18.87
	10 - 20	-2.8	-0.3	
	20 - 30	190.1	20.9	
	30 - 40	280	32.3	
	40 - 50	264.9	30.3	
	50 & up	320.6	37.9	
1810				18.61
	10 - 20	39	4	
	20 - 30	188.8	20.7	
	30 - 40	215.4	24	
	40 - 50	192.9	21.2	
	50 & up	361.6	43.9	
1820				21.1
	10 - 20	116.7	12.6	
	20 - 30	110.6	11.9	
	30 - 40	183.9	20.5	
	40 - 50	285.9	33.7	
	50 & up	413.5	52.9	
1830				21.83
	10 - 20	174.5	19	
	20 - 30	29.3	3	
	30 - 40	247.3	28	
	40 - 50	326	38.7	
	50 & up	375.1	45.9	
1840				17.61
	10 - 20	95.5	10	
	20 - 30	75.5	7.8	
	30 - 40	288.7	33.5	
	40 - 50	256.5	29.2	
	50 & up	223.3	24.9	
1850				18.06
	10 - 20	27.5	2.8	
	20 - 30	136.3	14.5	
	30 - 40	256.7	29.2	
	40 - 50	205.1	22.7	
	50 & up	362.6	44	

Table D-11. *Estimated death rates for Negro males 1800-60*
Relative underenumeration of each census year - 0%
Except U(1820) = 0.5%
Relative underenumeration of children each census year - 0%
Children's one-year death rate multiplied by 3

Decade starting	Ages at end of decade	Deaths per decade per thousand	Death rate per thousand	Crude death rate per thousand
1800				18.68
	10 - 20	-8.5	-0.8	
	20 - 30	190.1	20.9	
	30 - 40	280	32.3	
	40 - 50	264.9	30.3	
	50 & up	320.6	37.9	
1810				21.34
	10 - 20	112.9	11.9	
	20 - 30	188.8	20.7	
	30 - 40	215.4	24	
	40 - 50	192.9	21.2	
	50 & up	361.6	43.9	
1820				29.56
	10 - 20	314.2	37.7	
	20 - 30	110.6	11.9	
	30 - 40	183.9	20.5	
	40 - 50	285.9	33.7	
	50 & up	413.5	52.9	
1830				35
	10 - 20	443.9	57	
	20 - 30	29.3	3	
	30 - 40	247.3	28	
	40 - 50	326	38.7	
	50 & up	375.1	45.9	
1840				24.47
	10 - 20	262.3	30	
	20 - 30	75.5	7.8	
	30 - 40	288.7	33.5	
	40 - 50	256.5	29.2	
	50 & up	223.3	24.9	
1850				19.91
	10 - 20	80.5	8.4	
	20 - 30	136.3	14.5	
	30 - 40	256.7	29.2	
	40 - 50	205.1	22.7	
	50 & up	362.6	44	

Table D-12. *Estimated death rates for Negro males 1800-60*

Relative underenumeration of each census year - 0%

Except U(1820) = 0.5%

Relative underenumeration of children each census year - 10%

Decade starting	Ages at end of decade	Deaths per decade per thousand	Death rate per thousand	Crude death rate per thousand
1800				21.83
	10 - 20	87.4	9.1	
	20 - 30	190.1	20.9	
	30 - 40	280	32.3	
	40 - 50	264.9	30.3	
	50 & up	320.6	37.9	
1810				21.67
	10 - 20	125.5	13.3	
	20 - 30	188.8	20.7	
	30 - 40	215.4	24	
	40 - 50	192.9	21.2	
	50 & up	361.6	43.9	
1820				24.24
	10 - 20	196.4	22	
	20 - 30	110.6	11.9	
	30 - 40	183.9	20.5	
	40 - 50	285.9	33.7	
	50 & up	413.5	52.9	
1830				25.1
	10 - 20	249.1	28.2	
	20 - 30	29.3	3	
	30 - 40	247.3	28	
	40 - 50	326	38.7	
	50 & up	375.1	45.9	
1840				20.79
	10 - 20	177.3	19.3	
	20 - 30	75.5	7.8	
	30 - 40	288.7	33.5	
	40 - 50	256.5	29.2	
	50 & up	223.3	24.9	
1850				21.02
	10 - 20	115.5	12.2	
	20 - 30	136.3	14.5	
	30 - 40	256.7	29.2	
	40 - 50	205.1	22.7	
	50 & up	362.6	44	

Table D-13. *Estimated death rates for Negro males 1800-60*

Relative underenumeration of each census year - 0%

Except U(1820) = .0.5%

Relative underenumeration of children each census year - 10%

Children's one-year death rate multiplied by 3

Decade starting	Ages at end of decade	Deaths per decade per thousand	Death rate per thousand	Crude death rate per thousand
1800				28.27
	10 - 20	241.9	27.3	
	20 - 30	190.1	20.9	
	30 - 40	280	32.3	
	40 - 50	264.9	30.3	
	50 & up	320.6	37.9	
1810				31.16
	10 - 20	334.9	39.9	
	20 - 30	188.8	20.7	
	30 - 40	215.4	24	
	40 - 50	192.9	21.2	
	50 & up	361.6	43.9	
1820				39.65
	10 - 20	488.9	66.1	
	20 - 30	110.6	11.9	
	30 - 40	183.9	20.5	
	40 - 50	285.9	33.7	
	50 & up	413.5	52.9	
1830				45.43
	10 - 20	587.5	84.7	
	20 - 30	29.3	3	
	30 - 40	247.3	28	
	40 - 50	326	38.7	
	50 & up	375.1	45.9	
1840				34.56
	10 - 20	449.8	58	
	20 - 30	75.5	7.8	
	30 - 40	288.7	33.5	
	40 - 50	256.5	29.2	
	50 & up	223.3	24.9	
1850				29.43
	10 - 20	311.3	36.6	
	20 - 30	136.3	14.5	
	30 - 40	256.7	29.2	
	40 - 50	205.1	22.7	
	50 & up	362.6	44	

Table D-14. *Estimated death rates for Negro males 1800-60*

Relative underenumeration of each census year - 0%

Except U(1820) = 0.5%

Relative underenumeration of children each census year - 10%

Except C(1800) = 15%; C(1810) = 15%

Children's one-year death rate multiplied by 3

Decade starting	Ages at end of decade	Deaths per decade per thousand	Death rate per thousand	Crude death rate per thousand
1800				32.96
	10 - 20	337.7	40.3	
	20 - 30	190.1	20.9	
	30 - 40	280	32.3	
	40 - 50	264.9	30.3	
	50 & up	320.6	37.9	
1810				35.95
	10 - 20	419.6	52.9	
	20 - 30	188.8	20.7	
	30 - 40	215.4	24	
	40 - 50	192.9	21.2	
	50 & up	361.6	43.9	
1820				39.65
	10 - 20	488.9	66.1	
	20 - 30	110.6	11.9	
	30 - 40	183.9	20.5	
	40 - 50	285.9	33.7	
	50 & up	413.5	52.9	
1830				45.43
	10 - 20	587.5	84.7	
	20 - 30	29.3	3	
	30 - 40	247.3	28	
	40 - 50	326	38.7	
	50 & up	375.1	45.9	
1840				34.56
	10 - 20	449.8	58	
	20 - 30	75.5	7.8	
	30 - 40	288.7	33.5	
	40 - 50	256.5	29.2	
	50 & up	223.3	24.9	
1850				29.43
	10 - 20	311.3	36.6	
	20 - 30	136.3	14.5	
	30 - 40	256.7	29.2	
	40 - 50	205.1	22.7	
	50 & up	362.6	44	

Table D-15. *Estimated death rates for Negro females 1800-60*

Relative underenumeration of each census year - 0%

Except U(1820) = 0.5%

Relative underenumeration of children each census year - 0%

Decade starting	Ages at end of decade	Deaths per decade per thousand	Death rate per thousand	Crude death rate per thousand
1800				14.09
	10 - 20	-86.3	-8.3	
	20 - 30	155.8	16.8	
	30 - 40	253.2	28.8	
	40 - 50	253.2	28.8	
	50 & up	307	36	
1810				15.79
	10 - 20	-40	-3.9	
	20 - 30	171.7	18.7	
	30 - 40	227.4	25.5	
	40 - 50	217.5	24.2	
	50 & up	354.9	42.9	
1820				15.98
	10 - 20	50.6	5.3	
	20 - 30	73.8	7.8	
	30 - 40	163.5	18	
	40 - 50	273.9	32.1	
	50 & up	370	46	
1830				19.62
	10 - 20	151.9	16.3	
	20 - 30	-14.5	-1.4	
	30 - 40	241.1	27.2	
	40 - 50	338.4	40.5	
	50 & up	366.8	44.7	
1840				16.63
	10 - 20	84.5	8.8	
	20 - 30	69.7	7.2	
	30 - 40	279.1	32.2	
	40 - 50	246.2	27.9	
	50 & up	214.2	23.8	
1850				18.53
	10 - 20	41.1	4.2	
	20 - 30	141.1	15.1	
	30 - 40	230.5	25.9	
	40 - 50	224.1	25.1	
	50 & up	371.3	45.4	

Table D-16. *Estimated death rates for Negro females 1800-60*

Relative underenumeration of each census year - 0%

Except U(1820) = 0.5%

Relative underenumeration of children each census year - 0%

Children's one-year death rate multiplied by 3

Decade starting	Ages at end of decade	Deaths per decade per thousand	Death rate per thousand	Crude death rate per thousand
1800				8.45
	10 - 20	-279.3	-24.9	
	20 - 30	155.8	16.8	
	30 - 40	253.2	28.8	
	40 - 50	253.2	28.8	
	50 & up	307	36	
1810				13.1
	10 - 20	-124.4	-11.8	
	20 - 30	171.7	18.7	
	30 - 40	227.4	25.5	
	40 - 50	217.5	24.2	
	50 & up	354.9	42.9	
1820				19.47
	10 - 20	145	15.8	
	20 - 30	73.8	7.8	
	30 - 40	163.5	18	
	40 - 50	273.9	32.1	
	50 & up	370	46	
1830				30.83
	10 - 20	395.1	49	
	20 - 30	-14.5	-1.4	
	30 - 40	241.1	27.2	
	40 - 50	338.4	40.5	
	50 & up	366.8	44.7	
1840				22.63
	10 - 20	234.6	26.4	
	20 - 30	69.7	7.2	
	30 - 40	279.1	32.2	
	40 - 50	246.2	27.9	
	50 & up	214.2	23.8	
1850				21.31
	10 - 20	118.7	12.6	
	20 - 30	141.1	15.1	
	30 - 40	230.5	25.9	
	40 - 50	224.1	25.1	
	50 & up	371.3	45.4	

Table D-17. *Estimated death rates for Negro females 1800-60*

Relative underenumeration of each census year - 0%

Except U(1820) = 0.5%

Relative underenumeration of children each census year - 10%

Decade starting	Ages at end of decade	Deaths per decade per thousand	Death rate per thousand	Crude death rate per thousand
1800				17.01
	10 - 20	11.7	1.2	
	20 - 30	155.8	16.8	
	30 - 40	253.2	28.8	
	40 - 50	253.2	28.8	
	50 & up	307	36	
1810				18.77
	10 - 20	53.9	5.5	
	20 - 30	171.7	18.7	
	30 - 40	227.4	25.5	
	40 - 50	217.5	24.2	
	50 & up	354.9	42.9	
1820				19.06
	10 - 20	136.4	14.8	
	20 - 30	73.8	7.8	
	30 - 40	163.5	18	
	40 - 50	273.9	32.1	
	50 & up	370	46	
1830				22.86
	10 - 20	228.7	25.6	
	20 - 30	-14.5	-1.4	
	30 - 40	241.1	27.2	
	40 - 50	338.4	40.5	
	50 & up	366.8	44.7	
1840				19.79
	10 - 20	167.5	18.2	
	20 - 30	69.7	7.2	
	30 - 40	279.1	32.2	
	40 - 50	246.2	27.9	
	50 & up	214.2	23.8	
1850				21.51
	10 - 20	128	13.6	
	20 - 30	141.1	15.1	
	30 - 40	230.5	25.9	
	40 - 50	224.1	25.1	
	50 & up	371.3	45.4	

Table D-18. *Estimated death rates for Negro females 1800-60*

Relative underenumeration of each census year - 0%

Except U(1820) = 0.5%

Relative underenumeration of children each census year - 10%

Children's one-year death rate multiplied by 3

Decade starting	Ages at end of decade	Deaths per decade per thousand	Death rate per thousand	Crude death rate per thousand
1800				17.84
	10 - 20	34.8	3.5	
	20 - 30	155.8	16.8	
	30 - 40	253.2	28.8	
	40 - 50	253.2	28.8	
	50 & up	307	36	
1810				22.68
	10 - 20	153.8	16.6	
	20 - 30	171.7	18.7	
	30 - 40	227.4	25.5	
	40 - 50	217.5	24.2	
	50 & up	354.9	42.9	
1820				29.24
	10 - 20	360.3	44.5	
	20 - 30	73.8	7.8	
	30 - 40	163.5	18	
	40 - 50	273.9	32.1	
	50 & up	370	46	
1830				41.12
	10 - 20	550.8	76.9	
	20 - 30	-14.5	-1.4	
	30 - 40	241.1	27.2	
	40 - 50	338.4	40.5	
	50 & up	366.8	44.7	
1840				32.64
	10 - 20	429	54.5	
	20 - 30	69.7	7.2	
	30 - 40	279.1	32.2	
	40 - 50	246.2	27.9	
	50 & up	214.2	23.8	
1850				30.9
	10 - 20	340.8	40.8	
	20 - 30	141.1	15.1	
	30 - 40	230.5	25.9	
	40 - 50	224.1	25.1	
	50 & up	371.3	45.4	

Table D-19. *Estimated death rates for Negro females 1800-60*

Relative underenumeration of each census year - 0%

Except U(1820) = 0.5%

Relative underenumeration of children each census year - 10%

Except C(1800) = 15%; C(1810) = 15%

Children's one-year death rate multiplied by 3

Decade starting	Ages at end of decade	Deaths per decade per thousand	Death rate per thousand	Crude death rate per thousand
1800				22.43
	10 - 20	155.2	16.7	
	20 - 30	155.8	16.8	
	30 - 40	253.2	28.8	
	40 - 50	253.2	28.8	
	50 & up	307	36	
1810				27.35
	10 - 20	260.3	29.7	
	20 - 30	171.7	18.7	
	30 - 40	227.4	25.5	
	40 - 50	217.5	24.2	
	50 & up	354.9	42.9	
1820				29.24
	10 - 20	360.3	44.5	
	20 - 30	73.8	7.8	
	30 - 40	163.5	18	
	40 - 50	273.9	32.1	
	50 & up	370	46	
1830				41.12
	10 - 20	550.8	76.9	
	20 - 30	-14.5	-1.4	
	30 - 40	241.1	27.2	
	40 - 50	338.4	40.5	
	50 & up	366.8	44.7	
1840				32.64
	10 - 20	429	54.5	
	20 - 30	69.7	7.2	
	30 - 40	279.1	32.2	
	40 - 50	246.2	27.9	
	50 & up	214.2	23.8	
1850				30.9
	10 - 20	340.8	40.8	
	20 - 30	141.1	15.1	
	30 - 40	230.5	25.9	
	40 - 50	224.1	25.1	
	50 & up	371.3	45.4	

Table D-20. *Estimated birth rates for the Negro population 1800–60*

Correction factor for children, A = 0

Underenumeration of children in each census year = 0%

Year	Inc[a]	Diff[a]	Male births	Female births	Total births	Crude births	Refined births	Sex ratios at birth (M/F)
1800	1.032	1	24,934	22,453	47,387	46.5	222.7	.11
1810	1.032	1	34,002	30,674	64,675	46.8	224.6	.108
1820	1.026	1	43,097	38,917	82,014	45.9	209.4	.107
1830	1.033	1	60,114	56,954	117,068	50	225.6	.055
1840	1.018	1	68,152	65,385	133,537	45.8	226	.042
1850	1.018	1	74,524	73,962	148,486	40.8	183.3	1.008
1860	1.018	1	88,945	88,593	177,538	40	179.3	1.004

Note:

[a] See pp. 69–71, 78–9.

Table D-21. *Estimated birth rates for the Negro population 1800–60*

Underenumeration of children in each census year = 10%

Year	Inc[a]	Diff[a]	Male births	Female births	Total births	Crude births	Refined births	Sex ratios at birth (M/F)
1800	1.032	1	27,427	24,698	52,125	51.1	245	.11
1810	1.032	1	37,402	33,741	71,143	51.5	247.1	.108
1820	1.026	1	47,407	42,809	90,216	50.5	230.4	.107
1830	1.033	1	66,125	62,650	128,775	55	248.2	.055
1840	1.018	1	74,967	71,924	146,891	50.4	248.6	.042
1850	1.018	1	81,977	81,358	163,334	44.9	201.6	1.008
1860	1.018	1	97,840	97,452	195,292	44	197.2	1.004

Note:

[a] See pp. 69–71, 78–9.

Table D-22. *Estimated birth rates for the Negro population 1800-60*

Correction factor for children, A = 0.03

Underenumeration of children in each census year = 0%

Year	Inc[a]	Diff[a]	Male births	Female births	Total births	Crude births	Refined births	Sex ratios at birth (M/F)
1800	1.032	1	25,096	22,576	47,672	46.8	224	1.112
1810	1.032	1	34,223	30,842	65,065	47.1	226	1.11
1820	1.026	1	43,380	39,132	82,512	46.2	210.7	1.109
1830	1.033	1	60,505	57,266	117,772	50.3	227	1.057
1840	1.018	1	68,602	65,749	134,351	46.1	227.4	1.043
1850	1.018	1	74,906	74,277	149,183	41	184.2	1.008
1860	1.018	1	89,401	88,970	178,371	40.2	180.1	1.005

Note:

(a) See pp. 69-71, 78-9.

Table D-23. *Estimated birth rates for the Negro population 1800-60*

Underenumeration of children in each census year = 10%

Year	Inc[a]	Diff[a]	Male births	Female births	Total births	Crude births	Refined births	Sex ratios at birth (M/F)
1800	1.032	1	27,606	24,834	52,440	51.5	246.4	1.112
1810	1.032	1	37,646	33,926	71,572	51.8	248.6	1.11
1820	1.026	1	47,718	43,045	90,763	50.8	231.8	1.109
1830	1.033	1	66,556	62,993	129,549	55.3	249.7	1.057
1840	1.018	1	75,462	72,324	147,786	50.7	250.1	1.043
1850	1.018	1	82,396	81,704	164,101	45.1	202.6	1.008
1860	1.018	1	98,341	97,867	196,208	44.2	198.1	1.005

Note:

(a) See pp. 69-71, 78-9.

Table D-24. *Estimated birth rates for the Negro population 1800-60*

Correction factor for children, A = 0.1

Underenumeration of children in each census year = 0%

Year	Inc[a]	Diff[a]	Male births	Female births	Total births	Crude births	Refined births	Sex ratios at birth (M/F)
1800	1.032	1	25,481	22,867	48,348	47.4	227.2	1.114
1810	1.032	1	34,749	31,239	65,988	47.8	229.2	1.112
1820	1.026	1	44,050	39,639	83,689	46.9	213.7	1.111
1830	1.033	1	61,433	58,003	119,436	51	230.2	1.059
1840	1.018	1	69,670	66,608	136,278	46.7	230.7	1.046
1850	1.018	1	75,808	75,019	150,827	41.4	186.2	1.011
1860	1.018	1	90,477	89,859	180,336	40.6	182.1	1.007

Note:

[a] See pp. 69-71, 78-9.

Table D-25. *Estimated birth rates for the Negro population 1800-60*

Underenumeration of children in each census year = 10%

Year	Inc[a]	Diff[a]	Male births	Female births	Total births	Crude births	Refined births	Sex ratios at birth (M/F)
1800	1.032	1	28,029	25,154	53,183	52.2	249.9	1.114
1810	1.032	1	38,223	34,363	72,587	52.5	252.1	1.112
1820	1.026	1	48,455	43,603	92,058	51.6	235.1	1.111
1830	1.033	1	67,576	63,803	131,380	56.1	253.2	1.059
1840	1.018	1	76,637	73,269	149,905	51.4	253.7	1.046
1850	1.018	1	83,388	82,521	165,909	45.6	204.8	1.011
1860	1.018	1	99,525	98,845	198,370	44.7	200.3	1.007

Note:

[a] See pp. 69-71, 78-9.

Table D-26. *Estimated birth rates for the Negro population 1800-60*

Correction factor for children, A = 0

Underenumeration of children in each census year = 10%

Except C(1800) = 15%; C(1810) = 15%

Year	Inc(a)	Diff(a)	Male births	Female births	Total births	Crude births	Refined births	Sex ratios at birth (M/F)
1800	1.032	1	28,674	25,821	54,495	53.5	256.1	1.11
1810	1.032	1	39,102	35,275	74,377	53.8	258.3	1.108
1820	1.026	1	47,407	42,809	90,216	50.5	230.4	1.107
1830	1.033	1	66,125	62,650	128,775	55	248.2	1.055
1840	1.018	1	74,967	71,924	146,891	50.4	248.6	1.042
1850	1.018	1	81,977	81,358	163,334	44.9	201.6	1.008
1860	1.018	1	97,840	97,452	195,292	44	197.2	1.004

Note:

(a) See pp. 69-71, 78-9.

Table D-27. *Estimated birth rates for the Negro population 1800-60*

Underenumeration of children in each census year = 10%

Except C(1800) = 17%; C(1810) = 15%

Year	Inc(a)	Diff(a)	Male births	Female births	Total births	Crude births	Refined births	Sex ratios at birth (M/F)
1800	1.032	1	29,172	26,270	55,442	54.4	260.6	1.11
1810	1.032	1	39,102	35,275	74,377	53.8	258.3	1.108
1820	1.026	1	47,407	42,809	90,216	50.5	230.4	1.107
1830	1.033	1	66,125	62,650	128,775	55	248.2	1.055
1840	1.018	1	74,967	71,924	146,891	50.4	248.6	1.042
1850	1.018	1	81,977	81,358	163,334	44.9	201.6	1.008
1860	1.018	1	97,840	97,452	195,292	44	197.2	1.004

Note:

(a) See pp. 69-71, 78-9.

Table D-28. *Estimated manumissions 1800-60*

Same age-specific death rates for slave and free

Both sexes

Manumissions

Decade starting	10-20	20-30	30-40	40-50	50 & up	Relative underenumeration
1800	6,482	9,759	8,575	6,022	6,794	0 %
1810	-4,769	3,758	3,809	2,308	3,560	0 %
1820	2,543	10,848	8,388	5,019	5,329	0.5%
1830	294	5,650	6,471	4,592	3,752	0 %
1840	-4,276	3,838	3,906	933	-6,684	0 %
1850	-3,263	1,583	2,164	615	-655	0 %

Males

Manumissions

Decade starting	10-20	20-30	30-40	40-50	50 & up	Relative underenumeration
1800	2,131	4,535	4,191	2,986	3,548	0 %
1810	-3,737	1,652	1,862	1,138	2,003	0 %
1820	-396	5,000	4,195	2,678	2,462	0.5%
1830	-994	2,582	3,363	2,542	1,804	0 %
1840	-4,033	48	2,529	1,040	-3,333	0 %
1850	-3,123	-1,532	2,012	304	-838	0 %

Females

Manumissions

Decade starting	10-20	20-30	30-40	40-50	50 & up	Relative underenumeration
1800	4,346	5,195	4,361	3,028	3,235	0 %
1810	-1,036	2,083	1,962	1,195	1,548	0 %
1820	2,938	5,789	4,162	2,327	2,800	0.5%
1830	1,292	2,985	3,096	2,067	1,932	0 %
1840	-238	3,784	1,355	-122	-3,369	0 %
1850	-140	3,123	69	332	202	0 %

Table D-29. *Estimated manumissions 1800-60*

Free death rates are higher than the average for all Negroes by 10%

Both sexes

Manumissions

Decade starting	10-20	20-30	30-40	40-50	50 & up	Relative underenumeration
1800	6,339	10,179	9,045	6,351	7,508	0 %
1810	-4,764	4,498	4,468	2,749	4,916	0 %
1820	3,148	11,327	9,042	5,779	7,192	0.5%
1830	1,865	5,701	7,886	5,903	5,930	0 %
1840	-3,269	4,425	5,977	2,197	-5,117	0 %
1850	-2,849	2,935	4,083	1,821	2,569	0 %

Table D-30. *Estimated manumissions 1800-60*

Free death rates are higher than the average for all Negroes by 30%

Both sexes

Manumissions

Decade starting	10-20	20-30	30-40	40-50	50 & up	Relative underenumeration
1800	6,054	11,017	9,984	7,009	8,938	0 %
1810	-4,754	5,980	5,787	3,629	7,628	0 %
1820	4,358	12,284	10,349	7,299	10,918	0.5%
1830	5,007	5,803	10,717	8,525	10,287	0 %
1840	1,255	5,598	10,120	4,723	-1,983	0 %
1850	-2,022	5,640	7,919	4,234	9,017	0 %

Table D-31. *Estimated manumissions 1800-60*

Free death rates are higher than the average for all Negroes by 50%

Both sexes

Manumissions

Decade starting	10-20	20-30	30-40	40-50	50 & up	Relative underenumeration
1800	5,768	11,855	10,924	7,667	10,368	0 %
1810	-4,744	7,461	7,105	4,509	10,339	0 %
1820	5,568	13,241	11,656	8,818	14,644	0.5%
1830	8,150	5,905	13,547	11,147	14,643	0 %
1840	760	6,771	14,263	7,250	1,151	0 %
1850	-1,194	8,345	11,756	6,647	15,465	0 %

Table D-32. *Estimated manumissions 1800-60*

(Assuming 1,000 more immigrants 1800-03, 1808-60)

Both sexes

Manumissions

Decade starting	10-20	20-30	30-40	40-50	50 & up	Relative underenumeration
1800	6,661	9,974	8,562	6,042	6,812	0 %
1810	-4,555	4,223	4,084	2,435	3,580	0 %
1820	2,742	11,324	8,664	5,138	5,348	0.5%
1830	480	6,200	6,762	4,716	3,773	0 %
1840	-4,089	4,344	4,186	1,063	-6,661	0 %
1850	-3,087	2,034	2,430	738	-638	0 %

Male

Manumissions

Decade starting	10-20	20-30	30-40	40-50	50 & up	Relative underenumeration
1800	2,236	4,653	4,184	2,997	3,558	0 %
1810	-3,612	1,911	2,014	1,207	2,015	0 %
1820	-279	5,265	4,346	2,743	2,473	0.5%
1830	-882	2,890	3,525	2,611	1,816	0 %
1840	-3,920	342	2,686	1,113	-3,320	0 %
1850	-3,017	-1,270	2,158	375	-829	0 %

Female

Manumissions

Decade starting	10-20	20-30	30-40	40-50	50 & up	Relative underenumeration
1800	4,419	5,288	4,355	3,037	3,243	0 %
1810	-949	2,282	2,081	1,250	1,557	0 %
1820	3,019	5,993	4,282	2,379	2,809	0.5%
1830	1,367	3,221	3,220	2,120	1,941	0 %
1840	-164	3,992	1,475	-66	-3,360	0 %
1850	-70	3,309	185	383	209	0 %

Notes

1 *A Journey in the Seaboard Slave States in the Years 1853-1854* (New York: G.P. Putnam's Sons, 1904), Vol. II, p. 150.
2 U.S., Bureau of the Census, *Ninth Census of the United States. 1870. Population*, Vol. I, p. xix n.
3 Robert W. Fogel and Stanley L. Engerman, *Time on the Cross* (Boston: Little, Brown, 1974), Vol. II, pp. 101-13.
4 Concerning the 1850 count in Louisiana, for example (a state with a relatively high percentage of free Negroes) the superintendent of the census admitted to being puzzled by the mysterious disappearance of the free colored population. (J.D.B. DeBow, *Statistical View of the United States . . . Being a Compendium of the Seventh Census* (Washington: Beverly Tucker, 1854), p. 62.) Our efforts to correct for this apparent underenumeration are described in section 2.8.
5 Those that were recorded as mulattoes had their skin color reported by masters if they were slaves or determined by visual inspection of the census taker if they were free.
6 *Democracy in America* (New York: Alfred A. Knopf, 1945), Vol. I, p. 223.
7 See for example, Harry W. Richardson, *Regional Economics* (New York: Praeger, 1969), Chapter 9; or John R. Meyer, 'Regional Economics: A Survey', *American Economic Review*, LIII (March, 1963), 20-6.
8 August Lösh, *The Economics of Location* (New Haven: Yale University Press, 1954), p. 215.
9 Estimating migration for each state separately would have been prohibitively complex because of the necessity of allocating estimated white migrants from Canada and slaves smuggled from the Caribbean among the individual states (rather than among regions).
10 Georgia and Florida were relegated to the 'New' rather than the 'Old' South, since in 1800 both were beyond the area of major settlement.
11 Perhaps the two best known migration estimates are by Lebergott and Goldin. Focusing upon aggregate movements rather than upon movements by race, Stanley Lebergott used the ratio of population (aged 0-5) to females (aged 15-49) as a proxy for the rate of natural increase to derive rough estimates for the period after 1800. ('Migration in the U.S., 1800-1960: Some New Estimates', *Journal of Economic History*, XXX (December, 1970), pp. 839-47.) Claudia Goldin estimated migration for the slave population alone in the ante-bellum years, but

with little attempt to investigate such issues as likely international smuggling, population in unenumerated territories, or relative under-enumeration. (Goldin's procedures are detailed in Fogel and Engerman, *Time on the Cross,* Vol. II, pp. 43-8).

12 See for example Fogel and Engerman, *Time on the Cross,* Vol. 1, pp. 6, 247-57.

13 The estimated net outmigration for the Old South in the decade 1830-40, for example, indicates that 34 percent of the white exodus was in the age cohort 10-20 (at the end of the decade) while 44 percent of the Negro migration was in this same age category.

14 *Time on the Cross,* Vol. I, p. 48.

15 'The Treatment Received by American Slaves: A Critical Review of the Evidence Presented in *Time on the Cross*', *Explorations in Economic History,* XII (October, 1974), pp. 396-404.

16 Sutch's estimates for the 1850s suggest a similar preponderance of young migrants. See Richard Sutch, 'The Breeding of Slaves for Sale and the Westward Expansion of Slavery, 1850-1860', in Stanley L. Engerman and Eugene D. Genovese (eds.), *Race and Slavery in the Western Hemisphere* (Princeton: Princeton University Press, 1975), p. 181.

17 These rates exclude those who were in the age cohort 0-9 at the end of the ten-year period for reasons noted in section 5.2.

18 Since birth rates are expressed as a percentage of the enumerated popula-tion, only the *relative* underenumeration of children is important.

19 A massive research project is currently being conducted by Robert Fogel and others, designed to establish mortality and fertility trends between 1650 and 1910, as well as the causes of those trends. (For an outline of the project, see Robert W. Fogel *et al.,* 'The Economics of Mortality in North America, 1650-1910: A Description of a Research Project', *Historical Methods,* XI (Spring, 1978), 75-108.) Their major data source for the white population will be a genealogical sample drawn from the Genealogical Library of the Church of Jesus Christ of the Latter-day Saints in Salt Lake City. The sources for black data will be more diffuse, including plantation records, coast-wise slave manifests, church records, and unpublished census data. Critical questions include the represent-ativeness of the samples used and the validity of assumptions employed in various estimation techniques — questions that cannot be answered until the results are published and analysed by experts in the field.

20 U.S. Bureau of the Census, *Seventh Census of the United States. 1850,* p. xxxix. Despite such blatant imperfections, Fogel and Engerman draw a number of inferences from these data, using the unsubstantiated assumption that defects were uniformly diffused across regions, sexes, and age groups (with the exception of children). (*Time on the Cross,* Vol. II, p. 100.)

21 'Mortality Rates and Trends in Massachusetts Before 1860', *Journal of Economic History,* XXXII (March, 1972), p. 184.

22 Warren S. Thompson and P.K. Whelpton, *Population Trends in the United States* (New York: McGraw-Hill, 1933), p. 230; Conrad and I. Taeuber, *The Changing Population of the United States* (New York: Wiley, 1958), p. 269. Changing human stature at this time has been examined in Robert W. Fogel *et al.,* 'The Economic and Demographic Significance of Secular Changes in Human Structure: The U.S. 1750-

1960', Program on Long-Term Patterns of U.S. Economic Development, National Bureau of Economic Research, Report 1979.1, April 1979. For antebellum America, their major finding is a decline in the mean final height of both blacks and whites, a decline suggesting 'that both black and white cohorts born during the late antebellum era may have experienced deteriorating nutritional and health conditions' (27). As the authors are quick to emphasize, however, most of the associated data samples are small, the results are preliminary, and the height decline, even if representative for the population, could have been caused by such factors as rising foreign immigration.

23 One of the few careful studies of regional data for this period suggests a similar absence of secular change. See Maris A. Vinovskis, 'Mortality Rates and Trends in Massachusetts Before 1860', *Journal of Economic History,* XXXII (March, 1972), pp. 184-213.

24 Recent research on the height of slaves has, to date, done little to resolve the associated puzzles. See for example Fogel *et al.* (1978), and Richard H. Steckel, 'Slave Height Profiles from Coastwise Manifests', *Explorations in Economic History,* XVI (October, 1979), 363-80. Steckel has also used the records of 11 slave plantations to estimate the mortality rates for slaves in three age cohorts under the age of 15. ('Slave Mortality: Analysis of Evidence from Plantation Records', *Social Science History,* III (October, 1979), 86-114.) As the author himself notes, 'One should be cautious in attempting to extrapolate results from these data to the entire slave population. The number of plantations is small and little is known about the influence of plantation characteristics on mortality' (88).

25 Jack E. Eblen, 'New Estimates of the Vital Rates of the United States Black Population During the Nineteenth Century', *Demography,* XI (May, 1974), pp. 301-19. This article revised substantially some of Eblen's earlier work in 'Growth of the Black Population in *ante-bellum* America, 1820-1860', *Population Studies,* XXVI (July, 1972), pp. 273-89.

26 Eblen, 'New Estimates . . . ', p. 305.

27 Eblen quotes Henry S. Shryock *et al., The Methods and Materials of Demography* (Washington, D.C.: Government Printing Office, 1973), p. 109, which in turn reproduces a table of estimated underenumeration of the white population from Ansley J. Coale and Melvin Zelnik, *New Estimates of Fertility and Population in the United States* (Princeton: Princeton University Press, 1963).

28 One indication of the sensitivity of results to the smoothing techniques used is the extent to which Eblen's 1974 estimates are sharply different from his 1972 estimates. See Jack E. Eblen, 'Growth of the Black Population in *ante bellum* America, 1820-1860', *Population Studies,* XXVI (July, 1972), pp. 273-89.

29 Eblen's estimates for the Negro population are in the range of 30 per 1000. Estimates for the white population suggest that its crude death rate was certainly no more than 25 per 1000, and possibly as low as 18 per 1000. Compare, for example, the crude death rates implied by subtracting the rate of natural increase estimates of Table A-13 from the crude birth rate estimates of Table A-17.

30 'New Estimates . . . ', Tables 4, 5, and 6.

31 *Ibid.*, p. 311.
32 *Ibid.*, p. 312.
33 *Ibid.*, Tables 4 and 5.
34 *Ibid.*, p. 306.
35 Possible inaccuracies in infant death rate estimates are only one of several factors confounding accuracy. As outlined below, the accuracy of the age cohort counts and assumptions regarding the rate of growth of the infant cohort are also crucial.
36 Compare the European estimates of Table A-19 with the American estimates of Tables C-14 through C-19.
37 See Table A-17.
38 See Table A-17.
39 For a discussion of why 1850 death rates may be abnormally high for children, see notes 176 and 194.
40 The reasons for the decline in the ante-bellum white birth rate is the topic of a lively and unresolved debate. Much of Richard Easterlin's recent work on nineteenth-century America has attempted to explain declining fertility in terms of changing land availability. (See for example Easterlin [1976b], [1976c], and Easterlin, Alter and Condran [1978].) As Easterlin notes, this is an old idea, but is nevertheless a significant departure from the analysis of those who link fertility decline to some combination of urbanization, industrialization, education, and the changing costs and returns from child labor. Easterlin's focus has been upon the behavior of northern farm families. His major hypothesis includes an empirical assertion and a bequest model of farm behavior. Declining fertility is claimed to be strongly associated with various proxies for changing land availability (and weakly associated, if at all, with the variables emphasized by others). This linkage is explained by the desire of parents to give their children a proper start in life; specifically, that 'a farmer wishes to provide for each of his children as well as he himself was provided for' (1976c: 71). Attempts to verify the statistical association between declining fertility and changing land availability have found that the correlation ranges from quite strong in ante-bellum Ohio (Leet 1975, 1976, 1977), to quite weak in Upper Canada in the 1860s (McInnis 1977). The behavioral premises of Easterlin's model have been sharply criticized by Allan Bogue (1976), while other studies continue to find significant correlations between declining American fertility and the variables deemphasized by Easterlin. Maris Vinovskis (1976b), for example, finds a strong correlation with education. Even proximate causes of decline are a subject of dispute. Warren Sanderson traces much of the decline in the total fertility rate to a decrease in marital fertility rates (1979: 340), while Richard Steckel's study of regional differences in southern white fertility (1980) suggests that differences are primarily a reflection of differentials in the age and incidence of marriage and relatively independent of the practice of family limitation.
41 'New Estimates . . .', p. 312. Eblen's data are presented in Table 6, p. 309.
42 *Ibid.*, p. 312.
43 See Table A-17, and Tables C-14 through C-19.
44 This possibility is supported by Vinovskis's study of Massachusetts death rates at this time. See Maris A. Vinovskis, 'The Jacobson Life Table of

1850: A Critical Reexamination from a Massachusetts Perspective',
paper prepared for the Social Science History Association Meetings in
Philadelphia, October, 1976.

45 'New Estimates . . . ', p. 309.

46 U.S. Bureau of the Census, *Eighth Census of the United States. 1860.
    Population*, p. xv. For evidence of reliance upon these two numbers by
    historians, see Fogel and Engerman, *Time on the Cross*, Vol. II, p. 105.

47 Slavery was abolished by the constitutions of Vermont (1777), Ohio
    (1802), Illinois (1818) and Indiana (1816); by constitutional inter-
    pretation in New Hampshire; and by gradual abolition acts in Penn-
    sylvania (1780), Rhode Island (1784), Connecticut (1784 and 1797),
    New York (1799 and 1817) and New Jersey (1804) (Litwack, *North
    of Slavery*, p.3 n.1).

48 Fogel and Engerman note that rates of change in the Negro population
    of New York and New Jersey during this decade 'strongly suggest' that
    slaveowners in these states were selling their slaves to the South. (*Time
    on the Cross*, Vol. II, p. 36.) This does not answer the above question,
    but merely suggests the puzzle of why this phenomenon should be so
    concentrated in a single decade.

49 United Nations, *Methods of Estimating Basic Demographic Measures
    from Incomplete Data: Manual IV* (New York: United Nations, 1967).

50 The South has traditionally been viewed as having 'significantly' higher
    mortality than the North during this period. About the only hard evid-
    ence on this point is that life insurance companies typically charged an
    extra one percent premium on all southern policies — a premium that
    suggests those who should be best informed on the subject viewed the
    differential as being rather minor. The charge could also partially reflect
    a differential in selling costs. (See 'Life Insurance at the South', *DeBow's
    Commercial Review*, III (May, 1847), 362.) Our constancy assumption
    is, at best, an approximation for a reality that was undoubtedly diverse.
    The presumption is that the diversity was minor — or, more correctly,
    that if the true diversity were known, subsequent estimates would not
    be modified in any major way. One possible source of regional death
    rates are the data in the 1850 census. As noted in section 5.1, the evid-
    ence is overwhelming that those data are grievously flawed. This option
    was therefore rejected.

51 (1) New England, (2) Mid-Atlantic, (3) Northwest, (4) Old South, (5)
    New South, and (6) Far West.

52 See, for example, U.S. Bureau of the Census, *Historical Statistics of the
    United States* (Washington: 1961), p.1.

53 U.S. Bureau of the Census, *Ninth Census of the United States. 1870.
    Population*, pp. 1-74.

54 U.S. Bureau of the Census, *Negro Population in the United States,
    1790-1915* (Washington, 1918), pp. 44-5. The 1918 data differ only
    slightly from those in the 1870 study for the following years: 1820,
    1830, and 1840.

55 Even in the twentieth century this defect remains. The population re-
    ported in 1930, 1940, and 1950 has been estimated to be too low by
    0.7 per cent, 1.6 per cent, and 1.4 per cent, respectively. (*Historical
    Statistics of the United States*, p. 1.)

56 U.S. Bureau of the Census, *Seventeenth Census of the United States.
    1950. Population*, I, p. xi.

57 *Loc. cit.*
58 In the cases of Oregon and California, the estimation procedure cited above could not be used, given the absence of adjacent and enumerated territories. The alternative was to assume for both of these West Coast territories that population growth between 1840 and 1850 was proportional to their own recorded growth between 1850 and 1860.
59 U.S., Congress, House, *Message from the President of the United States to Both Houses of Congress,* 20th Congress, 2nd Session, 1828/29, House Doc. No. 2, p. 15.
60 A variety of experiments were conducted with this and other possible underenumeration estimates, checking the results for consistency with other estimates of the study. These suggested that 0.005 was at least a reasonable estimate, and considerably better than many other alternatives.
61 Relative underenumeration refers to the percentage of underenumeration.
62 See, for example, Harold Sinclair, *The Port of New Orleans* (New York: Doubleday, 1942), p. 210; Robert C. Reinders, 'The Free Negro in the New Orleans Economy, 1850-1860', *Louisiana History,* VI (Summer, 1965), p. 273.
63 J.D.B. DeBow, *Statistical View of the United States . . . Being a Compendium of the Seventh Census* (Washington: Beverly Tucker, 1854), p. 62.
64 The numbers in each parish were incorrectly totalled to 28,820. See Louisiana, Senate, *Report of the Committee Appointed to Apportion the Representation of the State,* 2nd Legislature, 1st Session, Sen. Doc. Appendix, 1854.
65 Part of the discrepancy may be explained by the fact that the 1850 data were collected during the summer. Free Negroes tended to leave New Orleans during that season in search of alternative occupations, possibly making them less accessible to census marshals. See, for example, Reinders, *op. cit.,* p. 272.
66 See pp. 20-1.
67 See pp. 20-1.
68 The derivation of D_K is discussed below.
69 See for example U. S. Bureau of the Census, *Historical Statistics of the United States* (Washington: 1960), p. 48.
70 A term repeatedly used by writers on the subject. See for example George Tucker, *Progress of the United States in Population and Wealth* (New York: Hunt's, 1855), p. 81; J. Potter, 'The Growth of Population in America, 1700-1860', in D. V. Glass and D. E. C. Eversley, *Population in History* (Chicago: 1965), p. 667; U. S. Bureau of the Census, *Historical Statistics of the United States* (Washington: 1961), p. 48; Ernest Rubin, 'Immigration and the Economic Growth of the United States, 1790-1914', Research Group for European Migration Problems, *Bulletin,* VII, No. 4 (Oct./Dec., 1959), p. 87.
71 Reporting of alien arrivals was required by the Act of 1798, but it expired two years later. (See *Historical Statistics of the United States* (1960), p. 48.)
72 'For 1820-23, a few arrivals by land borders were included', *loc. cit.*
73 Demographers are also 'fairly certain' that aliens traveling first or second

class were not counted. (See for example Brinley Thomas, *Migration and Economic Growth* [Cambridge: 1954], pp. 42–3.) This omission – if indeed cabin passengers were omitted – would seem to be relatively insignificant in the period prior to 1860.

74 U. S. Bureau of the Census, *Eighth Census of the United States. Population*, p. xviii. A minor qualification would seem to be Potter's suspicion (which remains largely undocumented) that 'with the sudden upsurge of immigration in the late 1840's, the ports were unable to record numbers accurately, at least in the early years', J. Potter, 'The Growth of Population in America, 1700–1860' in D.V. Glass and D. E. C. Eversley, *Population in History* (Chicago: 1965), pp. 666–7.

75 In 1850 the population of what are now the states of Washington and Oregon totalled only 1,201 and 12,093, respectively (U.S. Bureau of the Census, *Historical Statistics* (1960), p. 13).

76 J. Potter, 'The British Timber Duties, 1815–60', *Economica,* XXII (May, 1955), p. 132.

77 As Potter is the first to admit. See J. Potter, 'The Growth of Population in America, 1700–1860', p. 666n73.

78 That arrivals via this coastal route were counted is suggested by the fact that under the heading 'Country where born' immigration lists invariably included a number of passengers from 'British America'. See William J. Bromwell, *History of Immigration to the United States* (New York: Redfield, 1856), passim.

79 U. S. Bureau of the Census, *Eighth Census of the United States. 1860. Population*, p. xix. In addition, the count of immigrants 'may have included' alien passengers who died before arrival (*Historical Statistics of the United States* (1960), p. 49).

80 U. S. Bureau of the Census, *Eighth Census of the United States. 1860. Population*, p. xxi.

81 Marion Rubins Davis, 'Critique of Official United States Immigration Statistics', in Walter F. Willcox (ed.), *International Migrations* (New York, 1931), p. 648.

82 *Loc. cit.*

83 William S. Rossiter, *Increase of Population in the United States, 1910–1920,* U. S. Census Bureau Monograph No. I (Washington: 1922), p. 199.

84 Lester F. Ward, *Glimpses of the Cosmos* (New York: 1913), Vol. I, p. 189.

85 Conrad Taeuber and Irene B. Taeuber, *The Changing Population of the United States* (New York: 1958), p. 54.

86 Walter F. Willcox, 'Immigration into the United States', in Walter F. Willcox (ed.), *International Migrations,* Vol. II, p. 89.

87 *Loc. cit.*

88 Various writers have suggested that Willcox's estimates overstate emigration from the United States. See for example Ernest Rubin, 'Immigration and the Economic Growth of the United States, 1790–1914', Research Group for European Migration Problems, *Bulletin,* VII, No. 4 (Oct./Dec., 1959), p. 89.

89 J. Potter, 'The Growth of Population in America, 1700–1860', p. 668.

90 U.S. Bureau of the Census, *Eighth Census of the United States. 1860. Population*, p. xviii.

91 *Ibid.*, p. xxi.
92 See Table A-3.
93 See notes 73 and 79.
94 The insignificance of the latter flow is suggested by the limited entries under 'Born in U.S.A.' in Table A-4.
95 U. S. Bureau of the Census, *Eighth Census of the United States. 1860. Population*, p. xxi.
96 Transient aliens en route for British North America were 1.4 percent of total alien arrivals; those destined for other countries were 0.6 percent. The assumption was therefore made that transient aliens en route to foreign countries other than Upper and Lower Canada were 1.0 percent of total recorded alien arrivals.
97 Walter F. Willcox (ed.), *International Migrations* (New York: 1929), Vol. 1, pp. 627–8.
98 For data sources, see Table A-5.
99 Dominion Bureau of Statistics, *Census of Canada, 1871*, Vol. IV.
100 *Loc. cit.*
101 *Loc. cit.*
102 *Ibid.*, Vol. V.
103 See M. C. Urquhart and K. A. H. Buckley (eds.), *Historical Statistics of Canada* (Toronto, 1965) as follows: immigration data, p. 10; census data, p. 2; vital statistics, p. 37. Serious doubts do exist about the overall accuracy of census data prior to 1871, but the population data for Ontario and Quebec appear to be among the most reliable series. Langton's detailed criticism of the 1861 census, for example, notes in passing that 'I do not think that there is any reason to doubt the numbers living' (*ibid.*, p. 2).
104 Data sources are given in notes 97 and 98. Arrivals averaged 93 percent of departures in the 1827/35 period. The assumption was made that for the 1820/26 period, arrivals were 90 percent of departures.
105 The age distribution of immigrants suggests that their rate of natural increase was higher than that of the domestic population. (See Table A-6.) The above assumption will therefore overstate the domestic rate of natural increase and understate the secular decline in the aggregate rate of natural increase, insofar as the number of immigrants increases relative to the domestic population. At this juncture neither difficulty is critical. The sole objective is to estimate an average rate of natural increase for any given decade for the population as a whole.
106 Data for Upper Canada were available for 1840, but not for 1844.
107 If to the 1831 Catholic population one adds the recorded births minus deaths for the next 13 years, the implied 1844 population is 579,829 as compared with the census results of 572,439. If one deducts from the 1831 Catholic population (births minus deaths) for the preceding 6 years, the implied 1825 population is 346,119, as compared with the results achieved by the above extrapolation procedure of 353,206. See Table A-4.
108 An appendix describing the procedures used to overcome these difficulties is available from the authors on request.
109 Earl of Durham, *The Report and Despatches of the Earl of Durham on the Affairs of British North America* (London: 1839), p. 154. A minor difference is that Durham's estimate concerns the percentage

of immigrants that re-emigrate, whereas (Y) is an estimate of net immigration into the United States expressed as a percentage of immigrant arrivals.

110 See for example Tache's testimony quoted in M. C. Urquhart and K. A. H. Buckley, *Historical Statistics of Canada*, p. 10; or for a more recent view, A. R. M. Lower, 'The Growth of Population in Canada', in *Canadian Population and Northern Colonization: Symposium Presented to the Royal Society of Canada in 1961* (Toronto: 1962), p. 54.

111 Durham, *op. cit.*, p. 150.

112 With no apparent sources, Blodget (p. 75) simply stated in 1806 that annual gross immigration had 'not averaged more than 4,000 in the last ten years'; and net immigration was half that number. Seybert (p. 28) began by asserting that 10,000 per annum was an upper bound for immigration between 1795 and 1816, and then went on to 'suppose' (p. 29) an annual immigration rate of 6,000 per year between 1790 and 1810. Tucker (1855 edition, p. 82) began with a deflated version of Seybert's 1817 count of arriving passengers and assumed an identical number arrived annually between 1818 and 1820. A total count of 114,000 for the decade 1810-20 was then achieved by assuming no immigration during the War of 1812-14 and an annual immigration of 10,000 for 1811, 1815, and 1816. The last figure reflected Tucker's deference to Seybert's claim that immigration could not have exceeded 10,000, plus his own belief that it could not have been less. The 1860 Census estimate of gross immigration is based primarily on the work of Tucker and Seybert. The procedure used by the census to derive net immigration has been criticized elsewhere. (See above, pp. 33-4.)

113 As Thomas points out, British data collection was a by-product of legislation aimed at mitigating the appalling overcrowding on trans-atlantic vessels. 'These controls proved ineffective, as it was easy for vessels to evade inspection by sailing from out-of-the-way ports of the coast: thus in the early years the figures underestimate the number of persons who actually sailed from the United Kingdom' (Brinley Thomas, *Migration and Economic Growth* (Cambridge: 1954), p. 36).

114 Adam Seybert, *Statistical Annals . . . of the United States of America* (Philadelphia: 1818), p. 29.

115 *Loc. cit.* The ports were Boston, New York, Perth Amboy, Philadelphia, Wilmington (Del.), Baltimore, Norfolk, Charleston, Savannah, and New Orleans.

116 British data are also for the year ending December 31.

117 See for example George Tucker, *op. cit.*, pp. 81-3; Seybert, *op. cit.*, pp. 28-9; Marcus L. Hansen, *The Atlantic Migration 1607-1860* (Cambridge: 1940), pp. 77-8; C. Taeuber and I.B. Taeuber, *The Changing Population of the United States* (New York: 1958), p. 51; U.S., Bureau of the Census, *Eighth Census of the United States. 1860. Population*, I, xviii, *Niles' Register*, XIII (1817-1818), 35.

118 The Treaty of Amiens was not signed until 1802, but 'the rigor of military and naval supervision over commerce relaxed more than a year before', with the resulting transatlantic migration appearing to be 'phenomenally heavy' by previous standards (Hansen, *op. cit.*, p. 67).

119 *Ibid.*, pp. 68-9.

120 This is approximately one half the relative decline in shipping tonnage entering American ports (adjusted to the year ending December 31). (See Table A-10.) Between Canadian overland routes and lax American customs officials the determined immigrant encountered few insuperable barriers. For examples of how easily the Embargo Act was circumvented, see R. G. Albion and J. B. Pope, *Sea Lanes in Wartime* (New York: 1942), pp. 99-102. The tonnage of ships entering during 1808 would seem to be sufficient evidence for rejecting Hansen's assertion that 'Until the spring of 1809 all maritime activity and with it the passenger trade ceased' (Hansen, *op. cit.,* p. 69).

121 The Nonintercourse Act and Macon's Bill appear to have had a negligible effect on transatlantic commerce. Within Europe, blockades and the increased drain on manpower in the name of war suggest some reduction in the flow of international migration. See William J. Bromwell, *History of Immigration to the United States* (New York: 1856), p. 15.

122 See Table A-10. The British blockade of American ports that began in the late fall of 1812 was limited to the Chesapeake and Delaware Bays. The remainder of the eastern seaboard was gradually included, but New England ports remained open until the spring of 1814. The slowness of this blockade expansion plus available shipping data make suspect the claim of those who argue that all immigration ceased with the outbreak of hostilities. See for example George Tucker, *op. cit.,* p. 82; Hansen, *op. cit.,* p. 70; Jesse Chickering, *Immigration into the United States* (Boston: 1848), p. 58.

123 Much of the superficial complexity of the formulae for the years 1812 through 1814 is simply an attempt to change shipping tonnage data from their recorded year-end of September 20 to the desired year-end of December 31. The official immigration count for the year ending September 30, 1820 (8,385) was subjected to similar adjustments in the calculations of 1819 and 1820.

124 In the immediate post-war era, transatlantic commerce remained disrupted for some time. The flow of immigrants through the summer of 1815 was quite sparse, although some acceleration was apparent in the early fall. See Hansen, *op. cit.,* pp. 78-80.

125 See pp. 35-7. The close proximity of the War of 1812, with the implied continuance of some British-American animosities, suggests that re-emigration rates from Canada were somewhat below those achieved in the 1820s and 30s.

126 Most students of the subject have two impressions: (1) that prior to 1817 an annual rate of 10,000 represented the maximum inflow, and (2) that the rate of immigration in 1816 was rapidly approaching new highs. See Seybert, *op. cit.,* pp. 28-9; Hansen, *op. cit.,* pp. 80-3; *Niles' Register,* X (1816), 401.

127 Both British data on departures for the United States and contemporary American impressions suggest that the record levels of 1817 were sustained until the autumn of 1819. (See Table A-8; Seybert, *op. cit.,* p. 29; Hansen, *op. cit.,* pp. 90, 97, 103; Oscar Handlin, *Boston's Immigrants, 1790-1865* (Cambridge: 1941), p. 39; *Niles' Register,* XV (1818-19), 33; XVI (1819), 286; XVII (1819-20), 36.) Seybert's count of 22,240 passengers was multiplied by (1.05 x 0.86 = 20,083) and then deflated by 0.96. In the period 1820-30, inclusive, total alien

arrivals were 105 percent of arrivals at the ten ports enumerated by Seybert. In the same time period alien arrivals were 86 percent of total arrivals. (See Seybert, *op. cit.*, p. 29; Chickering, *op. cit.*, pp. 6-9; *Historical Statistics of the United States* (1960), pp. 57, 61.) The 0.96 deflation is an attempt to adjust for second passages and transient aliens. See pp. 33-5.

128 The implied sharp drop in the influx of transatlantic migrants in the autumn of 1819 is consistent with the impressions of contemporary observers. See *Niles' Register*, XVII (1819-1820), 36, 63; Matthew Carey, *Essays on Political Economy* (Philadelphia: 1822), pp. 451-2.

129 See for example the citations in note 117.

130 See Tables A-7, A-12 and A-13.

131 This immigration is calculated as a percentage of immigrants arriving at Montreal and Quebec City, using the percentages given in Table A-7. Total *net* immigration into the United States, 1820-60, is then the sum of (a) Canadian overland immigration, and (b) 96 percent of passenger arrivals at American seaports.

132 Recall that the western portions of New York, Pennsylvania and West Virginia are all included in this region.

133 See Table A-22.

134 See Table A-23.

135 The key assumption, as stated earlier, is that immigrants had a rate of natural increase equivalent to that of the domestic population after their arrival in America.

136 See Table A-14.

137 Francis A. Walker, 'Immigration and Degradation', *The Forum*, XI (August, 1891), 634-44.

138 As indicated in Table A-13, the first sharp decline in the American rate of natural increase predates the upsurge in immigration that occurred in the 1840s. For summaries of other empirical evidence challenging the Walker hypothesis see Brinley Thomas, *International Migration and Economic Development* (Paris, 1961), p. 49; J. J. Spengler, 'Effects Produced in Receiving Countries by Pre-1939 Immigration' in Brinley Thomas (ed.), *Economics of International Migration* (London, 1958), pp. 22-9.

139 See notes to Table B-5.

140 In July of 1804 Governor Claiborne wrote to James Madison that 'Slaves are daily introduced from Africa, many *direct* from *this* unhappy Country and others by way of the West India Islands' (Dunbar Rowland, *Official Letter Books of W.C.C. Claiborne* (Jackson, Miss.: State Department of Archives and History, 1917), Vol. II, p. 245). See also William E.B. DuBois, *Suppression of the African Slave-Trade to the United States* (New York: Longman, Green & Co., 1896), p. 89.

141 Ulrich B. Phillips, 'Racial Problems, Adjustments and Disturbances' in *The South in the Building of the Nation* (Richmond, 1901), Vol. IV, p. 217; Elizabeth Donnan, *Documents Illustrative of the History of the Slave Trade to America* (Washington: Carnegie Institution, 1935), IV, p. 665.

142 Dunbar Rowland, *op. cit.*, Vol. IV, pp. 381, 382, 409; Alcee Fortier *A History of Louisiana* (New York: Mangi, Joyant & Co., 1904), Vol. III, pp. 60-1; Henry C. Castellanos, *New Orleans As It Was* (New Orleans: L. Graham Co., 1905), pp. 300-1.

143 See W.E.B. DuBois, *op. cit.,* p. 90 n. 5; Noel Deerr, *The History of Sugar* (London: Chapman & Hall, 1949–50), II, p. 282. Smuggling may have been partially offset by exports. According to Senator William Smith of South Carolina, imports into Charleston 'were sold to the people of the Western States; Georgia and New Orleans, and a considerable quantity were sent to the West Indies, especially when the market became dull in Carolina' (U.S. Congress, Senate, *Annals of Congress,* 16th Cong., 2nd Sess., 1820/21, p. 76). The assertion that the Carolina market became 'dull' would seem somewhat questionable, given the upward trend in annual imports demonstrated in Table B-5.

144 *Statutes at Large,* II, 426; III, 450, 532, 600–1.

145 American Anti-Slavery Society, *Slavery and the Internal Slave Trade in the United States of North America* (London: Thomas Ward & Co., 1841), p. 20.

146 U.S. Congress, House, *Letter from the Secretary of the Treasury Transmitting Information . . . In Relation to Ships Engaged in the Slave Trade,* 15th Cong., 2nd Sess., 1818/19, House Doc. 107, p. 8. For other comments on lax enforcement, see *ibid.,* p. 5; Noel Deerr, *op. cit.,* II, p. 282; W.E.B. DuBois, *Suppression of the African Slave-Trade,* p. 111; Warren S. Howard, *Slavers and the Federal Law, 1837–1862* (Berkeley: University of California Press, 1963), p. 148; *Niles' Register,* XVII (1819/20), 356–60; Daniel P. Mannix and Malcolm Cowley, *Black Cargoes: A History of the Atlantic Slave Trade, 1518–1865* (New York: Viking, 1962), pp. 199–204.

147 See for example *Niles' Register,* XIII (1817/18), 32; Howard, *op. cit.,* p. 196; American State Papers, Committee on . . . the Illicit Introduction of Slaves, *Slaves Brought Into the United States from Amelia Island,* Miscellaneous Vol. II, No. 441, p. 458. For comments on the limited effectiveness of the British and American squadrons off the coast of Africa, see DuBois, *op. cit.,* pp. 143–7; 159; Mannix and Cowley, *op. cit.,* pp. 219–23, 286; Warren S. Howard, *op. cit.,* pp. 5, 41, 43, 59, 208; Philip D. Curtin, *The Atlantic Slave Trade: A Census* (Madison: Univ. of Wisconsin Press, 1969), p. 250; Peter Duigan and Clarence Clendenen, *The United States and the African Slave Trade, 1619–1862* (Stanford, Calif.: Hoover Institution on War, Revolution and Peace, 1963), p. 27.

148 Other estimates often based upon, or reflected in, one or more of the four noted may be found in DuBois, *op. cit.,* 85; Mannix and Cowley, *op. cit.,* p. 196; Ezra C. Seaman, *Essays on the Progress of Nations* (New York: Baker & Scribner, 1846), p. 403; Ernst von Halle, *Baumwollproduktion und Pflanzungswirtschaft in den Nordamerikanischen Südstaaten* (Leipzig: Duncker & Humblot, 1897), p. 49.

149 Curtin, *op. cit.,* p. 74.

150 Howard, *op. cit.,* p. 256.

151 L.C. Gray, *History of Agriculture in the Southern United States to 1860* (Washington: Carnegie Institution, 1933), Vol. II, pp. 648–50; W.E.B. DuBois, 'Enforcement of the Slave-Trade Laws', *American Historical Association Annual Report,* 1891, 173; Winfield H. Collins, *The Domestic Slave Trade of the Southern States* (New York: Broadway Publishing Co., 1904), p. 20; Deerr, *op. cit.,* II, p. 282; Mannix and Cowley, *op. cit.,* p. 196.

152 George Tucker, *Progress of the United States* (New York: Hunt's Merchants' Magazine, 1855), p. 53; Philip D. Curtin, *op. cit.,* pp. 73-4; J. Potter, 'The Growth of Population in America, 1700-1860', in D.V. Glass and D.E.C. Eversley, *Population in History* (Chicago: Aldine Publishing Co., 1965), p. 666; Reynolds Farley, *Growth of the Black Population: A Study of Demographic Trends* (Chicago: Markham Publishing Co., 1970), p. 30; Duigan and Clendenen, *op. cit.,* p.36.

153 See for example American Anti-Slavery Society, *Slavery and the Internal Slave Trade in the United States of North America* (London: Thomas Ward & Co., 1841), pp. 18-24.

154 U.S. Bureau of the Census, *Ninth Census of the United States. 1870. Population,* p. 336.

155 In 1820, when census data by sex were first collected, males constituted 50.7 percent of the total Negro population of the United States. By 1860, the percentage had fallen to 49.9. See Table B-1.

156 See for example Philip D. Curtin, 'Epidemiology and the Slave Trade', *Political Science Quarterly,* LXXXIII (June, 1968), 215; Reynolds Farley, *op. cit.,* p. 30. Curtin gives no source; Farley quotes George Dow who, on the strength of observing the carrying capacity of one Liverpool ship, concluded that 'The ships in this trade are usually fitted out to receive only one third women, or perhaps a smaller number . . .' (George F. Dow, *Slave Ships and Slaving* (Salem, Mass.: Marine Research Society, 1927), p. 147). For an example of how the carrying capacity ratio diverged from the sex ratio of slaves carried, see Great Britain, *Parliamentary Papers, (Accounts and Papers,* XXII), 1788, No. 565.

157 Of the slaves recaptured between 1808 and 1841 for which distinction by sex was made, 35,937 of 53,528 were males, or 67 percent. See Table B-21.

158 'The West Indies were nearer the source of supply, and consequently newly imported slaves came somewhat cheaper. On account of the density of population and high price of land the cost of rearing slaves to maturity was very much greater than in the South. Finally, the heavy labors of sugar planting made adult male slaves in the West Indies more economical than women and children, and there tended to be a preference for importing males, resulting in a large disproportion in numbers of the sexes' (Gray, *op. cit.,* I, p. 472). See also Curtin, *The Atlantic Slave Trade,* pp. 73, 92.

159 The actual count made was 1,095 men and 773 women, or 59 percent and 41 percent respectively. Calculated from data in Donnan, *op. cit.,* Vol. 3, pp. 153-5, 190-1, 385; Vol. 4, pp. 306-32, 385-96, 402, 428-9, 475-8, 491, 507, 633.

160 See Table B-9.

161 Thomas Jefferson, *Notes on the State of Virginia* (Philadelphia: R. T. Rawle, 1801), p. 282. For the reactions of another American president, see Charles Francis Adams (ed.), *Memoirs of John Quincy Adams* (Philadelphia: J.P. Lippincott, 1875), IV, p. 292.

162 See for example Frederic Bancroft, 'The Colonization of American Negroes, 1801-1865' in Jacob E. Cooke (ed.), *Frederic Bancroft, Historian* (University of Oklahoma Press, 1957), 163; Clement Eaton, *A History of the Old South* (New York: Macmillan, 1949), p. 377; John H. Franklin, *The Free Negro in North Carolina, 1790-1860*

(Chapel Hill: University of North Carolina Press, 1943), p. 237; Leon F. Litwack, *North of Slavery: The Negro in the Free States, 1790–1860* (Chicago: University of Chicago Press, 1961), p. 28.

163 Much has been made of the supposed mass exodus of Negroes to Canada following the passage of the Fugitive Slave Act in 1850. Estimates range as high as 30,000 for the decade 1850–60. (See Litwack, *op. cit.,* p. 249; Carter G. Woodson, *A Century of Negro Migration* (New York: Russell & Russell, 1918), p. xliii; Fred Landon, 'The Negro Migration to Canada After 1850', *Journal of Negro History,* V (January, 1920), 22.) Migration data considered in section 4.3 do support the hypothesis of some exodus at this time, but the likely magnitude would seem to be more in the 10,000 to 20,000 range. Even this magnitude is suspect if Canadian census data are accurate. In the ten-year period ending in January of 1861, the 'Colored Race' of Nova Scotia and New Brunswick increased by only 1,542; those 'Born in the United States' and residing in Quebec and Ontario increased by only 8,192. (Canada, Bureau of the Census, *Census of Canada. 1871*, Vol. IV, pp. 183, 207, 225, 235, 259, 291, 333, 350.)

164 In less stringent form, the key assumption is that whatever the time distribution for imports was for a given year, that distribution was centered at mid-year; i.e., for computational purposes, all slaves can be treated as arriving at mid-year.

165 See Table A-13.

166 Edward Wigglesworth, *Calculations on American Population* (Boston, 1775), pp. 5–6; Benjamin Franklin, *Poor Richard's Almanac,* 1750, reproduced in L.W. Labaree (ed.), *The Papers of Benjamin Franklin* (New Haven, 1959), IV, p. 441; Benjamin Franklin, *Observations Concerning the Increase of Mankind, Peopling of Countries, Etc.* (Boston, 1755), reproduced in John Bigelow (ed.), *The Complete Works of Benjamin Franklin* (New York, 1887), II, p. 225; T. R. Malthus, *An Essay on the Principle of Population* (London, 1878), p. 3.

167 Franklin in Labaree, *op. cit.,* III, p. 441; Malthus, *op. cit.,* p. 253. Modern demographers emphasize the same factors. See for example, W.H. Grabill, Clyde V. Kiser, and P. K. Whelpton, *The Fertility of American Women* (New York, 1958), p. 2; Warren S. Thompson, 'The Demographic Revolution in the United States', *Annals of the* For a discussion of the debate on why birth rates declined, see note 40. 1949), p. 62.

168 See for example Grabill, Kiser, and Whelpton, *op. cit.,* pp. 380–1; W. S. Thompson, *op. cit.,* 63; W. H. Bash, 'Changing Birth Rates in Developing America: New York State, 1840–1875', *Milbank Memorial Fund Quarterly.* XLI (April, 1963), 163; J. Potter, 'The Growth of Population in America, 1700–1860', in D. V. Glass and D. E. C. Eversley, *Population in History* (Chicago, 1965), pp. 677–8; Yasukichi Yasuba, *Birth Rates of the White Population in the United States, 1800–1860* (Johns Hopkins, 1961), passim.

169 See for example Potter (1961), 678, and Yasuba (1961), 135, 185–7. For a discussion of the debate on why birth rates declined, see note 40.

170 W. S. Thompson, *op. cit.,* 63; Grabill, Kiser, and Whelpton, *op. cit.,* p. 381; Norman E. Himes, *Medical History of Contraception* (Baltimore, 1936), pp. 224, 333, 370–2; A. J. Jaffee, 'Differential

Fertility in the White Population in Early America', *Journal of Heredity*, XXXI (September, 1940), 411.

171 Grabill, Kiser, and Whelpton, *op. cit.*, p. 2; Potter, *op. cit.*, p. 663. In 1800, 6 percent of the population lived in urban centers of 2,500 or more; in 1850, 15 percent (*Historical Statistics of the United States* (1960), p. 14). Potter suspects that whatever medical advances were achieved in this period had a negligible impact on the death rate (*op. cit.*, p. 679). For one of the few careful studies at the state level of secular trends in death rates at this time, see Maris A. Vinovskis, 'Mortality Rates and Trends in Massachusetts Before 1860', *Journal of Economic History*, XXXII (March, 1972), pp. 184-213. For recent work on this topic that still leaves the question of level and trend of the death rate for the nation as a whole in the ante-bellum period unresolved, see Fogel *et al.* (1978) and (1979); Meeker (1972), (1976), and (1977); and Steckel (1979a) and (1979b).

172 Wilson G. Smillie, 'The Period of Great Epidemics in the United States: 1800-1875', in Franklin H. Top (ed.), *The History of American Epidemiology* (St. Louis, 1952), pp. 52-8; John Allen Krout and Dixon Ryan Fox, *The Completion of Independence, 1790-1830* (New York, 1944), p. 304; Thurman B. Rice, *The Conquest of Disease* (New York, 1927), passim; U. S. Congress, House, *A History of the Travels of Asiatic Cholera in North America* by Ely McClellan, 43rd Cong., 2nd Sess., 1875, Exec. Doc. 95, passim. Yellow fever was most prevalent in southern ports because the mosquito which carried it preferred warmer climates. On occasion, however, the disease reached as far north as Quebec (Rice, *op. cit.*, p. 237).

173 Smillie, *op. cit.*, p. 58. See also Table A-15.

174 Samuel Blodget, *Economica* (Washington, 1806), p. 58. Despite the tenuous nature of Blodget's estimate, it has been frequently cited by more recent demographers. See for example W. S. Thompson, *op. cit.*, 62; Grabill, Kiser, and Whelpton, *op. cit.*, p. 7; Kuznets, *Modern Economic Growth*, p. 43.

175 E. B. Elliot, 'On the Law of Human Mortality that Appears to Obtain in Massachusetts', *Proceedings of the American Association for the Advancement of Science*, 1857, p. 59. Underreporting was assumed by Elliot to be roughly offset by the higher death rates of urban centers, the final result being advanced as representative for the whole of Massachusetts (*ibid.*, p. 52).

176 See Table A-16. Fragmentary data also exist for such urban centers as Baltimore, Charleston, Savannah, New Orleans, and Chicago. The major difficulties in calculating death rates from these statistics — aside from ascertaining the accuracy of the data — are to determine whether still-born are included or excluded, and to decide what urban population should be used as a denominator. Variations resulting from the inclusion of the surburban population are indicated in Table A-16. The reader should also bear in mind that 1850 death rates are inflated by a cholera epidemic which began in 1848, continued for a number of years, and ravaged most seaport towns. (See Table A-15; U.S. Congress, House, 1875, *op. cit.*, pp. 594, 633; Rice, *op. cit.*, p. 80.)

177 U.S. Bureau of the Census, *Seventh Census of the United States. 1850*, p. xli.

178 *Ibid.*, p. xxxix.
179 See Table A-13.
180 Compare Tables A-19, A-18, and A-17.
181 Although the number of people of age x at the beginning of a year is in general different from the average number of people aged x in that year, the following estimation procedure closely approximates the 'true' death rate when the true rate is low. Even when that rate is high, this technique will yield close approximations for the population as a whole.
182 Note that the subscript x is used with q to denote age-specific one-year death rates; i.e., q_x was previously defined as the proportion of people *of age* x who will not be alive one year hence.
183 Paul Jacobson, 'An Estimate of the Expectation of Life in the United States in 1850', *Milbank Memorial Fund Quarterly*, XXXV (April, 1957), 198. The problem of which life table to use for the ante-bellum period is not easily answered. The Jacobson table is constructed from data from that period. Although widely used by a number of scholars, it is not without its defects. (For a review of the widespread use and the flaws, see Vinovskis (1978:622).) The alternative is to use one or more of the model life tables from Coale and Demeny (1966), usually one of the Model West tables. (Meeker (1976), for example, uses a Model West table to estimate the life expectancy of southern blacks in the 1850s.) The Model West tables are a residual category for Coale and Demeny, constructed from 129 tables from countries that are primarily European, from data drawn mainly from the twentieth century. The U.S.A. input consists of 10 tables drawn from the period 1901–58. It is therefore far from clear how representative such model tables are for either the Negro or the white population of ante-bellum America. Several scholars have pointed out that even in the twentieth century, the age patterns of mortality of American Negroes do not conform to these model life tables (Demeny and Gingrich 1967; Zelnick 1969). Our decision was to anchor our study in data from the ante-bellum period, and modify the Jacobson table where necessary as best we would.
184 We first calculate the number of babies there were $t-x$ years ago when the x-year olds were born. This is

$$P_0^S[t-x] = (1+r)^{t-x} P_0^S[0].$$

The number that survive to year t is given by

$$P_x^S[t] = (1+r)^{t-x} P_0^S[0](1-q_0) \ldots (1-q_{x-1}) = P_x^S[0](1+r)^t.$$

185 $$1 - \frac{(1+r)(P^S[0] - P_0^S[0])}{P^S[0]} = 1 - \frac{P^S[1] - P_0^S[1]}{P^S[0]}$$

$$= 1 - \sum_x \frac{P_x^S[0](1-q_x)}{P^S[0]}$$

$$= \sum_x \frac{P_x^S[0]q_x}{P^S[0]}$$

186 These death rates exclude those of the population age 0-9 at $t+10$.

187 $U[t] = 0$ for all t except $t = 1820$; $U[1820] = 0.005$.

188 If the age-structure of immigrants closely matched that of the domestic population, then the age distribution of the resulting population would be similar to that of a closed population with a slightly higher growth rate. Unfortunately, this was not the case for America in the first half of the nineteenth century.

189 $I[2] \approx 200,000$; $I[3] \approx 650,000$; $I[4] \approx 1,500,000$; $I[5] \approx 2,700,000$.

190 The 1850 and 1860 census gave data for the age group 0-1, but the broader age category was still used for these years because of a concern that the youngest cohort was subject to serious underenumeration. See for example, Richard Sutch, 'The Breeding of Slaves for Sale and the Westward Expansion of Slavery, 1850-1860', p. 184nl4.

191 For the white population, $y = 9$ for $t = 1800, 1810, 1820$ and $y = 4$ for $t = 1830, 1840, 1850$.

192 Data for enumerated territories were taken directly from the original census. Data for unenumerated territories were estimated in the same manner as all age- and sex-specific data for these territories.

193 See section 5.2.

194 Research by Vinovskis suggests that 1850 death rates were abnormally high. This raises the possibility that the 'true' birth rate actually fell throughout the 1840s and 1850s, with the reversal in our data the product of exceptionally high infant mortality in 1850. See Maris A. Vinovskis, 'The Jacobson Life Table of 1850: A Critical Re-Examination from a Massachusetts Perspective', paper prepared for the Social Science History Association Meetings, October, 1976.

195 For each decade, a simple arithmetic average was taken of the crude birth rates calculated for the first and last year of that decade.

196 Farley, *Growth of Black Population*, p. 40.

197 Kenneth M. Stampp, *The Peculiar Institution* (New York: Alfred A. Knopf, 1963), p. 346; also Richard Sutch, 'The Breeding of Slaves. . .'

198 Ulrich B. Phillips, *American Negro Slavery* (New York: 1929), p. 362. This apparently contrasted sharply with the interests of Caribbean masters. See L.C. Gray, *op. cit.*, I, p. 472; P.D. Curtin, *The Atlantic Slave Trade*, pp. 73, 92.

199 L.C. Gray, *op. cit.*, II, p. 663; K. Stampp, *op. cit.*, pp. 245-51; Frederic Bancroft, *Slave Trading in the Old South* (Baltimore: J.H. Forst, 1931), pp. 68, 74, 84; William D. Postell, *The Health of Slaves on Southern Plantations* (Baton Rouge, 1951), pp. 111-16.

200 For a general statement on biological constraints, see Donald J. Bogue, *Principles of Demography* (New York: John Wiley, 1969), pp. 669-70. For empirical evidence on the Quebec Catholic population of the early nineteenth century, see Urquhart and Buckley, *Historical Statistics of Canada*, p. 54. The incidence of abortions, sterility, stillbirths and miscarriages among the American slave population are all unresolved issues. See Postell, *op. cit.*, pp. 117-18; Felice Swados, 'Negro Health on the Ante-Bellum Plantations', *Bulletin of the History of Medicine*, X (October, 1941), 468; Richard H. Shryock, 'Medical Practice in the Old South', *South Atlantic Quarterly*, XXIX (April, 1930), 175. Farley is among those who believe that 'The fertility rates of blacks must have reached a biological maximum before the Civil War' (*op. cit.*, pp. 2-3).

Although the supporting evidence is somewhat tenuous, recent research suggests a waiting time for slaves between mean age at menarche and mean age at first birth of approximately two-and-a-half years. (Trussell and Steckel [1978]). Reporting on his unpublished research on slave fertility, Steckel suggests that his findings indicate (a) that family limitation practices probably did not affect fertility among American slaves, and (b) that age at first birth was one or two years lower among slaves than among southern whites (Steckel [1980] 350).

201 For a compelling critique of Sutch's forced breeding thesis, see Stanley L. Engerman, 'A Critique of Sutch on "The Breeding of Slaves"' in Engerman and Genovese, *Race and Slavery*, pp. 527-30.

202 M. Zelnik, 'Fertility of the American Negro in 1830 and 1850', *Population Studies*, XX (July, 1966), 77-83.

203 *Ibid.*, 80. Farley suggests that Negro fertility probably did not decline before 1880, and estimates a crude birth rate for the Negro population as a whole of 54 per 1,000 for the period 1830-50 (Reynolds Farley, 'The Demographic Rates and Social Institutions of the Nineteenth Century Negro Population: A Stable Population Analysis', *Demography*, II, 395).

204 'Since the causal factor of disease was so little understood, very little was accomplished in arresting the various diseases that afflicted the south' (Postell, *op. cit.*, p. 13). Slaves may have been somewhat less susceptible to yellow fever than the white population. See Philip D. Curtin, 'Epidemiology and the Slave Trade', *Political Science Quarterly*, LXXXIII (June, 1968), 208-9; J.C. Nott, 'An Examination into the Health and Longevity of the Southern Sea Ports of the United States', *Southern Journal of Medicine and Pharmacy*, II (January, 1847, 129.

205 R.H. Shryock, *op. cit.*, 160-3; Postell, *op. cit.*, p. 4.

206 For conflicting opinions on the question of adequacy of the slave's diet, see Gray, *op. cit.*, I, p. 521; R.H. Shryock, *op. cit.*, 160; Postell, *op. cit.*, pp. 31-2, 85; Eugene D. Genovese, *The Political Economy of Slavery: Studies in the Economy and Society of the Slave South* (New York: Pantheon Books, 1965), pp. 44-5. The self-sufficiency of southern plantations with respect to food supplies is discussed in Robert E. Gallman, 'Self-Sufficiency in the Cotton Economy of the Antebellum South', *Agricultural History*, XLIV (January, 1970), 5-24; and in the same issue, Diane L. Lindstrom, 'Southern Dependence upon Interregional Grain Supplies: A Review of the Trade Flows, 1840-1860', 101-14. Although the adequacy of the slave's diet has been confirmed by recent research, such issues as caloric level and nutritional balance have been the subjects of a hotly contested debate. See especially Fogel and Engerman (1974), Chapter IV, and Paul A. David *et al.* (1976), Chapter VI. Further evidence on the adequacy of the slave's diet is provided by recent research on the height of slaves compared with that of the white population in Europe and America. (See Steckel [1979a] 378.)

207 R.H. Shryock, *op. cit.*, 175; F. Swados, *op. cit.*, 464; Stampp, *op. cit.*, p. 346; Postell, *op. cit.*, p. 122.

208 Farley, 'The Demographic Rates . . . ', 395.

209 For European rates, see Simon Kuznets, *Modern Economic Growth*, pp. 42-3; for Quebec rates, Urquhart and Buckley, *Historical Statistics of Canada*, p. 54. For fragmentary data on contemporary Negro death

rates, see M.F. Hendrix, 'Births, Deaths and Aged Persons in Claiborne County [Mississippi], 1822', *Journal of Mississippi History*, XVI (January, 1954), 38–46.

210 Gray, *op. cit.*, II, p. 650.

211 See Tables B-10 through B-13. This phenomenon appears to have been a commonplace among contemporary observers. *Niles' Register*, for example, noted that 'There is no doubt that the slaves with us are longer lived than the free Blacks — but a larger part of the apparent disproportion arises from the unpleasant and oppressive fact — that aged and infirm and wornout Negroes, from all parts of the state, are turned to Baltimore to live as they can, or die, if they must' (*Niles' Register*, Vol. XXXVII, January 16, 1830, p. 340).

212 Tables B-14 and B-15.

213 *Loc. cit.*

214 Alexis de Tocqueville, *The Republic of the United States of America* (New York: A.S. Barnes, 1851), I, p. 398. See also Gray, *op. cit.*, I, p. 523; Luther P. Jackson, *Free Negro Labor and Property Holding in Virginia, 1830-1860* (New York: Appleton-Century, 1942), p. 66; Richard C. Wade, *Slavery in the Cities: The South 1820-1860* (New York: Oxford Press, 1964), pp. 141-2; Carter G. Woodson, *Free Negro Heads of Families in the United States in 1830* (Washington, 1925), p. xl; Alice D. Adams, *The Neglected Period of Anti-Slavery in America 1808-1831* (Gloucester, Mass.: Peter Smith, 1964), p. 13. Berlin (1976) argues that the lot of free Negroes in the Lower South was, on the average, better than that of their counterparts in the Upper South.

215 Carter G. Woodson, *A Century of Negro Migration* (New York: Russell & Russell, 1918), pp. 82-3; Leon F. Litwack, *North of Slavery: The Negro in the Free States, 1790-1860* (Chicago: University of Chicago Press, 1961), passim; John H. Franklin, *From Slavery to Freedom* (New York: Alfred Knopf, 1947), pp. 231-2; Robert Ernst, 'The Economic Status of New York City Negroes, 1850-1863', *Negro History Bulletin*, XII (March, 1949), 131-2, 139-43; Roy Ottley and William J. Weatherby, *The Negro in New York* (New York: N.Y. Public Library, 1967), p. 65; Edward R. Turner, *The Negro in Pennsylvania, 1639-1861* (Washington: American Historical Association, 1911), pp. 127, 142, 251.

216 Such unions were apparently the exception in Charleston, but the class consciousness of Charleston free Negroes was seldom echoed in other southern communities. See E. Horace Fitchett, 'The Origin and Growth of the Free Negro Population of Charleston, South Carolina', *Journal of Negro History*, XXVI (October, 1941), 431; David Y. Thomas, 'The Free Negro in Florida Before 1865', *South Atlantic Quarterly*, X (October, 1911), 341; Luther P. Jackson, *op. cit.*, p. 181n26; John H. Russell, *The Free Negro in Virginia, 1619-1865*, Johns Hopkins University Studies in Historical and Political Science, 1913, p. 131; James M. Wright, *The Free Negro in Maryland, 1634-1860*, Columbia University Studies in Historical and Political Science, 1913, p. 131; 1921, p. 243.

217 Russell does suggest that at least in Virginia it was common for free Negro males to marry female slaves (Russell, *op. cit.*, p. 131).

218 See C. G. Woodson, *Free Negro Heads of Families*, p. xiii; Franklin, *Free Negro in North Carolina*, pp. 36-7.

219 In 1800, 43 percent of all free Negroes were in states north of the line formed by the northern borders of Tennessee, Virginia and Maryland; in 1850, the number had risen to 48 percent. Calculated from data in Table B-2.

220 U.S. Bureau of the Census, *Eighth Census of the United States. 1860. Population*, p. xv.

221 Eaton, *History of the Old South*, p. 109; L.P. Jackson, *op. cit.*, p. 172; J.M. Wright, *op. cit.*, pp. 44, 321; J.H. Franklin, *From Slavery to Freedom*, pp. 128-9.

222 For details of abolition dates for northern states see note 47.

223 See for example Eaton, *History of the Old South*, p. 109; Wright, *The Free Negro in Maryland*, p. 321; Franklin, *From Slavery to Freedom*, p. 146.

224 The simple decade average of the price of a prime field hand, deflated by a general price index, suggests the following pattern: 1810-19, $522; 1820-29, $774; 1830-39, $1052; 1840-49, $989; 1850-59, $1390. Prices from Alfred H. Conrad and John R. Meyer, *The Economics of Slavery* (Chicago: Aldine, 1964), p. 76; Warren and Pearson wholesale price index from U.S. Bureau of the Census, *Historical Statistics of the United States* (1960), pp. 115-16, Series E-1.

225 The extent to which the task of Negroes was complicated depended of course on whether their ability to save rose at the same rate as the price of slaves. This seems highly unlikely. Nothing in the historical evidence would begin to support the hypothesis that changes in their real income compensated for the approximate doubling of slave prices between 1810-19 and the 1830s. The continued importance of this source of manumissions is suggested by the fact that of the 1,353 petitions submitted in New Orleans to free slaves in the period 1827-51, 501 were filed by free Negroes (Robert C. Reinders, 'The Free Negro in the New Orleans Economy, 1850-1860', *Louisiana History*, VI (Summer, 1965), 282).

226 Wendell H. Stephenson, *A Basic History of the Old South* (Princeton: D. Van Nostrand, 1959), p. 88.

227 Russell, *The Free Negro in Virginia*, pp. 6, 71-82, 173-6; Eaton, *History of the Old South*, p. 271; Wright, *The Free Negro in Maryland*, p. 261; Alice D. Adams, *op. cit.*, pp. 249-52.

228 Jackson, *Free Negro Labor and Property Holding in Virginia*, p. 172.

229 Franklin, *From Slavery to Freedom*, p. 260.

230 See also W.H. Stephenson, *op. cit.*, p. 86; L.P. Jackson, *op. cit.*, p. 7; Gray, *op. cit.*, I, p. 526; J.H. Russell, *op. cit.*, pp. 75-82. For descriptions of various legal attempts to limit manumission (all of dubious effectiveness), see Charles S. Sydnor, 'The Free Negro in Mississippi Before the Civil War', *American Historical Review*, XXXII (July, 1927), 773-80; Ralph B. Flanders, 'The Free Negro in Ante-Bellum Georgia', *North Carolina Historical Review*, IX (July, 1932), 253-6; David Y. Thomas, 'The Free Negro in Florida Before 1865', *South Atlantic Quarterly*, X (October, 1911), 343; E. Franklin Frazier, *The Free Negro Family: A Study of Family Origins Before the Civil War* (Nashville: Fisk University Press, 1932), p. 38; Gray, *op. cit.*, I, p. 526; Franklin, *From Slavery to Freedom*, p. 215. Berlin (1976) has also argued (but without much supporting evidence) that in the Upper South as the nineteenth century

progressed, 'in most places, the number of slaves passing from slavery to freedom was a trickle compared to an earlier flood' (304), while in the lower South, 'manumission was generally paternal in origin and extremely selective' (311).

231 The basic equation is (45), p. 67.

232 As discussed at length in section 1.4, Eblen has calculated vital rates for this period using census data, life tables and a method of successive approximation. Two crucial issues remain unclear in his work. The first concerns the appropriateness of the life tables used. The second is the extent to which his final estimates are a product of his desire to repeat approximations until the end result has only the single merit of satisfying his desire for smoothness. See Jack Ericson Eblen, 'Growth of the Black Population in *ante bellum* America, 1820-1860', *Population Studies,* XXVI (July, 1972), 273-89; and 'New Estimates of the Vital Rates in the United States Black Population During the Nineteenth Century', *Demography,* XI (May, 1974), 310-19.

233 As with the white population estimates, the values for $r(t)$ appear in the birth rate tables under INC.

234 See above, p. 74.

235 The contrast between the first two decades of the century and later developments may be a product of estimation procedures used to overcome the scarcity of data prior to 1820.

236 Alfred H. Conrad and John R. Meyer, 'The Economics of Slavery in the Ante Bellum South', *Journal of Political Economy,* LXVI (April, 1958), 95-130.

237 Ideally the authors should have compared the marginal, not the average, return.

238 Conrad and Meyer do not cite specific sources for each number, but merely preface their data with the statement, 'Estimates of plantation expenses have been taken primarily from three excellent, exhaustive records of the available material: J.L. Watkins' *The Cost of Cotton Production,* Lewis C. Gray's *History of Agriculture in the Southern United States in 1860* and Kenneth Stampp's *The Peculiar Institution'* (104). Saraydar (1964) was the first to point out that their actual sources for land prices were two observations in Gray's book.

239 Gray (1933), Vol. I, 542.

240 *The Southern Cultivator* (Athens, Atlanta), 1846, IV, 11. The $6 figure with accompanying source is cited by Gray (1933), Vol. I, 542.

Bibliography

Adams, Alice D. 1964. *The Neglected Period of Anti-Slavery in America 1808-1831*. Gloucester, Mass.: Peter Smith.

Adams, Charles Francis (ed.). 1875. *Memoirs of John Quincy Adams*. Philadelphia: J.P. Lippincott.

Albion, Robert G. and Jennie B. Pope. 1942. *Sea Lanes in Wartime*. New York: W.W. Norton.

American Anti-Slavery Society. 1841. *Slavery and the Internal Slave Trade in the United States of North America*. London: Thomas Ward & Co.

American Colonization Society. *The African Repository*.

American State Papers, Committee on . . . the Illicit Introduction of Slaves. 1826. *Slaves Brought Into the United States from Amelia Island*. Miscellaneous Vol. II, No. 441.

Aydelotte, William O. 1966. 'Quantification in History'. *American Historical Review*, LXXI (April), 803-25.

Bancroft, Frederic. 1931. *Slave Trading in the Old South*. Baltimore: J.H. Forst.

1957. 'The Colonization of American Negroes, 1801-1865', in Jacob E. Cooke (ed.), *Frederic Bancroft, Historian*. Norman: University of Oklahoma Press, pp. 145-269.

Bash, W.H. 1963. 'Changing Birth Rates in Developing America: New York State, 1840-1875'. *Milbank Memorial Fund Quarterly*, XLI (April), 161-82.

Berlin, Ira. 1976. 'The Structure of the Free Negro Caste in the Antebellum United States'. *Journal of Social History*, IX (Spring), 297-318.

1980. 'Time, Space, and the Evolution of Afro-American Society on British Mainland North America'. *American Historical Review*, LXXXV (February), 44-78.

Bigelow, John (ed.). 1887. *The Complete Works of Benjamin Franklin*. New York: Putnam's.

Blodget, Samuel. 1806. *Economica: A Statistical Manual for the United States of America*. Washington, D.C.: printed for author.

Bogue, Allan G. 1976. 'Population Change and Farm Settlement in the Northern United States: Discussion'. *Journal of Economic History*, XXXVI (March), 76-81.

Bogue, Donald J. 1969. *Principles of Demography*. New York: John Wiley.

Bromwell, William J. 1856. *History of Immigration to the United States*. New York: Redfield.

Carey, Matthew. 1822. *Essays on Political Economy.* Philadelphia: H.C. Carey & I. Lea.

Castellanos, Henry C. 1905. *New Orleans As It Was.* New Orleans: L. Graham Co.

Chickering, Jesse. 1848. *Immigration into the United States.* Boston: C.C. Little and J. Brown.

Coale, Ansley J. and Paul Demeny. 1966. *Regional Model Life Tables and Stable Populations.* Princeton: Princeton University Press.

Coale, Ansley J. and Melvin Zelnik. 1963. *New Estimates of Fertility and Population in the United States.* Princeton: Princeton University Press.

Collins, Winfield H. 1904. *The Domestic Slave Trade of the Southern States.* New York: Broadway Publishing Co.

Conrad, Alfred H. and John R. Meyer. 1958. 'The Economics of Slavery in the Ante Bellum South'. *Journal of Political Economy,* LXVI (April), 95-130.

1964. *The Economics of Slavery.* Chicago: Aldine.

Curtin, Philip D. 1968. 'Epidemiology and the Slave Trade'. *Political Science Quarterly,* LXXXIII (June), 190-216.

1969. *The Atlantic Slave Trade: A Census.* Madison: University of Wisconsin Press.

David, Paul A. *et al.* 1976. *Reckoning With Slavery.* New York: Oxford University Press.

Davis, Marion Rubins. 1931. 'Critique of Official United States Immigration Statistics', in Walter F. Willcox (ed.), *International Migrations.* New York: National Bureau of Economic Research, 645-60.

DeBow, J.D.B. 1854. *Statistical View of the United States . . . Being a Compendium of the Seventh Census.* Washington: Beverly Tucker.

Deerr, Noel. 1949-50. *The History of Sugar.* London: Chapman & Hall.

Demeny, Paul and Paul Gingrich. 1967. 'A Reconsideration of Negro-White Mortality Differentials in the United States'. *Demography,* IV, Number 2, 830-7.

Dominion Bureau of Statistics. 1871. *Census of Canada.*

Donnan, Elizabeth. 1935. *Documents Illustrative of the History of the Slave Trade to America.* Washington, D.C.: Carnegie Institution.

Dow, George F. 1927. *Slave Ships and Slaving.* Salem, Mass.: Marine Research Society.

DuBois, William E.B. 1891. 'Enforcement of the Slave-Trade Laws'. *American Historical Association Annual Report,* 163-74.

1896. *Suppression of the African Slave-Trade to the United States.* New York: Longman, Green & Co.

Duigan, Peter and Clarence Clendenen. 1963. *The United States and the African Slave Trade, 1619-1862.* Stanford, Calif.: Hoover Institution on War, Revolution and Peace.

Durham, John George Lampton, 1st earl. 1839. *The Report and Despatches of the Earl of Durham on the Affairs of British North America.* London: Ridgways.

Easterlin, Richard A. 1971. 'Does Human Fertility Adjust to the Environment?' *American Economic Review,* LXI (May), 399-407.

1975. 'An Economic Framework for Fertility Analysis'. *Studies in Family Planning,* VI (March), 54-63.

1976a. 'The Conflict between Aspirations and Resources'. *Population and Development Review,* II (September/December), 417-25.

1976b. 'Factors in the Decline of Farm Family Fertility in the United States: Some Preliminary Research Results'. *Journal of American History*, LXIII (December), 600-14.

1976c. 'Population Change and Farm Settlement in the Northern United States'. *Journal of Economic History*, XXXVI (March), 45-75.

1977. 'Population Issues in American Economic History: A Survey and Critique', in Robert E. Gallman (ed.), *Recent Developments in the Study of Business and Economic History: Essays in Memory of Herman E. Krooss, Research in Economic History*. Greenwich, Conn.: JAI Press, Supplement 1, 131-58.

1978. 'The Economics and Sociology of Fertility: A Synthesis', in Charles Tilly (ed.), *Historical Studies of Changing Fertility*. Princeton; Princeton University Press, 57-133.

1980. 'Population', in Glenn Porter (ed.), *Encyclopedia of American Economic History*. New York: Charles Scribner's Sons, 167-82.

Easterlin, Richard A, George Alter and Gretchen A. Condran. 1978. 'Farms and Farm Families in Old and New Areas: The Northern States in 1860', in Tamara K. Hareven and Maris A. Vinovskis (eds.), *Family and Population in Nineteenth Century America*. Princeton: Princeton University Press, 22-84.

Eaton, Clement. 1949. *A History of the Old South*. New York: Macmillan.

Eblen, Jack E. 1972. 'Growth of the Black Population in *ante bellum* America, 1820-1860'. *Population Studies*, XXVI (July), 273-89.

1974. 'New Estimates of the Vital Rates in the United States Black Population During the Nineteenth Century'. *Demography*, XI (May), 301-19.

Elliot, E.B. 1857. 'On the Law of Human Mortality that Appears to Obtain in Massachusetts'. *Proceedings of the American Association for the Advancement of Science*. Eleventh Meeting, Montreal, Quebec. Cambridge, Mass.: Joseph Lovering, 1958, pp. 51-82.

Engerman, Stanley L. 1975a. 'Comments on the Study of Race and Slavery', in Stanley L. Engerman and Eugene D. Genovese (eds.), *Race and Slavery in the Western Hemisphere*. Princeton: Princeton University Press, 495-530.

1975b. 'A Critique of Sutch on "The Breeding of Slaves", in Stanley L. Engerman and Eugene D. Genovese (eds.) *Race and Slavery in the Western Hemisphere: Quantitative Studies*. Princeton: Princeton University Press, 527-30.

Ernst, Robert, 1949. 'The Economic Status of New York City Negroes, 1850-1863', *Negro History Bulletin*, XII (March), 131-2, 139-43.

Farley, Reynolds. 1965. 'The Demographic Rates and Social Institutions of the Nineteenth Century Negro Population: A Stable Population Analysis'. *Demography*, II, 386-98.

1970. *Growth of the Black Population: A Study of Demographic Trends*. Chicago: Markham.

Ferenczi, Imre. 1929. *International Migrations*. Vol. 1. Edited by Walter F. Willcox. New York: National Bureau of Economic Research.

Fitchett, E. Horace. 1941. 'The Origin and Growth of the Free Negro Population of Charleston, South Carolina'. *Journal of Negro History*, XXVI (October), 421-37.

Flanders, Ralph B. 1932. 'The Free Negro in Ante-Bellum Georgia'. *North Carolina Historical Review*, IX (July), 250-72.

Fogel, Robert W. 1977. 'Cliometrics and Culture: Some Recent Developments in the Historiography of Slavery'. *Journal of Social History*, XI (Fall), 34-51.

 et al. 1978. 'The Economics of Mortality in North America, 1650-1910: A Description of a Research Project'. *Historical Methods*, XI (Spring), 75-108.

 et al. 1979. 'The Economic and Demographic Significance of Secular Changes in Human Structure: The U.S. 1750-1960'. Program on Long-Term Patterns of U.S. Economic Development. National Bureau of Economic Research. Report 1979.1 (April).

Fogel, Robert W. and Stanley L. Engerman. 1974. *Time on the Cross: The Economics of American Negro Slavery*. Boston: Little, Brown.

 1979. 'Recent Findings in the Study of Slave Demography and Family Structure'. *Sociology and Social Research*, LXIII (April), 566-89,

Fortier, Alcee. 1904. *A History of Louisiana*. New York: Mangi, Joyant & Co.

Franklin, Benjamin. 1755. *Observations Concerning the Increase of Mankind, Peopling of Countries, Etc.* Boston: S. Kneeland.

Franklin, John H. 1943. *The Free Negro in North Carolina, 1790-1860*. Chapel Hill: University of North Carolina Press.

 1947. *From Slavery to Freedom*. New York: Alfred Knopf.

Frazier, E. Franklin. 1932. *The Free Negro Family: A Study of Family Origins Before the Civil War*. Nashville: Fisk University Press.

Gallman, Robert E. 1970. 'Self-Sufficiency in the Cotton Economy of the Antebellum South'. *Agricultural History*, XLIV (January), 5-24.

Genovese, Eugene D. 1965. *The Political Economy of Slavery: Studies in the Economy and Society of the Slave South*. New York: Pantheon.

Glass, D.V. and E. Grebenik. 1965. 'World Population, 1800-1950', in M.M. Postan and H.J. Habakkuk (eds.), *The Cambridge Economic History of Europe*. Cambridge, England: Cambridge University Press, Vol. VI, 60-138.

Grabill, Wilson H., Clyde V. Kiser and P.K. Whelpton. 1958. *The Fertility of American Women*. New York: Wiley.

Gray, L.C. 1933. *History of Agriculture in the Southern United States to 1860*. Washington, D.C.: Carnegie Institution.

Great Britain. *Parliamentary Papers. Accounts and Papers.*

Handlin, Oscar, 1941. *Boston's Immigrants, 1790-1865*. Cambridge, Mass.: Harvard University Press.

Hansen, Marcus L. 1940. *The Atlantic Migration, 1607-1860*. Cambridge, Mass.: Harvard University Press.

Hazard's Register of Pennsylvania.

Hazard's United States Commercial and Statistical Register.

Hendrix, M.F. 1954. 'Births, Deaths and Aged Persons in Claiborne County [Mississippi], 1822'. *Journal of Mississippi History*, XVI (January), 38-46.

Higgs, Robert. 1973. 'Mortality in Rural America, 1870-1920: Estimates and Conjectures'. *Explorations in Economic History*, X (Winter), 177-95.

 1979. 'Cycles and Trends of Mortality in 18 Large American Cities, 1871-1900'. *Explorations in Economic History*, XVI (October), 381-408.

Himes, Norman E. 1936. *Medical History of Contraception*. Baltimore: Williams & Williams.

Howard, Warren S. 1963. *Slavers and the Federal Law, 1837-1862.*
 Berkeley: University of California Press.
Hunt's Merchants' Magazine.
Jackson, Luther P. 1942. *Free Negro Labor and Property Holding in Virginia,
 1830-1860.* New York: Appleton-Century.
Jacobson, Paul. 1957. 'An Estimate of the Expectation of Life in the United
 States in 1850'. *Milbank Memorial Fund Quarterly,* XXXV (April),
 197-201.
Jaffee, A.J. 1940. 'Differential Fertility in the White Population in Early
 America'. *Journal of Heredity,* XXXI (September), 407-11.
Jefferson, Thomas. 1801. *Notes on the State of Virginia.* Philadelphia:
 R.T. Rawle.
Krout, John Allen and Dixon Ryan Fox. 1944. *The Completion of Independ-
 ence, 1790-1830.* New York: Macmillan.
Kuznets, Simon. 1966. *Modern Economic Growth: Rate, Structure, and
 Spread.* New Haven: Yale University Press.
Labaree, L.W. (ed.). 1959. *The Papers of Benjamin Franklin.* New Haven:
 Yale University Press.
Landon, Fred. 1920. 'The Negro Migration to Canada After 1850'. *Journal
 of Negro History,* V (January), 22-36.
Lebergott, Stanley. 1970. 'Migration in the U.S., 1800-1960: Some New
 Estimates'. *Journal of Economic History,* XXX (December), 839-47.
Leet, Don R. 1975. 'Human Fertility and Agricultural Opportunities in
 Ohio Counties: From Frontier to Maturity, 1810-1860', in David C.
 Klingaman and Richard K. Vedder, *Essays in Nineteenth Century
 Economic History: The Old Northwest.* Athens: Ohio University
 Press, 138-58.
 1976. 'The Determinants of the Fertility Transition in Antebellum
 Ohio'. *Journal of Economic History,* XXXVI (June), 359-78.
 1977. 'Interrelations of Population Density, Urbanization, Literacy, and
 Fertility'. *Explorations in Economic History,* XIV (October),
 388-401.
'Life Insurance at the South'. 1847. *DeBow's Commercial Review,* III (May),
 358-75.
Lindstrom, Diane L. 1970. 'Southern Dependence upon Interregional Grain
 Supplies: A Review of the Trade Flows, 1840-1860'. *Agricultural
 History,* XLIV (January), 101-14.
Litwack, Leon F. 1961. *North of Slavery: The Negro in the Free States
 1790-1860.* Chicago: University of Chicago Press.
Lösh, August. 1954. *The Economics of Location.* New Haven: Yale
 University Press.
Louisiana, Senate. 1854. *Report of the Committee Appointed to Apportion
 the Representation of the State.* 2nd Leg., 1st sess., Sen. Doc.
Lower, A.R.M. 1962. 'The Growth of Population in Canada', in Vincent
 W. Bladen (ed.), *Canadian Population and Northern Colonization:
 Symposium Presented to the Royal Society of Canada in 1961.*
 Toronto: University of Toronto, 43-70.
McClellan, Ely. 1875. *A History of the Travels of Asiatic Cholera in North
 America.* U.S., Congress, House, 43rd Cong., 2nd sess., Exec. Doc. 95.
McInnis, R.M. 1977. 'Childbearing and Land Availability: Some Evidence
 from Individual Household Data', in Ronald Demos Lee *et al.,
 Population Patterns in the Past.* New York: Academic Press, 201-27.

Malthus, T.R. 1878. *An Essay on the Principle of Population*. London: Reeves & Turner.

Mannix, Daniel P. and Malcolm Cowley. 1962. *Black Cargoes: A History of the Atlantic Slave Trade, 1815-1865*. New York: Viking.

Massachusetts, Secretary of State. *Annual Reports Relating to the Registry and Return of Births, Marriages, and Deaths*.

Meeker, Edward. 1972. 'The Improving Health of the United States, 1850-1915'. *Explorations in Economic History*, IX (Summer), 353-73.

    1976. 'Mortality Trends of Southern Blacks, 1850-1910: Some Preliminary Findings'. *Explorations in Economic History*, XIII (January), 13-42.

    1977. 'Freedom, Economic Opportunity, and Fertility: Black Americans, 1860-1910'. *Economic Inquiry*, XV (July), 397-412.

Meyer, John R. 1963. 'Regional Economics: A Survey'. *American Economic Review*, LIII (March), 19-54.

Niles' Register.

Nott, J.C. 1847. 'An Examination into the Health and Longevity of the Southern Sea Ports of the United States'. *Southern Journal of Medicine and Pharmacy*, II (January), 121-46.

Olmsted, Frederick. 1904. *A Journey in the Seaboard Slave States in the Years 1853-1854*. New York: G.P. Putnam's Sons.

Ottley, Roy, and William J. Weatherby. 1967. *The Negro in New York*. New York: N.Y. Public Library.

Phillips, Ulrich B. 1901. 'Racial Problems, Adjustments and Disturbances', in F.L. Riley (ed.), *The South in the Building of the Nation*. Richmond: Southern Historical Publication Society, Vol. 4, 194-241.

    1929. *American Negro Slavery*. New York: Appleton.

Postell, William D. 1951. *The Health of Slaves on Southern Plantations*. Baton Rouge: Louisiana State University Press.

Potter, J. 1955. 'The British Timber Duties, 1815-60'. *Economica*, XXII (May), 122-36.

    1965. 'The Growth of Population in America, 1700-1860', in D.V. Glass and D.E.C. Eversley, *Population in History*, Chicago: Aldine, 631-88.

Reinders, Robert,C. 1965. 'The Free Negro in the New Orleans Economy, 1850-1860'. *Louisiana History*, VI (Summer), 273-86.

Rice, Thurman B. 1927. *The Conquest of Disease*. New York: Macmillan.

Richardson, Harry W. 1969. *Regional Economics*. New York: Praeger.

Rossiter, William S. 1922. *Increase of Population in the United States, 1910-1920*. U.S. Census Bureau Monograph No. 1, Washington, D.C.

Rowland, Dunbar. 1917. *Official Letter Books of W.C.C. Claiborne*. Jackson, Miss.: State Department of Archives and History.

Rubin, Ernest. 1959. 'Immigration and the Economic Growth of the United States, 1790-1914'. Research Group for European Migration Problems, *Bulletin*, VII, No. 4 (October/December), 87-95.

Russell, John H. 1913. *The Free Negro in Virginia, 1619-1865*. Johns Hopkins University Studies in Historical and Political Science, XXI, No. 3.

Sanderson, Warren C. 1978a. 'New Estimates of the Decline in the Fertility of White Women in the United States, 1800-1920'. Unpublished paper, Center for Research in Economic Growth, Memorandum No. 225, Department of Economics, Stanford University.

1978b. 'New Interpretations of the Decline in the Fertility of White Women in the United States, 1800-1920'. Unpublished paper, Center for Research in Economic Growth, Memorandum No. 224, Department of Economics, Stanford University.

1979. 'Quantitative Aspects of Marriage, Fertility and Family Limitation in Nineteenth Century America: Another Application of the Coale Specifications'. *Demography*, XVI (August), 339-58.

Saraydar, Edward. 1964. 'A Note on the Profitability of Ante-Bellum Slavery'. *Southern Economic Journal*, XXX (April), 325-53.

Seaman, Ezra C. 1846. *Essays on the Progress of Nations*. New York: Baker & Scribner.

Seybert, Adam. 1818. *Statistical Annals . . . of the United States of America*. Philadelphia: T. Dobson.

Shattuck, Lemuel. 1893. *Bills of Mortality, 1810-1849, City of Boston*. Boston: Registry Department.

Shryock, Henry S. *et al.* 1973. *The Methods and Materials of Demography*. Washington, D.C.: Government Printing Office.

Shryock, Richard H. 1930. 'Medical Practice in the Old South'. *South Atlantic Quarterly*, XXIX (April), 160-78.

Sinclair, Harold. 1942. *The Port of New Orleans*. New York: Doubleday.

Smillie, Wilson G. 1952. 'The Period of Great Epidemics in the United States: 1800-1875', in Franklin H. Top (ed.), *The History of American Epidemiology*. St. Louis: Mosby, 52-73.

Spengler, J.J. 1958. 'Effects Produced in Receiving Countries by Pre-1939 Immigration', in Brinley Thomas (ed.), *Economics of International Migration*. London: Macmillan, 17-51.

Stampp, Kenneth M. 1963. *The Peculiar Institution*. New York: Alfred A. Knopf.

Steckel, Richard H. 1979a. 'Slave Height Profiles from Coastwise Manifests'. *Explorations in Economic History*, XVI (October), 363-80.

1979b. 'Slave Mortality: Analysis of Evidence from Plantation Records'. *Social Science History*, III (October), 86-114.

1980. 'Antebellum Southern White Fertility: A Demographic and Economic Analysis'. *Journal of Economic History*, XL (June), 331-50.

Stephenson, Wendell H. 1959. *A Basic History of the Old South*. Princeton: D. Van Nostrand.

Sutch, Richard. 1974. 'The Treatment Received by American Slaves: A Critical Review of the Evidence Presented in *Time on the Cross*'. *Explorations in Economic History*, XII (October), 335-429.

1975. 'The Breeding of Slaves for Sale and the Westward Expansion of Slavery, 1850-1860', in Stanley L. Engerman and Eugene D. Genovese (eds.). *Race and Slavery in the Western Hemisphere*. Princeton: Princeton University Press, 173-210.

Swados, Felice. 1941. 'Negro Health on the Ante-Bellum Plantations'. *Bulletin of the History of Medicine*, X (October), 460-72.

Sydnor, Charles S. 1927. 'The Free Negro in Mississippi Before the Civil War'. *American Historical Review*, XXXII (July), 769-88.

Taeuber, Conrad and Irene B. Taeuber. 1958. *The Changing Population of the United States*. New York: Wiley.

Taylor, George Rogers. 1966. 'Beginnings of Mass Transportation in Urban America: Part I'. *Smithsonian Journal of History*, I (Summer), 35-50.

Thomas, Brinley. 1954. *Migration and Economic Growth*. Cambridge, England: Cambridge University Press.

1961. *International Migration and Economic Development*. Paris: Unesco.

Thomas, David Y. 1911. 'The Free Negro in Florida Before 1865'. *South Atlantic Quarterly*, X (October), 335–45.

Thompson, Warren S. 1949. 'The Demographic Revolution in the United States'. *Annals of the American Academy of Political and Social Science*, CLVII (March), 62–9.

Thompson, Warren S. and P. K. Whelpton. 1933. *Population Trends in the United States*. New York: McGraw-Hill.

Tocqueville, Alexis de. 1851. *The Republic of the United States of America*. New York: A.S. Barnes.

1945. *Democracy in America*. New York: Alfred A. Knopf.

Trussell, James and Richard Steckel. 1978. 'The Age of Slaves at Menarche and Their First Birth'. *Journal of Interdisciplinary History*, VIII (Winter), 477–505.

Tucker, George. 1855. *Progress of the United States in Population and Wealth*. New York: Hunt's.

Turner, Edward R. 1911. *The Negro in Pennsylvania, 1639–1861*. Washington, D.C.: American Historical Association.

United Nations. 1953. *The Determinants and Consequences of Population Trends*. New York: United Nations.

1967. *Methods of Estimating Basic Demographic Measures from Incomplete Data: Manual IV*. New York: United Nations.

Urquhart, M.C. and K.A.H. Buckley (eds.). 1965. *Historical Statistics of Canada*. Toronto: Macmillan.

U.S. Bureau of the Census. 1790. *First Census of the United States*.

1800. *Second Census of the United States*.

1810. *Third Census of the United States*.

1820. *Fourth Census of the United States*.

1830. *Fifth Census of the United States*.

1840. *Sixth Census of the United States*.

1850. *Seventh Census of the United States*.

1860. *Eighth Census of the United States*.

1870. *Ninth Census of the United States. Population*, Vol. I.

1918. *Negro Population in the United States, 1790–1915*. Washington, D.C.

1950. *Seventeenth Census of the United States*.

1960. *Historical Statistics of the United States: Colonial Times to 1957*. Washington, D.C.

1975. *Historical Statistics of the United States: Colonial Times to 1970*. Washington, D.C.

U.S., Congress, House. 1818/1819. *Letter from the Secretary of the Treasury Transmitting Information . . . In Relation to Ships Engaged in the Slave Trade*. 15th Cong., 2nd sess., House Doc. 107.

1828/29. *Message from the President of the United States to Both Houses of Congress*, by John Quincy Adams. 20th Cong., 2nd sess., House Doc. No. 2.

1875. *A History of the Travels of Asiatic Cholera in North America*, by Ely McClellan. 43rd Cong., 2nd sess., Exec. Doc. 95.

U.S., Secretary of the Treasury. *Annual Statement of the Commerce and Navigation of the United States*.

Vinovskis, Maris A. 1972. 'Mortality Rates and Trends in Massachusetts Before 1860'. *Journal of Economic History*, XXXII (March), 184–213.

1976a. 'The Jacobson Life Table of 1850: A Critical Reexamination from a Massachusetts Perspective'. Paper prepared for the Science History Association Meetings in Philadelphia, October.

1976b. 'Socioeconomic Determinants of Interstate Fertility Differentials in the United States in 1850 and 1860'. *Journal of Interdisciplinary History*, VI (Winter), 375–96.

1978. 'Recent Trends in American Historical Demography: Some Methodological and Conceptual Considerations'. *Review of Sociology*, IV, 603–27.

von Halle, Ernst. 1897. *Baumwollproduktion und Pflanzungswirtschaft in den Nordamerikanischen Südstaaten.* Leipzig: Duncker & Humblot.

Wade, Richard C. 1964. *Slavery in the Cities: The South 1820–1860.* New York: Oxford University Press.

Walker, Francis A. 1891. 'Immigration and Degradation'. *The Forum*, XI (August), 634–44.

Ward, Lester F. 1913. *Glimpses of the Cosmos.* New York: G.P. Putnam.

Wigglesworth, Edward. 1775. *Calculations on American Population.* Boston: John Boyle.

Willcox, Walter F. 1931. 'Immigration into the United States', in Walter F. Willcox (ed.), *International Migrations.* New York: National Bureau of Economic Research, 85–122.

Willcox, Walter F. (ed.) *International Migrations.* Vol. 1 by Imre Ferenczi. New York: National Bureau of Economic Research.

Woodson, Carter G. 1918. *A Century of Negro Migration.* New York: Russell & Russell.

1925. *Free Negro Heads of Families in the United States in 1830.* Washington, D.C.: The Association for the Study of Negro Life and History.

Wright, James M. 1921. *The Free Negro in Maryland, 1634–1860.* Columbia University Studies in History, Economics and Public Law, XCVII.

Yasuba, Yasukichi. 1961. *Birth Rates of the White Population in the United States, 1800–1860.* Johns Hopkins University Studies in Historical and Political Science, LXXIX.

Zelnick, Melvin. 1966. 'Fertility of the American Negro in 1830 and 1850'. *Population Studies*, XX (July), 77–83.

1969. 'Age Patterns of Mortality of American Negroes: 1900–02 to 1959–61'. *Journal of the American Statistical Association*, LXIV (June), 433–51.

Index